Praise for *CMMI® Survival Gu*

"Traveling down the CMMI road can be difficult and time-consuming. Garcia and Turner have given us a practical roadmap that addresses the key points to learn as well as the many potholes to avoid. Their *Survival Guide* is a most valuable resource for the journey. It will help immeasurably in achieving the process improvement that you seek."

Dr. Howard Eisner, Distinguished Research Professor,
George Washington University

"Helps you get to the 'red meat' of the CMMI quickly and with minimum pain."

Donald J. Reifer, President, Reifer Consultants, Inc.

"The best words I can offer potential readers is that you must have this book, not on your shelf, but with you for repeated reading to glean new ideas or reinforce old ones you gained from the past readings....If you have ever been directly involved in a process improvement initiative or if you are starting one, this book can only help you to do a better job. And while [the authors] may not have written this book explicitly for experienced consultants, I found it a great reference even for those of us who helped start this industry, because it provides clear and useful answers to those tough questions we are asked all of the time."

Tim Kasse, CEO and Principal Consultant,
Kasse Initiatives LLC

"This book contains practical (working) tips for the 'getting started' phase of process improvement, which is the hardest one in the road to improving one's processes."

Agapi Svolou, Principal of Alexanna, LLC, and
SEI CMMI Transition Partner

"The authors have done an outstanding job in providing guidance for process improvement from a practical perspective. Instead of focusing on a single technique or approach, they have provided a variety of methods for process improvement implementation and have framed their discussion with rich context from lessons learned. The concepts described in this book will be useful to both those starting CMMI implementations and to those who are well into their journey but are still looking for ways to lessen the pain and provide value-added improvements. Reading the book is like being in the audience during a live presentation by SuZ and Rich—they wrote the book as they would present the information to a live audience."

Bill Craig, Director, Software Engineering Directorate,
AMRDEC, RDECOM

"I have been involved in process improvement since the early 90's and many of the mistakes that I made could have been prevented if this book had been available then."

Claude Y. Laporte, Professor, ETS Université du Québec

"Primarily, the book is *practical*. The guidance presented is geared toward someone who is not exactly sure *why* they need process improvement, but is presented with the fact that they *must* do it. Very often these are smaller organizations, with limited resources, and uncertain support from above. As I read the book, I thought almost immediately of a couple of organizations with which I am familiar who could use this kind of tutelage. There are real, and useful, techniques in this book that I believe can help these kinds of organizations prioritize and establish reasonable plans for improving the processes in the organization. I also like the sidebars and personal observations. Discussions of experience can really help organizations through the various pitfalls that are part of developing and deploying processes. It makes the book more of a 'real life' guide, and not a theoretical exercise. Finally, the book is an enjoyable read. The conversational style of the book (and the humor) make it much easier to read than many of the books I have read in the past."

Alexander Stall, Principal Process Improvement Engineer,
Systems and Software Consortium

CMMI® Survival Guide

CMMI® Survival Guide

Just Enough Process Improvement

Suzanne Garcia
Richard Turner

✦✦Addison-Wesley

Upper Saddle River, NJ • Boston • Indianapolis • San Francisco
New York • Toronto • Montreal • London • Munich • Paris • Madrid
Capetown • Sydney • Tokyo • Singapore • Mexico City

Carnegie Mellon
Software Engineering Institute

The SEI Series in Software Engineering

The publisher offers discounts on this book when ordered in quantity bulk purchases and special sales, which may include electronic versions and/or custom covers and content particular to your business, training goals, marketing focus, and branding interests. For more information, please contact:

> U.S. Corporate and Government Sales
> (800) 382-3419
> corpsales@pearsontechgroup.com

For sales outside of the U.S., please contact:

> International Sales
> international@pearsontechgroup.com

Visit us on the Web: www.awprofessional.com

Library of Congress Cataloging-in-Publication Data

Garcia, Suzanne.
　CMMI survival guide : just enough process improvement / Suzanne Garcia, Richard Turner.
　　p. cm.
　Includes bibliographical references and index.
　ISBN 0-321-42277-5 (pbk. : alk. paper)
　1. Production management.　2. Quality control.　3. Capability maturity model (Computer software)　I. Turner, Richard, 1954–　II. Title.

　TS155.G23 2006
　658.5'03—dc22　　　　　　　　　　　　　　　　　　　　　　　　　　　　2006022109

ISBN: 0-321-42277-5
Text printed in the United States on recycled paper at R.R. Donnelley in Crawfordsville, Indiana.
First printing, October 2006

Contents

List of Figures

List of Tables

Foreword

It is a delight for me to provide an introduction to this work. Despite our efforts to make the CMMI V1.2 documents complete, there is always great value in a guide like this. So although our release may not *require* a survival guide, you are in for a treat from these two. SuZ and Rich are two of the most creative folks in process improvement and have combined their talents to produce a wonderful, readable how-to approach to both the use of CMMI and the general conduct of process improvement.

In this book they provide a holistic, helpful, and humorous distillation of their experiences, tools, techniques, and observations. They step outside the traditional process improvement box and discuss the critical psychological, social, and management issues that must be overcome to be successful with CMMI in any environment, large or small. Their concept of survival is anchored in business value, practical strategies, and useful tools. For these reasons, the *CMMI Survival Guide* can be used by everyone from the executive suite to the delivery staff.

As I write this, I am conscious of the exceptional progress applying CMMI around the world. Currently 62 percent of more than 1,500 appraisals are conducted at development sites outside the United States. We have seen translations of all or parts of the CMMI model into Japanese, Chinese, French, Dutch, German, and Portuguese. This international expansion, crossing cultures and business environments, increases the need for the flexible, business-driven approach in the *CMMI Survival Guide*.

In addition to the international expansion, CMMI is expanding coverage of organizational needs for process discipline. Those who find they are providing services or acquiring technology rather than doing engineering development are finding that some adjustment in CMMI is needed to capture the best practices in their day-to-day environment. Two CMMI "constellations" are being developed to address these needs, and others likely will follow. Because this book focuses on the process improvement initiative and its successful outcome, it is equally valuable regardless of which constellation of CMMI is used.

We have just completed version 1.2 of CMMI based on well over 1,000 comments and suggestions. The three themes that drove this update were to

- Simplify the material
- Expand the coverage to include hardware elements, and provide basic coverage of key practices across the work environment
- Increase the confidence in appraisal results

We are extremely pleased that *CMMI Survival Guide* uses V1.2 as its basis.

For the last ten years it has been my pleasure to work with SuZ and Rich, both with improvement teams and at many conferences around the world. They have seen the challenges that change agents face within the organization and as advisors from afar. Change is never easy, but these two can help you prevent having "speed bumps" turn into "road closures" on your improvement journey!

Mike Phillips
CMMI V1.2 Program Manager
The Software Engineering Institute
July 2006

Preface

Adopting CMMI (or any other process improvement initiative) can seem like navigating a jungle full of unknown dangers, pitfalls, and false paths. No matter where you are in your process improvement journey, there are a lot of reasons why you might need a CMMI survival guide. If you are just starting out, you'll need to survey the territory, consult maps, talk to other explorers, look into hiring guides, and maybe reconsider whether you really need to take that trip after all. If you are already committed, but feel like you're lost or stuck or going around in circles, your outlook may be reduced to simple survival. On the other hand, if you have begun to see past the dangers and into the possibilities, you may want some additional tools and techniques to get the most out of your journey. For all of you, we are pleased to present this compendium of knowledge and experience about the process improvement jungle in the hope that it can make your trip more efficient, valuable, and satisfying.

We have three goals for this volume: We'd like to calm the nervous, help the little guy, and make process improvement more agile. Let's look at each of these.

Calming the nervous

We've heard lots of nervous concerns about CMMI. It's as though Dante's "Abandon all hope ye who enter here" somehow were added to the CMMI shingle. Consider (if you will) the following common perceptions about CMMI:

- CMMI is big and intimidating. Who wants to wade through a 700-page-plus book to try to understand it?
- Our [choose one: customer/acquiring company/prime] told us we have to use it.
- We thought we were immune to process improvement because we don't build software. Now they tell us CMMI applies to us.

- It costs so much to implement. We don't have that kind of overhead funding available.
- It seems to take such a long time before return on investment is achieved.
- It was written by and for large, government-driven businesses. It can't possibly be useful—or usable—for small companies and organizations or limited projects.
- We want to be agile, and CMMI is über-high ceremony.
- We'll wait until it's absolutely, positively unavoidable—and then we'll bite the bullet and buy our way in.

Fortunately, most of this anxiety is based on misperceptions rising from a somewhat old-fashioned, traditional role for process improvement. While we can't counter every fear, we can provide suggestions for ways to mitigate many of the scary risks.

Helping the little guy

We believe that small businesses and organizations are particularly under-served by current resources. Our experience tells us that process improvement, when approached sensibly, can benefit many smaller organizations. For that reason, we've included examples from smaller environments. Our approach to incremental process improvement, driven by specific business value rather than simply seeking a maturity level, is especially appropriate for resource-strapped smaller organizations. If your business fits into this category, we hope the book will help you find the confidence to actively adopt new methods that have worked so well in other, larger places.

Making process improvement more agile

One response to traditionally process-heavy approaches, at least in the software industry, has been the agile methods movement. Methods such as Extreme Programming and Scrum have gained attention as approaches that are designed for easier implementation. Some argue that methods like these are incompatible with models like CMMI; others have found ways to use elements of both in complementary ways.

In this book, we'll take a somewhat different approach and describe ways in which process improvement itself can take advantage of the agile philosophy and practices. We describe a more lightweight, focused, and time-constrained process improvement life cycle that we believe captures the flexibility and responsiveness of agile development methods.

Through years of interaction with diverse organizations, we've seen the many ways that models and methods are used effectively to promote business value, and nearly as many ways that they can be used unproductively. So we've written this book to share approaches that have worked and identify a few that haven't. You can judge for yourself what might be achievable when you attempt to improve project management, engineering, or support practices in your own business environment.

The book's format is intended to support readers who need a quick scan of the territory as well as those who are looking for actual techniques and templates. We believe that no one has all the answers. Many of our techniques are ones we have learned from others, and wherever possible, we'll tell you where to find more in-depth information.

If you are just hearing about CMMI, model-based improvement, or agile methods, we hope that this book will provide a coherent set of steps and techniques to get you started on your path to improved practices.

For those of you who are against the wall and under orders to adopt a model or method, we believe you will find fresh ways to approach your mandate, making the experience productive for you and your organization.

And for all of you who pick up this book, we hope you'll find it enjoyable enough that you actually finish reading it! As we explore this material with you, it's the most ambitious goal we've set for ourselves.

Organization

In general, we are writing to you in much the way we would talk with you: directly and with a bit of wry humor thrown in. The organization of the book, based on an extended adventure analogy, is straightforward. There is increasing detail as you read, with earlier chapters being prologue to later chapters, thus providing good "management-level" reading. At the end of each chapter, we collect any references to other books or material. Occasionally we relate (mostly) real stories that we hope illustrate the subject through examples.

The book is divided into five parts:

- Part I: Scouting the Territory. We describe process improvement from a practical standpoint, describing why we think it is worth pursuing, how it is helpful, and why it isn't as easy as it sounds.
- Part II: Mapping the Route. We provide some specific guides that can make process improvement more organized and often more effective.
- Part III: Surviving the Passage. We present a case study for those who like "reality shows" and describe ways in which survival of a process improvement initiative is analogous to physical survival as taught by the U.S. Army.
- Part IV: Experiencing the Journey. This is the section where the rubber meets the road. We discuss the specifics of executing a process improvement initiative and use CMMI to lead by example.
- Part V: Outfitting Your Expedition (PI Resources). This is our tools-and-techniques section, where we can go into more detail about some of the tools we've mentioned in previous chapters. We also provide a complete bibliography.

A note about the illustrations for the part introductions: These woodcuts were executed by artist and designer Witold Gordon in 1926 for an illustrated edition of Marco Polo's *The Travels of Marco Polo (The Venetian)*, translated by William Marsden and corrected by Manuel Komroff. We thought these wonderful art deco pieces were particularly appropriate, because process improvement is both an adventure and a journey of discovery.

Acknowledgments

We'd like to thank the many people who have influenced our ideas, philosophies, writing, and practice.

In particular, SuZ would like to acknowledge Eileen Forrester, whose passion for researching technology transition methods spurred me in directions I would never have gone on my own; Roger Bate, whom I have always respected and enjoyed working with, and whose trust in me to lead the Systems Engineering CMM project started me on a whole new path in my career journey; Chuck Myers, my perennial tutorial partner, whose creativity and depth of insight never cease to amaze me; Mike Konrad, who allowed me many growth opportunities to explore the CMMs space and to try new approaches, even when he wasn't sure they would work; Mark Paulk, who was the one who moved me from complaining about maturity models to actually working on and improving them; Eamonn McGuinness, who allowed me much freedom in experimenting with process improvement techniques in a *very* small organization; Agapi Svolou, whose continual enthusiasm for my ideas and techniques humbles and inspires me; John Foreman, who allowed me to explore many of my adoption ideas with small companies on the TIDE project; Sandra Cepeda, my steadfast partner in consulting on the Huntsville CMMI pilots, who never tried to turn me into an appraiser (much as she wanted to); Bill Craig, whose sponsorship of the CMMI Huntsville pilots led to many of the insights shared herein.

Bill Peterson, whose continual support of my many ideas in the process improvement area and of me personally is unparalleled; Watts Humphrey, whose passion to improve the outcomes and practices of software engineers and whose continual willingness to share his knowledge and perspectives give me hope for the future of the software engineering discipline; Caroline Graettinger, who had no idea what she was getting when she hired me back into the Software Engineering Institute (SEI), yet has never once complained; Jerry Weinberg, whose coaching and mentoring at critical points throughout my career have enabled the "writing side" of me to come out; all the participants in the 2004 Weinberg Writer's Workshop, whose encouragement and productive criticism gave me the desire to write prose again; the participants of Consultant's Camp, whose many insights have influenced and guided me in so many directions none of us would expect; and my family, the Poehlman clan, whose love and support has never failed, no matter how weird I've gotten!

Rich would like to particularly mention Jim Armstrong, Hillary Davidson, Rich McCabe, Ken Nidiffer, Bill Smith, and Alex Stall of the Systems and Software Consortium who, whether they knew it or not, acted as sounding boards for much of this material; Mark Schaeffer of the U.S. Department of Defense, who challenged the community to develop CMMI in the first place; Roger Bate, Mike Phillips, Bob Rassa, Hal Wilson, the CMMI Steering Group, and the CMMI teams that have struggled to make the model useful and extensible while remaining stable enough for wide adoption; Kristen Baldwin and the Tri-Service Assessment Initiative team for their work in focusing on causal chains in evaluating programs in vitro.

Vic Basili, Kathleen Dangle, and Michelle Shaw of the Fraunhofer Center at the University of Maryland, who were pioneers in bringing maturity models to smaller organizations; Tim Kasse, who renewed my confidence in the process improvement support industry with his fervent, yet rational, approach to process consulting; Alistair Cockburn, who truly understands the role of communication and humbles me with his eclectic intellect; Don Reifer for his phenomenal support in nearly everything I do; and Barry Boehm, my partner in investigating the agile world, for his insight and wisdom into seeing beyond the methods and into the future.

And from both of us, immeasurable thanks to Michael and Jo, our partners in life and love, whose patience and support during the process of writing this book were key to its completion. There are no words that can sufficiently thank them for their contributions. We love you more than you know.

SuZ Garcia
Rich Turner
September 2006

CMMI® Survival Guide

Illustration from *The Travels of Marco Polo*
by Witold Gordon (1885–1968)

Part I

Scouting the Territory

I am always doing that which I cannot do, in order that I may learn how to do it.
Pablo Picasso (1881–1973)

Man can learn nothing unless he proceeds from the known to the unknown.
Claude Bernard, *French physiologist* (1813–1878)

*I prepared excitedly for my departure, as if this journey had a mysterious significance. I had decided to change my mode of life. "'til now,"
I told myself, "you have only seen the shadow and been well content with it; now, I am going to lead you into the substance."*
Nikos Kazantzakis, *Zorba the Greek*

Unless commitment is made, there are only promises and hopes; but no plans.
Peter F. Drucker

Before you make any decisions about process improvement and CMMI, you need to scout out the territory—or, if you prefer, sense the gestalt of process improvement—so you have a context as you read further. It is important to understand the rationale behind this type of effort. Without this context, much of the benefit of CMMI or other approaches can be difficult to grasp, and so is much less compelling to you or your management.

In this first part, we act as your reconnaissance scout, providing a manager's-eye view of the process improvement wilderness. We briefly discuss its history, provide a rationale for your journey, and broadly describe the kind of activities you'll need to master if you are to return safe and enlightened. We highlight some specific locations you may wish to visit—that is, describe several process models and improvement approaches, all of which can work if applied intelligently and diligently.

All this preparation is not intended to confuse you, but to provide a broader context and more choice in developing your own process improvement strategy. If, after completing Part I, you think that model-based improvement could be useful to you, proceed to Parts II and III, where we'll get into the details of model-based improvement that will result in added business value for your organization. Then, if you're really hooked, reading Parts IV and V will take you deeper into the "how-tos" of process improvement.

But, you ask, why would I want to start this journey in the first place? What's the reward, the business case? Well, that's a great setup for the next section—so let's get on with the business at hand and talk about the benefits of process improvement.

Chapter 1

Why We Think Process Is Important

Why is process such a critical element to the success of an organization or business? This isn't a new question, so a bit of history is in order.

1.1 A short history of process improvement

Process improvement has a long history in manufacturing. Operations research, efficiency studies, and similar activities have all tried to "get the fat" out of industrial processes for more than a century. It was only in the 1980s, however, that process was specifically applied to thought labor as opposed to mechanical or physical labor. Software development was a primary target. As more and more products and systems depended on computers to fulfill their requirements, and as software development organizations had greater and greater cost and schedule overruns, something had to be done to get these software folks on track. In this instance, the process-related activities were not so much about increasing efficiency as about incorporating discipline into routine activities—that is, making sure everything that was supposed to be done was done, and that there was sufficient repeatability in the tasks to make future work predictable. This process repeatability and predictability came to be called capability maturity. Process became the means to structure the work of developing software—a highly cerebral task likened to writing books or music and often referred to as being more art than science. And if there was one thing businesses (and governments) couldn't deal with, it was the vagaries and whims of artists. So software process improvement was born, and the Capability Maturity Model for Software (SW-CMM) was developed. After a rough start, but with some help from government acquisition organizations, software process improvement was poked, prodded, tried, evaluated, and—lo and behold—declared good. By the mid-1990s, somewhat unpredictably, the SW-CMM's five-level worldview became the dominant gestalt in software engineering process improvement—particularly in U.S. defense-related work.

At this point, however, as in nearly all cases of successful approaches, folks began to think that the elegant ideas represented in the SW-CMM could be applied to their particular problem: "Hey, if process could bring predictability to this most ephemeral activity, it could surely be applied to all sorts of thought-related tasks. Let's build a CMM for [fill in the blank]!"[†] The result of this technology transition was an explosion of models—some good, some bad—that purported to help guide process improvement in any number of areas. To counter this unruly multiplication of models, the U.S. Defense Department enlisted the Software Engineering Institute at Carnegie Mellon University, the developer of the SW-CMM, to lead a group of engineers and develop a new model that incorporated systems, software, and product engineering into a common and extensible framework. And so was born CMMI (Capability Maturity Model Integration), a second generation of CMMs that officially extended process improvement beyond the software development domain.

There are other process improvement approaches in addition to CMM-based initiatives. Total Quality Management, Lean Aerospace Initiative, Six Sigma, and Business Process Reengineering are all essentially process-based approaches. The number of methods begs the question "Why should businesses be interested in process?"

[†] We have been known to refer to these as YAMMs (Yet Another Maturity Model). If you studied computer science in the '70s, you'll appreciate the allusion. If you didn't, don't worry—you're probably just as well off not knowing. . . .

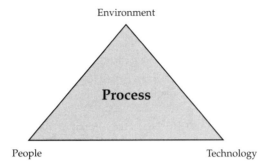

Figure 1-1: *A holistic view of the role of process*

1.2 The role of processes in business

It's clear that good processes are not the only thing you need to succeed, but many people, including us, assert that they are a necessary element for that success. Figure 1-1 illustrates our view of the role of process engineering within an organization.[†]

The triangle in Figure 1-1 characterizes the primary components of business performance. The three points of the triangle are all in flux and must be synchronized if your organization is to operate successfully:

- **People** bring changing skills and motivations to the work.
- **Technology** (tools and techniques that make work more efficient and effective) evolves constantly.
- The **Environment** within which the business operates changes as markets, competition, and products adjust to economic influences and the general zeitgeist.

How do you go about balancing these three elements? More important, how do you mitigate problems in one or more of them? That's where process engineering comes in. Well-thought-out and appropriate processes can create synergy among these elements and help push the organization forward.

[†] Garcia, Suzanne. "Standardization as an Adoption Enabler for Project Management Practice." In *IEEE Software*, vol. 22, no. 5 (Sept./Oct. 2005), pp. 22–29.

They can also compensate when one or more of them is out of synch with the others. Here are a couple of examples:

- An aerospace corporation has very sophisticated **technology** in its cost-estimation system. Unfortunately, the skilled **people** required to take advantage of its sophistication are not available due to retirement, attrition, or assignment elsewhere caused by the business **environment.** Having inexperienced people run the system can waste a lot of money and effort, as well as produce questionable results. If **processes** for using the capability are developed that are geared toward the available skill level, some of the benefit of the technology can be realized.

- A commercial software integrator finds its **environment** in chaos because several of its major customers have changed their information technology infrastructures. At the same time, other customers are increasing their demands for more functionality from their existing technology. The need to shift **people** around increases, as the demands change between maintaining legacy systems and configuring new software and hardware. Issues can arise around competency with both new **technology** and old tools, and around team performance. Appropriate **processes** that are technology neutral can cushion the impact, particularly if they are common across all customers. As team members migrate on short notice and teams are formed and dissolved, common processes speed team startup and new-member assimilation by answering basic questions about what tasks are required and how the team should execute them.

Effective processes can also provide buffers between difficult elements in the normal business environment and the people and technologies of the organization. For example, in a business environment with very complex contracting requirements, well-defined processes can guide employees who rarely use those contracting procedures.

Note that in the above discussion, we have emphasized "appropriate, well-thought-out" processes. Failing to meet those two criteria often gets organizations in trouble, and that trouble relates to the triangle as well. Processes need to be appropriate for the environment, people, and technologies being used. They should be created carefully with the participation of process performers so as to share ownership and take advantage of any synergies that may exist.

Meeting these criteria makes establishing one process for all occasions unlikely. Although some level of standardization is helpful, the key is discovering what *set* of standard processes will accommodate the range of environments you encounter. We know of very few organizations that deal with a single environment in terms of how their processes are performed.

So good, flexible, well-engineered processes compensate and integrate the varying influences of people, technology, and environment on the conduct of business in a rapidly changing world. Good practices may not guarantee success, but bad processes can easily result in poor performance and failure.

Chapter 2

Why Process Improvement Helps

We've described process as one way of getting a handle on activities that deal with creative thought, and as the mediator among your enterprise's people, technology, and environment. It helps us order our thinking by defining common activities and artifacts. Process is also a means to capture and transfer the knowledge we gain in developing a particular product or service.

We learn about a process nearly every time we execute it. By taking time and effort, we can apply our knowledge to make the process better. Innovative ways to improve the productivity or predictability of a process may come to mind. Processes need to fit the task, so as the specific circumstances we are dealing with change, our processes need to respond. There are also times when we need to create new processes. We'll almost never make them exactly right the first time.

All this leads us to the idea of improving processes. We want our processes to be the perfect balance of discipline and agility[†] so they enable us to create

---

[†] *Discipline* generally is defined as compliance or strong guidance. *Agility* is the flexibility to take advantage of or react quickly to limit the impact of unforeseen changes. You can find more about this in *Balancing Agility and Discipline*, by Barry Boehm and Richard Turner (Boston: Addison-Wesley, 2004).

the most value with the least cost. This is rarely accomplished in a "one step to greatness" paradigm. The usual method is a stepwise refinement of the process, although in some cases, radical changes can require radically different processes.

This section addresses the "whys," and some of the high-level "hows," of process improvement. Each section deals with one of our fundamental tenets of process improvement. These tenets are reflected in various ways throughout the rest of the book.

2.1 Process improvement is about learning

Processes are a means of capturing knowledge and passing it on to others. Knowledge can be explicit and written or tacit and observed. Process improvement can be thought of as identifying and deploying knowledge over larger and larger groups. Right now, some individuals within your organization know ways of doing their jobs that are more effective than the ways their peers use. This individual knowledge is an asset that is not intentionally or explicitly available to others. If the individual writes up guidance that can be shared, the knowledge becomes available to others, but there is no real organizational intention of using it. Process improvement helps incorporate that intention into the way the organization works.

Most process improvement models have levels or stages that can be used as targets for improvement initiatives. From a learning perspective, all the models describe the scope of knowledge deployment within an organization. The following stages of learning map well to maturity levels for any CMM:

- *Individual learning.* Knowledge resides within individuals and may be informally shared with others in an ad hoc fashion.
- *Group learning.* Knowledge is explicitly collected and shared within groups such as teams or projects, supporting better performance within the group.
- *Organizational learning.* Group-based knowledge is collected and standardized, and mechanisms exist that encourage its use across related groups.
- *Quantitative learning.* The organizational knowledge transfer and use are measured, and decisions are made based on empirical information in addition to qualitative information. Shared knowledge is deep and wide enough to determine where quantitative methods make sense within the organization.

- *Strategic learning.* Knowledge collection, transfer, and use are rapid across the organization; strong, deep, and wide channels for applying innovation are available, and their use is intrinsic in the organization's behavior.

The first four stages generally focus on improving the operational effectiveness of the organization. Operations, as used here, are not limited to managing the manufacturing plant's resources or maintaining the software; we mean improving the effectiveness of the day-to-day operations of whatever it is you're doing. For many software organizations, improving operational effectiveness is mostly about improving the processes they use in software product development. The fifth stage is a bit different. It's about *using* what you know about your operational capabilities to respond flexibly and effectively to changes in your environment: market changes, organizational changes, key personnel changes, and so on. One of the reasons we believe maturity models are so popular is that most individuals and groups recognize the learning stages reflected here as reasonable and appropriate. Another reason is that maturity models explicitly contain mechanisms for encouraging the improvement of the targeted processes with relation to this learning viewpoint.

2.2 Process improvement should be driven by business value

Your business status, objectives, and goals are major inputs into making process improvement work for you. To be most effective, you need to identify and rank the business processes that are most critical to achieving your goals.

Sometimes, this kind of analysis and reflection helps identify key targets for improvement. If your company is essentially a consulting firm, for example, the most critical processes might be those associated with responding to customers, identifying new clients, or generating proposals. On the other hand, if you build products, processes for handling quality control or meeting critical delivery timelines might warrant investigation. If your goals involve growth, looking at how your existing way of doing business will scale up may identify processes that need to be changed radically to meet the projected expansion of staff and business.

One of the reasons the Capability Maturity Models have been so widely applied is that they can help focus you on the things that have historically been critical success factors in their particular domain. Other aids in identifying critical factors include domain competency models like the *Project Management Body of Knowledge Guide*[1] and domain standards such as those published by industry organizations like the IEEE (Institute of Electrical and Electronics Engineers) and SAE (Society of Automotive Engineers), as well as international standards bodies like ISO (International Organization for Standardization).

Regardless of how you do the analysis, the key issue is to target processes where improvement seems most likely to yield a strong return on investment. Be careful, however, not to miss the interaction of processes. Often, there are enabling processes that support the processes you want to improve. If your version control for products is out of whack, changing your customer delivery system may result only in delivering the wrong product faster—not necessarily an improvement in business value. Or improving the performance of your order management system could overload your order processing or shipping processes and lead to delays rather than shorter schedules. This interaction is a key reason planning and executing process improvement efforts is more complex than it may seem.

2.3 Process improvement can be valuable for organizations of all sizes

Often, small businesses and organizations assert that process improvement works only for the big guys—that you have to have large overhead resources and dedicated process people to be effective. Fortunately, this is often not the case at all. We agree that the traditional approaches to process improvement (a la CMMs) have tended toward larger efforts—but if you think about it, they evolved through application within larger projects (such as the aerospace world of satellites, shuttles, and ground stations) and very naturally reflected that environment. Conway's law concerning the structure of a developed system reflecting the organizational structure of its developers can come into play for human systems, too.[2] And we believe it has.

Consider for a moment the evolution of agile software development methods. They have been harangued for being unscalable, but because they were a product of small internal IT development projects, they reflect the ways things were accomplished in those shops. Despite their heritage, however, they are now being selectively applied in very large settings with promising, if varied, success. The success usually depends on how creative the folks are who apply them. In a similar way, creative and energetic people (like us) have found ways to apply process improvement in such a way that consideration is given to the size of your organization, making process improvement an asset to enterprises of any size.

Almost every technique or approach we describe in this book can be applied to small organizations. Additional information on process improvement in smaller settings is available in the CMMI adoption pages of the Software Engineering Institute (SEI) Web site (www.sei.cmu.edu/cmmi/adoption/acss).

2.4 You have choices in your improvement approach

One thing that makes doing process improvement challenging is that there are many ways to approach it. These approaches usually are called process improvement life cycles, and almost all of them have been successful somewhere. The question is, which approach will be most successful for you?

In the following sections, we *very* briefly describe a few of these life cycles. These are the ones we've worked with or seen working successfully in multiple contexts. Understand that this is a personal, selective, and noninclusive list; you can choose among dozens of life cycles, and you have many sources for learning about how to use each one. If you look into the ones we identify and decide that none of them fits your situation, you will find resources in Chapter 15 that offer even more choices.

The last life cycle in this section, DLI, is a bit different from the others and is our synthesis of what we've seen work from other life cycles. It is elaborated more fully in Part 2.

2.4.1 IDEAL

The IDEAL model is a process improvement life cycle developed by the SEI to provide organizations with a high-level set of activities that they can follow to execute an improvement program. It is a variation on a basic Plan-Do-Check-Act (PDCA) cycle, also known as a Shewhart cycle.[3] Each of the letters in *IDEAL* stands for one phase of the life cycle:

I=Initiation. The fundamental sponsorship and business reasons for engaging in improvement are established within the organization, and resources are prepared to begin the improvement effort.

D=Diagnosis. The organization attempts to understand the gaps between its intended process state and its current processes. This gap analysis should be based on the process needs of the organization, which in turn are based on the organization's business goals.

E=Establishment. The infrastructure for the process improvement effort is set up, and the resources for engaging in effective process improvement activities are established.

A=Action. The process improvement teams engage in activities to make improvements in the processes that were identified in the Diagnosis phase as being necessary to improve the organization.

L=Learning or Leveraging. The organization looks across the improvement activities that have taken place and learns from what went well and what didn't go well so as to improve its approach to the next cycle of improvement.

Figure 2-1 shows a graphical depiction of the IDEAL cycle. The SEI Web site contains a substantial amount of information on the phases of IDEAL. Start

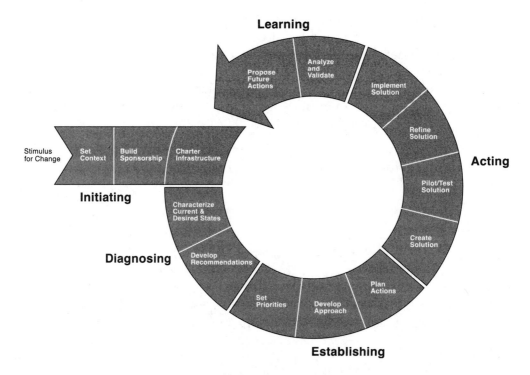

Figure 2-1: *IDEAL cycle*

at www.sei.cmu.edu/ideal to get to free SEI resources related to IDEAL. You will also find presentations related to IDEAL at conferences devoted to systems and software process improvement, such as the Systems and Software Engineering Process Group (SEPG) conference. Chapter 15 lists several annual conferences that may provide useful information for you.

2.4.2 Six Sigma

Jeannine Sivy and Eileen Forrester at the SEI describe Six Sigma as "an approach to business improvement that includes a philosophy, a set of metrics, an improvement framework, and a toolkit of analytical methods. Its philosophy is to improve customer satisfaction by eliminating and preventing defects, resulting in increased profitability. Sigma (Ω) is the Greek symbol used to represent the statistical value known as standard deviation, or the amount of variation in a process. The measure six sigma (6Ω), from which the overall approach derives its name, refers to a measure of process variation (six standard deviations) that translates into an error or defect rate of 3.4 parts per million, or 99.9997 percent defect free. In the Six Sigma approach, defects are defined as anything in a product or service, or any process variation that prevents the needs of the customer from being met."[4]

One of the primary improvement frameworks associated with Six Sigma is DMAIC (Define, Measure, Analyze, Improve, Control), which is illustrated in Figure 2-2.

As you probably guessed, this is another PDCA cycle variant, with more emphasis on the Do-Check part of the cycle.

Some organizations use Six Sigma methods and tools to help implement their process improvement strategy. The SEI technical report *Results of SEI Independent Research and Development Projects and Report on Emerging Technologies and Technology Trends*[5] summarizes a study conducted by the SEI on using Six Sigma to enable successful technology transition. The primary technology under study was CMMI, so you may find some useful ideas in the Six Sigma section of this report.

One thing that makes Six Sigma techniques attractive in conjunction with CMMI-based improvement is that Six Sigma constantly and consistently emphasizes alignment of the improvement tasks/approaches with business goals, so it acts as an amplifier for one of the philosophies of CMMI that is sometimes hard to see in the details of the model.

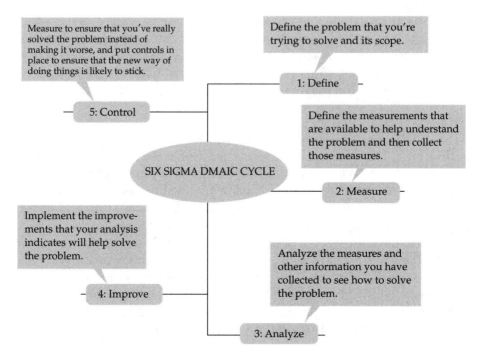

Figure 2-2: *Summary of Six Sigma DMAIC cycle*

2.4.3 QIP

The Quality Improvement Paradigm (QIP) is an improvement approach that has evolved over a period of 25 years of experience with improving software in the NASA Software Engineering Laboratory, a joint effort of the University of Maryland, Computer Sciences Corporation, and NASA Goddard Space Flight Center.[6] Developed by Dr. Victor Basili of the University of Maryland, QIP builds a continually improving organization based upon identifying and assessing against its own evolving goals.[7] QIP, as illustrated in Figure 2-3, is a cyclical process for organizational improvement that focuses practitioners on understanding how quantitative measures *across* projects contribute to larger organizational goals.[8]

QIP is a two-feedback loop process (project and organization loops) that is a variation of the scientific method.[9] It consists of six fundamental steps:

1. Characterize the project and its environment with respect to models and metrics.

2. Set quantifiable goals for successful project performance and improvement.

3. Choose the appropriate process models, supporting methods, and tools for the project.

4. Execute the processes, construct the products, collect and validate the prescribed data, and analyze the data to provide real-time feedback for corrective action.

5. Analyze the data to evaluate current practices, determine problems, record findings, and make recommendations for future project improvements.

6. Package the experience in the form of updated and refined models and other forms of structured knowledge gained from this and previous projects, and save it in an experience base to be reused by future projects.

The QIP uses two tools that are key to its successful implementation: the Goal/Question/Metric (GQM) paradigm and the Experience Factory Organization (EFO). GQM supports QIP by providing a systematic approach for tailoring and integrating goals with models according to the specific needs of the project and organization. The EFO is an organizational structure, separate and distinct from the project, that performs the experience-building activities specified by the QIP in steps 5 and 6.

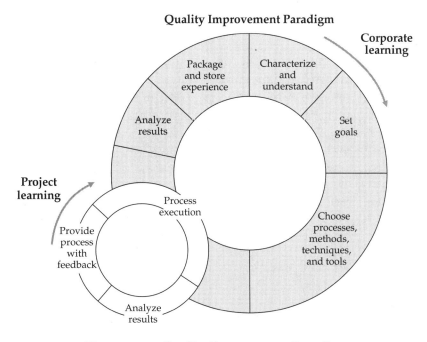

Figure 2-3: *Quality Improvement Paradigm*

QIP prescribes a foundational mechanism within the organization that represents what is expected from a CMMI Maturity Level 5 organization. Level 5 organizations can manipulate process to achieve various product characteristics through the use of a process and an organizational structure to:

- Understand processes and products
- Measure and model the project and the organization
- Define and tailor process and product qualities explicitly
- Understand the relationship between process and product qualities
- Feed back information for project control
- Experiment with methods and techniques
- Evaluate successes and failures
- Learn from experience
- Package and reuse successful experience

Because QIP drives the process improvement efforts through an understanding of the business—product and process problems, business goals, local experiences with methods, and so on—the motivation for the process improvement initiative is the same as the motivation for organizational success.

2.4.4 Agile methods

Surprisingly, agile software development methods—long seen as an anathema to "process mature" organizations—have a lot to offer when it comes to process improvement. Although not specifically aimed at organizational processes, the principles of agile methods provide mechanisms that help meet several typical process improvement goals, particularly at the team or project level. First, their insistence on short cycle times and iteration, if applied to process improvement, fulfills the need to show value early in the process. Second, many methods include a post-iteration analysis or "reflection" on what went well, what didn't, and how the team could do it differently in the future. Because data on the velocity of the work and the productivity of the team is maintained, changes can be evaluated empirically to validate their benefit. Quick application of process changes and feedback mean that "wrong" directions are caught early and useful changes can be propagated quickly.

For summaries of popular agile methods (as well as summaries of plan-driven methods such as CMMI and TSP), *Balancing Agility and Discipline,* by Barry Boehm and Richard Turner, is a good place to start.[10]

2.4.5 DLI

For many organizations, IDEAL is a favored life cycle. It was developed explicitly for supporting model-based process improvement, and it provides more detail than many other life-cycle models, which is useful for many people. We also have encountered people who find the *Initiating* phase of IDEAL to be more than they are ready to invest in. In fact, the question they often ask is "How can I prove to myself and my management that investing in the infrastructure recommended by IDEAL will be worth it?" Our answer to that question is a precursor life cycle to IDEAL that can help you navigate the initial choices you need to make even before you commit to building a process improvement infrastructure. Based on some of the agile principles, DLI (Decision-based Lifecycle for Improvement) takes you through a trial use of the model to see just how it helps solve the problems and meet the goals of your business. In this way, it provides information you need to make a decision as to whether to stop, continue, or redirect your process improvement initiative.

Figure 2-4 illustrates the DLI stages. In Chapter 4 we describe the DLI model in much more detail.

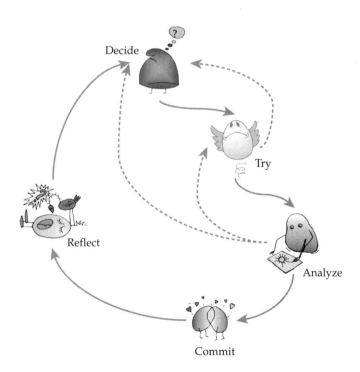

Figure 2-4: *A Decision-based Lifecycle for Improvement*

2.5 You have choices in your reference model

As we mentioned in the introduction to Part I, you can use several models or standards as a reference in designing, implementing, and evaluating your organizational processes. Some are specific to certain domains or businesses, and some are very general. Some are explicit in their guidance, and others are more abstract. All have constituencies that support (and sometimes proselytize) their use.

Although having a reference model to guide you in your improvement effort is not absolutely necessary, in our experience, it usually is a good idea. Using a model:

- Provides a common framework and language to help you communicate across your organization and with other organizations
- Leverages years of experience as to critical success factors for the processes within their scope
- Limits "tunnel vision" by reminding you of the big picture
- Allows you to concentrate on improving more than creating
- Generally is supported by training, consulting, and ancillary literature
- Provides an arbiter for disagreements

In this section, we briefly describe some of the most widely used references. In Chapter 5, we discuss what you need to know to choose the one that best fits your business and operating environment. Like our description of lifecycles, this is a selective, noninclusive list based on our experiences.

2.5.1 No reference model

You can choose to forgo a reference model and still have a successful process improvement initiative. It may be that your particular work environment is unique or is not sufficiently addressed in any of the common reference models. You can readily apply to your particular needs many of the techniques and approaches we discuss throughout the book. Even without a model, however, it usually is good to have some way of disciplining your thought processes. Six Sigma, Total Quality Management, Business Process Reengineering, and the Quality Improvement Paradigm are examples of proven, documented approaches that don't require a reference model.

2.5.2 CMMI

CMMI-DEV is the latest in the evolution of capability maturity models from the Software Engineering Institute (SEI) at Carnegie Mellon University in the United States. SEI is a research organization that receives its core funding from the U.S. Department of Defense and is chartered to improve the performance of the software industry.

At its simplest, CMMI-DEV (CMMI for Product Development) is

- A framework of management, engineering, and support best practices organized into 22 topics called Process Areas
- An approach to improving the capability of any of the 22 Process Areas by incrementally applying a set of Generic Practices that enhance the functioning of an individual process
- Best thought of as a set of "process requirements" that help guide an organization that is defining and implementing processes related to the 22 topics
- *Not* a predefined, implementable, "as is" process definition

CMMI is a terrific product, albeit a bit on the voluminous side and strongly aligned to product development in its initial version. It has rapidly become a popular international improvement framework; as of May 2006, over 50,000 people from all over the world have been through the three-day "Introduction to CMMI" course.[†] Although we use CMMI in many of our examples in this book, we want to stress that it is not the only process improvement paradigm. We discuss others in the next few paragraphs and will discuss CMMI in much more detail in the next chapter and in Part II. If the material on CMMI is intriguing, a good starting place for managers and other "non-process-savvy" people to learn more is *CMMI Distilled,* by Dennis Ahern, Aaron Clouse, and Richard Turner.[11] The full-blown model is available for download from the SEI Web site and in *CMMI: Guidelines for Process Integration and Product Improvement,* 2d ed., by Mary Beth Chrissis, Mike Conrad, and Sandy Shrum.[12]

Organizations can be appraised against CMMI, using a team led by an authorized lead appraiser who can assign capability or maturity ratings. The results can be posted at an SEI-refereed Web site to share with current and

---

[†] To keep up with current adoption statistics, access the SEI's public transition aids site and look for the "CMMI Today" folder that contains the most recent public briefing slides on CMMI: https://bscw.sei.cmu.edu/pub/bscw.cgi/0/395854.

potential customers (not to mention the soon-to-be-envious competition). The SEI administers authorization programs for lead appraisers and Introduction to CMMI instructors. Using authorized instructors and lead appraisers ensures that you are getting authentic SEI services from SEI partners who have gone through appropriate training and mentoring for their role.

2.5.3 ISO 9000 Series

The International Organization for Standardization (ISO, after its name in French) is a nongovernmental, worldwide organization that coordinates the development of international standards for a broad variety of disciplines and domains. ISO 9000 is a series of quality-management and quality-control standards. It has been applied to manufacturing, printing, electronics, steel, computing, legal services, financial services, retailing, aerospace, construction, pharmaceuticals, publishing, telecommunications, health care, hospitality, and dozens of other business sectors and domains.

ISO 9001 establishes a set of requirements (called *normative clauses*) for a quality-management system.[13] Businesses develop their own quality processes that meet these requirements. After the quality system is up and running, several audits are conducted (both internal and external) to make sure all requirements are met. If the system passes the audit by an official Registrar, the organization is certified and registered, and may use this certification in its marketing and advertising. A company doesn't have to complete certification to use 9000 to improve its quality processes, of course, but most companies do identify certification as a goal.

Information about ISO is available at www.iso.org. Although the standards are available only from ISO, a wealth of consulting organizations, auxiliary publications, and conferences support ISO 9000. There is even a book that covers using ISO 9001 (and a few other standards) with CMMI: *Systematic Process Improvement Using ISO 9001:2000 and CMMI,* by Boris Mutafelija and Harvey Stromberg.[14]

2.5.4 ISO 15504/12207/15288

There is also a set of ISO standards related to software and system development that organizations can use to support their process assessment and improvement efforts.

ISO 12207 focuses on software development and management.[15] ISO 15288 focuses on system development and management.[16] ISO 15504 is an assessment and evaluation standard that allows the use of a Process Reference Model (PRM) as the basis of assessment.[17] Either 12207 or 15504 could be used as the PRM for ISO 15504. Other models are also used as the PRM for 15504, usually nationally created standards such as Mexico's MoProSoft.[18] The SEI is working with the ISO 15504 team to achieve PRM status for CMMI.

If you are involved in a marketplace that recognizes these standards, familiarity with them and ability to cite compliance with them could be an advantage for you. In the United States, the source for official ISO standards documents is ANSI (American National Standards Institute). You will find consulting and appraisal resources fairly easily by searching the Internet, but the penetration of these standards across the world marketplace is quite spotty. In some regions, you will find a great deal of support for them; in others, you will have trouble finding the resources you need.

Also, because of the fairly tight controls ISO puts on intellectual-property rights for the standards, you won't find as many books on the market that explain and help you learn about them in comparison with some of your other choices.

2.5.5 ITIL

The Information Technology Infrastructure Library (ITIL) is a collection of documents that addresses the whole range of internal information technology service management and delivery activities.[19] Developed in the United Kingdom, it has gained extensive popularity in business and government, particularly in the traditional IT business processing environment. ITIL truly is a library. There are seven sets of documents, each set addressing a particular facet of IT. The current sets are Service Support, Service Delivery, Planning to Implement Service Management, Information and Communications Technology (ICT) Infrastructure Management, Applications Management, Security Management, and The Business Perspective. The ITIL is managed by the UK Office of Government Commerce (OGC).[20]

ITIL currently does not have an organizational certification or evaluation method. Rather, *individuals* can be certified as to their knowledge and understanding of the library through official examinations at three levels: Foundation, Practitioner, and Manager. These certifications are administered by Examination Institutes regulated by the OGC. More information is available at http://www.itil.co.uk.

2.5.6 COBIT

Control Objectives for Information and related Technology (COBIT) is an IT governance framework and supporting tool set. It supports the establishment of processes to control and govern IT-related activities.[21] COBIT is maintained by the IT Governance Institute (ITGI), a not-for-profit, externally funded research institute that studies how IT policy interacts with and supports business strategy, technical risk, and corporate control. ITGI was established by the Information Systems Audit and Control Association (ISACA), a not-for-profit professional organization that formerly was the EDPA Auditors Foundation, founded in 1969.

COBIT is structured hierarchically. There are four Domains, each divided into Processes, with each Process further divided into Control Objectives. Below the Control Objectives are around 1,600 Control Practices. The Control Objectives are stated in terms of a condition and so are auditable. No specific evaluation method is associated with COBIT, although several auditing methods are suitable. More information about COBIT is available at www.ITGI.org and www.ISACA.org.

2.5.7 "Interoperable" process improvement

As you may guess from the brief survey of selected reference models in the preceding sections, there is a good chance that in your business environment, more than one of the references mentioned (or some that weren't mentioned) will be of interest to you. You may even have to be audited or appraised against more than one of these. You are not alone in facing this challenge. In the same way that many of your software systems now need to interoperate with other systems that were not originally conceived to work with yours, your processes will need to interoperate with more than one reference model or standard. SuZ has started calling this need *interoperable process improvement*, whereas the Systems and Software Consortium refers to it as *multi-compliant frameworks*. Other terms you may hear include *transparent process architecture* and *unified process improvement architecture.*

You have three ways to approach dealing with multiple standard reference models:

- Deal with each individually—that is, map your processes onto ISO 9001 requirements; next, map them onto CMMI; and then map them onto whatever else you're asked to interoperate with.

- Make your internal processes the unifying reference—that is, each of your processes would contain tagging that shows all the different areas of all the standards you are dealing with.
- Make one of the standards you work with the unifying reference—that is, map each of the other standards to the selected standard and then map your processes to that standard as the unifying reference.

We believe that the third choice is the one that holds the most promise long term. Figure 2-5 provides a diagram illustrating what this might look like.[†]

For this approach to work, the unifying reference has to be detailed enough that it covers most of the content in the other standards you use. It also needs to be publicly available so that you can easily map the other standards to it. We favor (huge surprise!) CMMI for this reference. Here are a few reasons we think this approach is fruitful:

- CMMI normative (the content you get audited or appraised against) and informative content is publicly available at detailed levels and covers much of the content in standards commonly referenced.

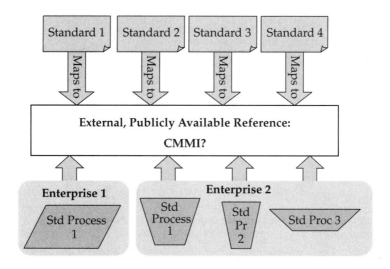

Figure 2-5: *Interoperable process improvement with CMMI as the unifying reference*

[†] Thanks to Pat Kirwan and Urs Andelfinger for the animated discussions that led to clarifying this concept. The initial work on Unified Process Improvement Architecture made it possible to see and coherently discuss the issues around working with multiple standards.

- Public mappings of different standards to CMMI are available from multiple sources, making it possible to review/validate them.

- Because of the different audiences, purposes, and levels of detail of the different standards, you'll never be able to say, "If I do *x* on this standard, it automatically covers *y* on this other one." But being able to say, "If I do *x* on CMMI, I probably should look at how that affects *y* in the related clause of *<standard>*" is still a valuable way to cut down on how much of each standard you have to look at to satisfy yourself that you're progressing toward compliance where it's needed.

- When (not if) changes to one of the standards occurs, you can do an impact analysis via the reference (CMMI), and you can count on others needing to do that too, so there is a high likelihood that you'll be able to find articles, assets on public Web sites, and the like to help you through the change. If the changes don't change the mapping, you still look in the same place in your own process for content related to that standard; if the mappings change, you know that you may have to change the way you implement that element of the standard.

- When (not if) changes to CMMI occur, you can look at the changes implied in your own processes, and also look to see whether those changes alter your mapping to other standards and proceed accordingly.

One critical principle is that your process users should *not* have to understand or use terminology related to all the different standards you're working with. This is the responsibility of the staff working on improvement.

We don't want to duplicate the material you can find in other good sources on this subject. If you will need to deal with multiple standards, take some time to check the current literature; we expect that the approach we describe is only one of many ideas you will see on this subject.

1. Project Management Institute. *A Guide to the Project Management Body of Knowledge (PMBOK® Guide).* 3d ed. (Newton Square, Penn.: Project Management Institute, 2000).

2. Conway, Melvin E. "How Do Committees Invent?" In *Datamation,* April 1968, pp. 28–31.

3. McFeeley, Robert. *IDEAL: A User's Guide for Software Process Improvement.* CMU/SEI-96-HB-001. (Pittsburgh: Carnegie Mellon University, 1996).

4. Bergey, John, Jeannine Sivy, Eileen Forrester, et al. *Results of Independent Research and Development Projects and Report on Emerging Technologies and Technology Trends.* CMU/SEI-2004-TR-018. (Pittsburgh: Carnegie Mellon University, 2004), pp. 33–42.

5. Bergey, John et al., *Results of SEI Independent Research and Development Projects and Report on Emerging Technologies and Technology Trends,* CMU/SEI-2004-TR-018. (Pittsburgh: Carnegie Mellon University, 2004).

6. Basili, V., and S. Green. "Software Process Evolution at the SEL." In *IEEE Software,* July 1994, pp. 58–66.

7. Basili, V. "The Experience Factory and its Relationship to Other Improvement Paradigms." In *Proceedings of the Fourth European Software Engineering Conference (ESEC) in Garmish-Partenkirchen, Germany.* The Proceedings appeared as lecture notes in *Computer Science,* September 1993.

8. Shull F., C. Seaman, and M. Zelkowitz. "Quality Time: Victor R. Basili's Contributions to Software Quality." In *IEEE Software,* January 2006, pp. 16–18.

9. Basili, V., G. Caldiera, F. McGarry, R. Pajerski, G. Page, and S. Waligora. "The Software Engineering Laboratory—An Operational Software Experience Factory," In *Proceedings of the Fourteenth International Conference on Software Engineering,* May 1992.

10. Boehm, Barry, and Richard Turner. *Balancing Agility and Discipline.* (Boston: Addison-Wesley, 2004).

11. Ahern, Dennis, et al. *CMMI Distilled: A Practical Introduction to Integrated Process Improvement.* 2d ed. (Boston: Addison-Wesley, 2004).

12. Chrissis, Mary Beth, et al. *CMMI: Guidelines for Process Integration and Product Improvement.* 2d ed. (Boston: Addison-Wesley, 2006).

13. ISO 9001:2000(E). *Quality Management Systems—Requirements. International Organization for Standardization.* Dec. 15, 2000. 3d ed.

14. Mutafelija, Boris, and Harvey Stromberg. *Systematic Process Improvement Using ISO 9001:2000 and CMMI.* (Boston: Artech House Publishing, 2003).

15. ISO/IEC 12207. 1995 Information Technology—Software Life Cycle Processes, Edition 1.0, International Organization for Standardization/International Electrotechnical Commission, Aug. 1, 1995; ISO/IEC 12207/Amd1:2002 Information technology—Software life cycle processes—Amendment 1. International Organization for Standardization/International Electrotechnical Commission, May 1, 2002; ISO/IEC 12207/Amd1:2002 Information technology—Software life cycle processes—Amendment 1, International Organization for Standardization/International Electrotechnical Commission, May 1, 2002.

16. ISO/IEC 15288:2002. Systems engineering—System life cycle processes. International Organization for Standardization/International Electrotechnical Commission. Nov. 1, 2002.

17. ISO/IEC TR 15504-5:1999. Information technology—Software Process Assessment—Part 5: An assessment model and indicator guidance. International Organization for Standardization/International Electrotechnical Commission (technical report), May 1, 1999.

18. Oktaba, Hanna. *MoProSoft: modelo de procesos para la industria de software,* pp. 251–260. (Cartagena: C.F.C.E., 2003).

19. BS ISO/IEC 20000-1:2005. Information technology. Service management. Specification. British Standard/International Organization for Standardization/International Electrotechnical Commission. ISBN 0-580-40470-6; BS ISO/IEC 20000-2:2005. Information technology. Service management. Code of practice. British Standard/International Organization for Standardization/ International Electrotechnical Commission. ISBN 0-580-41125-7.

20. www.ogc.gov.uk (ITIL managing organization).

21. ISACA. *Control Objectives for Information and Related Technology (COBIT).* 4th ed. (Rolling Meadows, IL: ISACA, 2005). Available at www.isaca.org.

Chapter 3

Why Process Improvement Isn't Trivial

Lest you misinterpret anything we have discussed so far, be aware that process improvement (PI) is not trivial. First, it is an intentional activity—that is, if you start a PI project, it won't run on autopilot; you have to pay attention to it.

Second, many collateral activities have to go on to support a PI initiative. These initiatives do require resources, for example, and unless you personally have control of sufficient resources, you will have to establish and sustain sponsorship for the activity from someone who does. You have to establish some modicum of infrastructure for measurement and deployment of improvements, even in a small organization. That may be a single person paying attention to improvement issues part time, or it may be a group that gets together on a regular basis to prioritize and deal with process issues. Larger organizations will probably need to stand up some sort of official process improvement group, and that means more resources. You will most likely cross some organizational boundaries, so negotiation with other groups may become necessary.

The object, of course, is to minimize the amount of infrastructure and overhead so that your PI initiative can be as lean and effective as you want your business processes to be.

This chapter provides a summary of the primary cost and effort challenges associated with a process improvement effort. In Part IV, we'll give you some guidance on how to deal with these challenges successfully.

3.1 Building and sustaining sponsorship

The challenge of building and sustaining sponsorship is one that every organization faces, but it's one area where the solutions tend to be fairly specific to the context and culture of the particular setting.

The sponsorship we're talking about is the people who have purview over the policies, processes, and resources associated with what you want to improve. Getting those people to agree to sponsor PI actively—through allocating resources, supporting policy changes, and reinforcing the changes made with the improved processes—is the first challenge. The second challenge is keeping them interested and supportive when things get moving.

This is one area where small settings *may* have an advantage, *if* your senior management is supportive of process improvement. If the CEO or CTO favors process improvement, it's usually a very short walk to find the project manager who will make the changes needed to improve a project's practices.

The larger and more diverse the organization (in terms of geography, business sector, customer, or culture), the more of a challenge sustaining sponsorship is likely to be. Usually, to be successful, a process improvement effort requires both the sponsorship of a manager whose span of control encompasses all the parts of the organization affected by the improvement and the sponsorship of the intervening managers in the organizational hierarchy. Some people call this intervening level of sponsorship the "middle-management black hole," because many improvement efforts seem to disappear between the senior manager and the parts of the organization meant to participate in them. In Part 4, we explore some of the particular challenges you may run into and some strategies for dealing with these kinds of sponsorship challenges.

3.2 Managing an appraisal life cycle

Appraising your processes—evaluating the gap between your current processes and the way you want your processes to work—is one of the activities that you must perform on a regular basis if you are to have confidence that you are improving, not just changing. Most organizations find it useful to appraise their processes against external benchmarks of best practices relevant to their business as an objective way to measure their improvement (what we call *reference models* in Chapter 2). CMMI is our personal favorite of several models that are used to help organizations benchmark their processes.

Note that the title of this section is "*Managing* an appraisal life cycle" as opposed to "Conducting appraisals." We don't assume that you will have in-house capability to conduct appraisals when you're getting started. There are different forms of appraisal, some external and some internal. External appraisals are often used to inform supplier decisions or to make marketing claims. Many organizations want to have confidence that the processes of the suppliers they are dealing with are capable of performing to their expectations. External appraisals usually are a fairly expensive activity; that's the first challenge of managing an appraisal life cycle. External appraisals involve hiring external consultants who are qualified appraisers and involving internal staff in both preparing for the appraisal and participating on the appraisal team.

Internal appraisals typically are less expensive and time consuming than external ones, and after you know what you're doing, they can be quite effective. When you're just getting started, however, you're often in the position of *not* knowing what you're doing, in relation either to the model you've chosen to benchmark against or the appraisal approach you're planning to use. This is one of the places where getting external expertise can have a high payoff.

Most organizations employ a mix of external and internal appraisals: external ones when they are ready to or need to "prove" to outsiders how far their improvement has progressed, and internal ones to help them decide what to address next to get the most business value for the organization or to understand how close they are to an external benchmark they need to achieve.

The improvement challenge here is finding and retaining the skills and resources (both external and internal) to plan, perform, and communicate about the appraisals needed for your business context.

3.3 Developing and sustaining process improvement infrastructure

No matter which improvement life cycle or model you choose, you need to accept the fact that a long-term organizational improvement effort will require a sustainable infrastructure of people and other critical resources. This is the capital-investment aspect of improvement. When you're building a manufacturing facility, you accept the fact that you will have to pay for the building, the tooling, the design of the manufacturing line, and the selection and training of the people who will manage the plant before you produce a single item from that line. We're not trying to say that an improvement effort is as big as building a manufacturing plant, but both efforts share the attribute of requiring some level of investment before you can expect to see much benefit, and both require maintenance and sustainment of that infrastructure if you want to continue seeing benefit from their operation.

One difference between the DLI life cycle and some other PI life cycles is that the first three stages (Decide, Try, Analyze) are geared toward getting results without a large infrastructure already in place (at least for the first time through the cycle). This allows you to learn a little bit about the improvement process before committing resources to your PI infrastructure.

Some of the typical infrastructure elements you will need for a long-term effort include a measurement system; a Process Asset Library (PAL) or other knowledge repository; and training materials, some of which you may be able to acquire and some of which you'll probably have to develop internally. We give you guidance on these and other infrastructure elements you may need in Part 4.

3.4 Deploying new and improved processes

The real work of process improvement is about understanding your current processes and making changes in them that will make them work better for you. If you're an engineer, this is akin to improving a product that's been released. You need to understand what needs to change to improve the product (the requirements), and you need to design, implement, and test the changes that will meet the requirements. You do the same thing with processes. If you've ever built or evolved a product, you know that this simple set of steps breaks down into an often amazing number of details that have to be done correctly, at the right time in iterative cycles, to enable everything to integrate in a way that will actually be an improvement.

As shown in Figure 3-1, designing and deploying new or improved processes is like building a product, in that you should, for each iteration

- define requirements for the process. What does this process need to accomplish? Some of these requirements can come from the gaps you find between your processes and an external benchmark, such as CMMI; others come from the business needs of the organization.

- design the process. Usually, you do this through a process-definition exercise, which usually has both a graphical "mapping" type of component and a more text-based component.

- implement the process. This is often discussed in terms of piloting the process—making sure that the first people using the process understand it and are appropriate to use it, and that the right support mechanisms are in place to get feedback on the new process.

- validate the process. The results from the pilot provide feedback on the utility and appropriateness of the process in its first use. Often, you will extend the pilots into other parts of the organization after the feedback from the initial pilot has been incorporated into the process definition and support elements so that the process can be deployed to its target audience. In some cases, you may have to go back to the drawing board for a process redesign.

- deploy the process. Now you can communicate the process to the target audience, making sure that they have the support tools needed to perform it and verifying that your incentives system encourages (or at minimum doesn't discourage!) use of the process.

So if you've built products before, what's the big challenge in developing and deploying new processes? The fundamental difference between product development and process deployment is that process deployment is all about getting *people* in an organizational setting to change their behavior as individuals and groups. The skills that we learn for designing particular products generally are not the same as the ones we need for enabling people

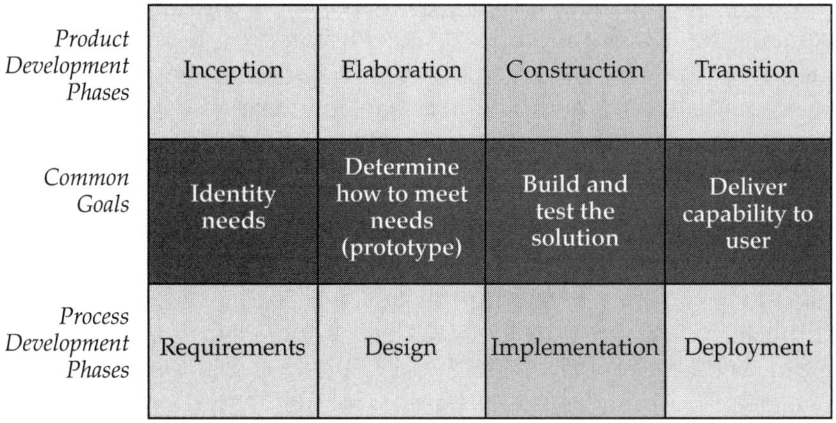

Product Development Phases	Inception	Elaboration	Construction	Transition
Common Goals	Identity needs	Determine how to meet needs (prototype)	Build and test the solution	Deliver capability to user
Process Development Phases	Requirements	Design	Implementation	Deployment

Figure 3-1: *Product versus process development phases*

to change to a new set of behaviors. Most of those skills come from the psychology, sociology, and anthropology disciplines, which typically are not well represented in business and engineering organizations. In later chapters, we expose you to some models and techniques we've found useful in helping people change their behavior.

3.5 Developing and measuring realistic goals

A key area of discussion in any endeavor in which capital (human or otherwise) is invested is concise definition of goals and mechanisms used to measure progress. Unfortunately, measuring something as invasive and complex as process improvement has proved challenging. In large companies, it is almost impossible to separate benefits gained in PI from the variances in personnel, task complexity, customer, domain, or any other number of contributors to project outcome. In smaller environments, however, it may be easier to identify where and how PI contributes to the business.

Our best advice is to develop goals around business values that resonate with all levels of your organization. Goals for improving organizational performance and quality generally are more useful than those associated with strict cost savings. It may take some time to achieve financial returns, and if those returns are not achieved, the PI program could be in jeopardy before it has a chance to provide its real benefits.

Often, goals are set around achieving some organizational maturity level by some certain date. This is a two-edged sword. First, it makes the process improvement the focus rather than the outcome of the processes being performed. It also invites the dangerous level-chasing syndrome. This teaching-to-the-test strategy has resulted in companies spending large amounts of resources to get a grade without actually doing the work to improve their processes. Although these companies may be able to fly a Level X banner, they usually don't perform significantly better than their "less certified" competition.

Our best references for describing the business value of process improvement in the software arena are Don Reifer's book *Making the Software Case*[1] and the SEI technical report *CMMI Impact Study,* by Dennis Goldenson and Diane Gibson.[2] The impact study is part of an ongoing SEI project to measure ROI for CMMI use, so updates will come out periodically.

3.6 Advantages and disadvantages of different-size improvement efforts

The activities just described—building and sustaining sponsorship, managing an appraisal life cycle, developing and sustaining process improvement infrastructure, deploying new and improved processes, and developing and measuring realistic goals—provide a nice way of segmenting the cost, effort, and skills required for an improvement effort. It is worth noting that the scale of cost and effort for these different aspects of improvement is influenced by many factors. One factor that is easy to visualize is the size of the organization that is the focus of the improvement effort. Table 3-1 summarizes differences in the challenge for very small settings and for large settings.

Table 3-1: *Size-Based Advantages and Disadvantages*

	Small	Large
Building/sustaining sponsorship	*Advantage:* It's a short walk from the sponsor's office to the implementing manager! *Disadvantage:* If the senior managers aren't bought in, there is very low probability that the PI will succeed.	*Advantage:* Senior managers often have powerful incentives for complying with their goals. If PI is one of those goals, there will likely be support from them and from their organizations. *Disadvantage:* Typically, many "reinforcing" sponsors are needed between senior managers and the focus of the improvement effort, requiring a great deal of effort to sustain the sponsorship.

(continued)

Table 3-1: *Size-Based Advantages and Disadvantages* (Continued)

	Small	Large
Managing an appraisal life cycle	*Advantage:* A single appraisal event often covers a large percentage of the organization's actual performance. *Disadvantage:* Appraisal-related cost generally is a high percentage of the operating budget.	*Advantage:* Appraisal-related cost generally is a low percentage of the operating budget. *Disadvantage:* A single appraisal event often covers a very small percentage of the organization's actual performance.
Developing and sustaining PI infrastructure (including defining processes)	*Advantage:* A simpler infrastructure (for example, Excel spreadsheets instead of commercial appraisal tools) usually is sufficient. *Disadvantage:* Tool and training costs are a high percentage of the operating budget.	*Advantage:* Tool and training costs usually are a low percentage of the operating budget. *Disadvantage:* Often, multiple infrastructures that percolate from the bottom up are not integrated and cause redundant costs to be incurred. Also, managing a complex infrastructure is a nonlinear increase from a simpler one.

Table 3-1: *Size-Based Advantages and Disadvantages* (Continued)

	Small	Large
Deploying new/improved processes	*Advantage:* There are fewer people to deploy to before you've done a complete deployment. *Disadvantage:* Employee turnover means a higher-percentage cost for training new employees in comparison with larger organizations.	*Advantage:* Resources are likely to be available for creating high-volume deployment mechanisms (such as Web-based training). *Disadvantage:* There are many people whose behavior needs to change, which increases the time and cost of deployment activities in total.
Developing and measuring realistic goals	*Advantage:* Goals are much more "present" in most small organizations, and the impact of process improvement may be easier to see. *Disadvantage:* Reduced resources in smaller organizations may lead to goals that are not significant enough to maintain sponsorship.	*Advantage:* Most large organizations migrate their corporate goals down into their operating organizations, leading to particular clarity for the manager. *Disadvantage:* Goals may be so specific that they do not lend themselves to the broader results of process improvement.

3.7 Project management issues

Many aspects of managing an improvement effort are related most easily to managing a project. Most of the models that people use to improve their processes include some guidance on managing projects. Project management content is prevalent in these models because many organizations exhibit problems in managing projects. Soooooo . . . you need to manage your improvement project, but if you were already good at managing projects, you probably wouldn't need the model to help you. Yup, that's the crux of the issue and one of the reasons project management made it into this chapter.

We won't spend many pages elaborating on basic project management practices and processes, for two reasons:

- There's probably more good literature available on managing projects than there is for almost any other subject covered in this book. (We include some of our favorites in Part 5.)
- Each model that you might choose to work with treats project management differently (though there isn't a huge amount of variation). It makes sense to try out the project management approaches that the model you choose suggests.

What isn't covered in most of the books about project management is the idea of "above the line/below the line" planning. SuZ's friend and colleague Chuck Myers uses this concept to explain one of the important nuances in managing an improvement project.

Above-the-line planning is the planning of the tasks that come out of events such as model gap analyses and from suggested practices from a model. These tasks include things such as "Create an estimation procedure for critical attributes of a project" or "Create the appraisal plan for the year for the organization." Often, these tasks are directly traceable to some element of the model you're using, and their completion indicates the closing of some gap between your organization's practices and the practices of the model.

Below-the-line planning is the planning of the more nebulous tasks that go along with things like building sponsorship and helping people adopt the new practices. Some of the tasks in the below-the-line section of the plan include things like "Perform informal communications about CMMI with new staff members" or "Have meetings with all the project leaders once every two weeks to get an idea of where barriers to adoption are showing up."

Judging completion of these tasks is often the first challenge, because many of them are ongoing and/or recurring. And after you do "complete" one of these tasks, there isn't necessarily something new that's been created or something tangible, such as an event, to mark the completion. Often, completion is marked by something like the absence of complaints about some new procedure or improved timeliness of certain process steps being completed.

Which of these types of tasks is more important to plan and manage? The answer depends on which part of your improvement journey you're on and what kinds of problems you're encountering or are anticipating. In our opinion, the best solution is to plan and manage both. Forgetting to do either one will result in a lack of progress or slower progress than you want or need.

Of the two types, the above-the-line tasks are the easier to plan and manage, because they have the more tangible, visible outcomes. But trying to manage *only* above-the-line tasks rarely works. Also, most of the visible schedule slips that occur when you don't get explicit with below-the-line tasks can be attributed to lack of planning and lack of visibility of related below-the-line tasks.

3.8 Common pitfalls for PI initiatives

Over the years, we have discovered various PI initiative pitfalls—generally by falling into them ourselves or by pulling others out. In this section, we list the ones we've seen most often, in the hope that foreknowledge can help you avoid most of them. Most of the techniques we present in the rest of the book address one or more of these pitfalls either directly or indirectly. Although most of the pitfalls aren't deadly, they certainly can raise your costs, lengthen your schedule, and increase your risk, as well as possibly damage your professional reputation.

Common pitfalls we've seen are

- Trying to do too much too fast
- Not understanding what it takes for people to be willing and able to adopt new practices
- Lack of understanding about how to deal with culture change
- Lack of objectivity in initial gap analysis (common when a self-taught group tries to perform a model-based gap analysis)
- Underestimating how long or how much it takes to perform the tasks related to a process improvement project

- Becoming too inwardly focused and forgetting that the ultimate goal is to improve your product and performance for your customers.
- Having no baseline data to compare progress against
- Setting goals that are not measurable (remember that *measurable* can include a binary yes/no)
- Setting goals that are in no way achievable based on the organization's current state
- Measuring things that will lead to a different result from the desired behavior
- Ignoring the history of previous change attempts within the organization
- Endorsement by senior management, but no active commitment or engagement

3.9 Summary of Part I

In this first part of our journey, we have presented some basic information about process improvement in general and about what we see as the primary challenges that any organization faces as it approaches a serious process improvement effort. We've also provided some ideas about how some of the challenges of process improvement may play out differently in organizations of different sizes. If you're ready to move forward, Part II will help you understand some of the many choices you have available to you at the start of your process improvement effort.

---

1. Reifer, Donald J. *Making the Software Business Case: Improvement by the Numbers.* (Boston: Addison-Wesley, 2002).

2. Goldenson, Dennis, and Diane Gibson. *Demonstrating the Impact and Benefits of CMMI: An Update and Preliminary Results.* CMU/SEI-2003-SR-00. (Pittsburgh: Carnegie Mellon University, 2003).

Illustration from *The Travels of Marco Polo*
by Witold Gordon (1885–1968)

Part II

Mapping the Route

*In preparing for battle I have always found that plans are useless,
but planning is indispensable.*
Dwight D. Eisenhower (1890–1969)

A man who does not plan long ahead will find trouble right at his door.
Confucius

*It is not the brains that matter most, but that which guides
them—the character, the heart, generous qualities, progressive ideas.*
Fyodor Dostoyevsky (1821–1881), *Russian novelist*

*The shortest route is not the most direct one, but rather the one where the most
favorable winds swell our sails: that is the lesson that seafarers teach.*
Friedrich Nietzsche (1844–1900)

You've scouted out the territory and have decided it is worthwhile to take this journey—that is, the benefits outweigh the costs, and the risks are manageable. But now what? Do you just plunge ahead into the bush without preparation? Do you know what to take along? Where do you start? For that matter, where are you headed? Even the most experienced adventurer takes time to plan, and so should you.

In this part of the book, we take a practical look at the basics of process improvement. We identify and describe how to use our favorite guidance: CMMI. We discuss the tasks you'll need to perform along your journey, and even provide a highly refined and specially drawn process improvement map: a life cycle that we feel works well in small organizations (or even for the big guys) before they are ready to apply scarce resources to building an improvement infrastructure.

We understand that no two organizations or projects are just alike, so nearly everyone will take a different path. It is our belief, however, that the path you plan early may not turn out to be the right one. Rather than plow through the obstacles, it is better to be more agile, react to the surroundings, and set a new course. In fact, when there isn't enough information to plan very far in advance, you probably will have to try a few directions and see which ones seem to meet your needs best. That's why our DLI life cycle is a bit different from some of the more traditional approaches.

So step up, grab the map and your calipers, and let's begin charting your course to process improvement rewards.

Chapter 4

CMMI As Your Guide

Because the title of this tome is *CMMI Survival Guide,* it is obvious that we believe CMMI is an important and useful tool for process improvement. Putting its name recognition and support infrastructure aside, it is the most flexible and most widely useful of all the improvement models we've worked with. In this chapter, we discuss some of the characteristics of CMMI that lead us to this opinion. If you've already chosen a model other than CMMI, you can skip this chapter.

4.1 Why CMMI?

To begin, we provide a defense of our preference for CMMI (other than Rich's having been one of the authors). Essentially, we have confidence in CMMI's historical foundations and are satisfied that its scope meets the needs of many, if not most, organizations.

4.1.1 Pedigree

CMMI is the latest in a line of development-oriented models. It draws on the initial work that led to the CMM for Software, which goes back to at least 1985, but also includes ideas from several other sources. It was developed by a team of more than 200 authors, reviewers, and analysts over a period of 2 years. Mark Schaeffer in the U.S. Office of the Secretary of Defense began the CMMI project as a response to the growing concern about the proliferation of models being used within the defense community. He chartered SEI and a team from industry, government, and academia to bring as wide a perspective as possible to the development of an integrated, extensible process improvement framework. Drafts and versions were put out for review to the entire process improvement community, and thousands of comments were received, considered, and processed.

The CMMI project had both initial and longer-term objectives. The initial objective (which was achieved in 2000 with the release of version 1.0 of the CMMI-SE/SW and CMMI-SE/SW/IPPD models) was to integrate three specific process improvement models: software, systems engineering, and integrated process and product development.[†]

The longer-term objective was to lay a foundation for the potential future addition of other disciplines (such as acquisition and services) into CMMI. With the release of version 1.2 of CMMI-DEV (CMMI for Product Development, which encompasses all the content of the former CMMI-SE/SW/IPPD/SS), and the constellations for acquisition and services that will follow soon, these objectives are on their way to fulfillment as well.

CMMI is not a de jure standard (one that is released by an acknowledged national or international standards organization) in the same sense as ANSI/ISO standards. The level of adoption it has achieved, however, has put it in the category of a de facto standard (one that is generally accepted and used even though it is not released by an official national or international standards organization).

4.1.2 Process coverage

Figure 4-1, used as part of CMMI introductory training, provides an idea of the scope of the topics covered by CMMI-DEV in terms of the aspects of an organization's work.[1]

The current configuration of CMMI primarily focuses on product development as "the work" of the organization, so people trying to use it to improve

---

[†] For version 1.1 of CMMI, the designation *CMMI-SE/SW* stands for the CMMI model that contains the disciplines of systems engineering and software, whereas the designation *CMMI-SE/SW/IPPD* stands for the model that adds to it the materials for integrated process and product development.

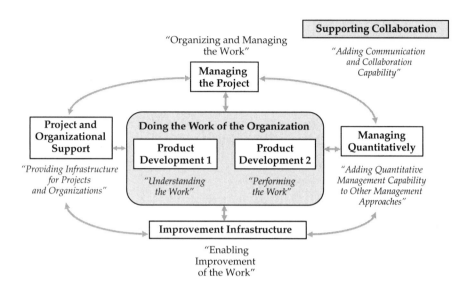

Figure 4-1: *The work areas of an organization supported by CMMI*

their financial accounting practices probably would find interpretation to be challenging. Work is going on at the SEI to incorporate other aspects of organizational work into the CMMI framework, however. Right now, a Services constellation (the term being used for the clustering of model elements related to a particular focus) and an Acquisition constellation are being designed, in addition to the existing Product Development constellation.

Regardless of the constellation, you can see from Figure 4-1 that the CMMI perspective is that "doing the work" is only one part of what goes on in an organization. For the organization to be successful doing the work, the other elements shown in the diagram also need to function appropriately. The model's practices are meant to provide useful guidance for performing, supporting, managing, and improving the work being done in the organization.

4.2 CMMI primer

The CMMI Product Suite contains an enormous amount of information and guidance to help an organization improve its processes. But how does this information help? To answer this question, we start by noting that essentially two kinds of materials are contained in the CMMI models:

1. Materials to help you improve and evaluate the content of your processes—information that is essential to your technical, support, and managerial activities.
2. Materials to help you improve process performance—information that is used to increase the capability of your organization's activities.

We start with a brief look at each of these types. As we discuss the materials, you can refer to Table 4-1 for a list of Process Areas arranged by process category.

Table 4-1: *CMMI-DEV Process Areas*

Process Area	Purpose
Engineering	
Product Integration (PI)	Assemble the product from the product components; ensure that the product, as integrated, functions properly; and deliver the product.
Requirements Development (RD)	Produce and analyze customer, product, and product-component requirements.
Requirements Management (REQM)	Manage the requirements of the project's products and product components and identify inconsistencies between those requirements and the project's plans and work products.
Technical Solution (TS)	Design, develop, and implement solutions to requirements. Solutions, designs, and implementations encompass products, product components, and product-related life-cycle processes either singly or in combination, as appropriate.
Validation (VAL)	Demonstrate that a product or product component fulfills its intended use when placed in its intended environment.
Verification (VER)	Ensure that selected work products meet their specified requirements.

Table 4-1: *CMMI-DEV Process Areas* (Continued)

Process Area	Purpose
Process Management	
Organizational Innovation and Deployment (OID)	Select and deploy incremental and innovative improvements that measurably improve the organization's processes and technologies. The improvements support the organization's quality and process-performance objectives as derived from the organization's business objectives.
Organizational Process Definition (OPD)	Establish and maintain a usable set of organizational process assets and work environment standards.
Organizational Process Focus (OPF)	Plan and implement organizational process improvement based on a thorough understanding of the current strengths and weaknesses of the organization's processes and process assets.
Organizational Process Performance (OPP)	Establish and maintain a quantitative understanding of the performance of the organization's set of standard processes in support of quality and process-performance objectives, and provide the process performance data, baselines, and models to quantitatively manage the organization's projects
Organizational Training (OT)	Develop the skills and knowledge of people so they can perform their roles effectively and efficiently.
Project Management	
Integrated Project Management (IPM)	Establish and manage the project and the involvement of the relevant stakeholders according to an integrated and defined process that is tailored from the organization's set of standard processes.

(continued)

Table 4-1: *CMMI-DEV Process Areas* (Continued)

Process Area	Purpose
Project Monitoring and Control (PMC)	Provide an understanding of the project's progress so that appropriate corrective actions can be taken when the project's performance deviates significantly from the plan.
Project Planning (PP)	Establish and maintain plans that define project activities.
Quantitative Project Management (QPM)	Quantitatively manage the project's defined process to achieve the project's established quality and process-performance objectives.
Risk Management (RSKM)	Identify potential problems before they occur so that risk-handling activities can be planned and invoked as needed across the life of the product or project to mitigate adverse impacts on achieving objectives.
Supplier Agreement Management (SAM)	Manage the acquisition of products from suppliers.
Support	
Causal Analysis and Resolution (CAR)	Identify causes of defects and other problems, and take action to prevent them from occurring in the future.
Configuration Management (CM)	Establish and maintain the integrity of work products using configuration identification, configuration control, configuration status accounting, and configuration audits.
Decision Analysis and Resolution (DAR)	Analyze possible decisions using a formal evaluation process that evaluates identified alternatives against established criteria.
Measurement and Analysis (MA)	Develop and sustain a measurement capability that is used to support management information needs.

Table 4-1: *CMMI-DEV Process Areas* (Continued)

Process Area	Purpose
Process and Product Quality Assurance (PPQA)	Provide staff and management with objective insight into processes and associated work products.

4.2.1 Process content

CMMI provides guidance for your managerial processes. For example, CMMI recommends establishing and maintaining a plan for managing your work, and ensuring that everyone involved is committed to performing and supporting the plan. That certainly seems reasonable. And when you plan, you should establish exactly how you develop and maintain cost, schedule, and product estimates. If you ever want or need to justify your estimate to a customer, you'll find this information invaluable. When you do the work that you plan, you compare the performance and progress with the plan and take corrective actions if you find actual and planned results out of sync. CMMI provides information on managing project risk, working with suppliers, and creating and managing teams as well.

CMMI guidance on technical matters includes expectations for the basic activities in developing, elaborating, and managing requirements, as well as developing and implementing technical solutions that meet those requirements. The guidance reminds you that integrating product components depends on good interface information, and needs to be planned and verified. In today's world, integration is one of the issues cited most often in project failure. CMMI recommends that the products and services you develop be consistent with the requirements agreed to, and that they satisfy the customer's actual needs in its environment through verification and validation practices. If you verify only that the product works in *your* environment, what happens if your environment is different from your customer's? (Nothing good, we assure you!)

Support processes for technical and managerial activities are also addressed within the model. CMMI recommends that you manage the versions and configurations of your intermediate work products, as well as end products and services. That could come in handy if you have a hard-disk crash on your favorite software development machine. You should have methods of ensuring that the processes you have defined are being followed and that the products you are developing meet the quality specifications you have established. If you didn't think that these processes were important to the success of your project, why would you have bothered to ask people to follow them?

Measurement is another common activity CMMI addresses. You need to decide what information is important to you in making decisions. Then you need to establish ways to measure and track that information. It will greatly raise the probability of obtaining the data if you ensure that the information is also useful to the practitioners who supply it. If the information isn't useful to the collectors, the quality of the data will never be what you expect or need, because people usually only collect data that they understand and see a use for.

CMMI draws on hundreds of years of experience when it recommends planning ways to formally resolve issues early in the project; you're not caught having to improvise when an important conflict arises. CMMI then provides guidance on figuring out the root cause of serious problems with your products or key processes.

One characteristic often missed by newcomers to CMMI is that the PAs generally do not line up one-for-one with your processes. So don't think you have to define a process for each PA. Your processes should be based on how you do business. CMMI provides a checklist of related critical success factors that you can compare to your process implementation to identify gaps.

4.2.2 Improving the capability of your processes

Now let's look at improving the processes that you've established. The improvement information in CMMI models includes suggesting the creation of a viable, improvable process infrastructure. To build this infrastructure, CMMI includes ways to get your organization to focus more on defining and following its processes. Through training and standardization, you can make sure that everyone knows their roles and how to execute them in the process. By following CMMI practices, you learn to use the measurement data you collect effectively to improve your process performance, innovate when processes need to evolve, and ensure your ability to meet changing needs.

Processes need to be planned just like projects, and it helps if the organization has given some weight and validity to this activity through policy. CMMI recommends that you make sure that resources are available for trained, empowered people to perform the process. Those with an interest in the outcomes of a particular process need to be identified and involved. Work products and the process documentation should be controlled, and the progress against the plan for performing that process should be tracked as well. Someone should be responsible for objectively evaluating that the process is being followed, and management should be briefed periodically on the process performance.

Processes become more capable when there is enough information about project performance that they can be standardized across the organization and their performance can be monitored against historical data. This way, you can detect variation in performance early enough to address it less expensively. Ultimately, the process should be improving continuously through identifying the root causes of variability and innovative ways to fulfill its objectives. Generic Practices are the model construct used to communicate this improvement within a process. Generic Practices are arranged into a set of Generic Goals that essentially define capability and maturity levels.

If this seems a bit confusing, you are not alone. We recommend *CMMI Distilled*[2] for a more complete (and probably more understandable) discussion of this topic.

4.3 Some choices to think about in using CMMI

If you've decided that CMMI is the model you should (or must) use, there are some decisions about CMMI you will have to make before you dive into your process improvement effort. While many of these things are covered in other books about the model, we want to highlight a few that we feel are key.

This section focuses on several decisions we have particular opinions about. Our choices may be different from other authors' choices, but we believe that describing them will be useful to you. These choices revolve around:

- Which representation to use (there are two)
- How rigorously you want or need to adopt the model
- At what point you want to introduce Generic Practices, one of the elements of the model

4.3.1 The staged/continuous choice

You will hear people advocate (sometimes passionately) for one or the other of two representations that are expressed in CMMI version 1.2. One choice is the *staged representation;* the other is the *continuous representation.* In some ways, this is more of an *appraisal* choice than an *implementation* choice because the model content is almost the same in each representation, and the place where you see the results of using one representation over the other most clearly is in appraisal results.

So if you are appraised against the staged representation, your result would be a Maturity Level rating, which could range from 1 to 5, and a set of findings and recommendations that provide more detail on where you have gaps between your Maturity Level and the next one above you. A Maturity Level is a predetermined cluster of related Process Areas that meet a specified set of goals (some specific and some generic) for that Maturity Level. Each higher Maturity Level subsumes the one(s) below it. So Maturity Level 3 includes all the goals and Process Areas associated with both Maturity Level 3 and Maturity Level 2. (There are no Process Areas or goals at Maturity Level 1.)

If you are appraised against the continuous representation, your result would be a profile chart of all the Process Areas within your improvement scope, showing the Capability Level (from 0 to 5) for each Process Area that was rated. You also would get a set of findings and recommendations that provide more detail on the gaps within each Process Area from your current Capability Level to the ones above you. Figure 4-2 shows an example Capability Level profile.

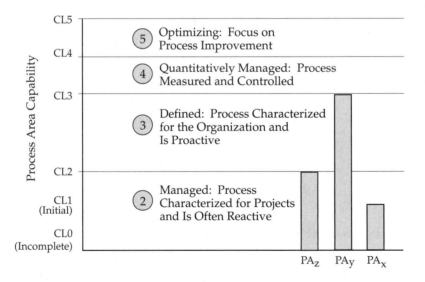

Figure 4-2: *Notional CMMI Capability Profile*

Even though this is primarily an appraisal choice, it can have implications for your implementation, depending on how you approach it. If you choose the staged representation as the one you work with primarily, assuming that you start your improvement at Maturity Level 1 (the default level, where anyone who hasn't been appraised at a higher Maturity Level is assumed to be working), you would have a predetermined set of six Process Areas, mostly covering topics related to project management and support, that you would be expected to work on. You would be trying to meet the Specific Goals of each Process Area, and you would also be trying to meet the Capability Level 2 Generic Goal for each of the Process Areas.

If you choose to work primarily with the continuous representation, you would choose a set of Process Areas you want to work with initially. That set could be six, or one, or three, or ten. (Most organizations start with fewer rather than more.) You would establish which Capability Level Generic Goal you want to achieve for each one of these Process Areas, depending on some inherent dependencies in the model, as well as on your improvement goals and how they translate into Capability Levels. You could represent your set of Process Areas and your desired Capability Level for them in a profile, such as the example shown in Figure 4-3.

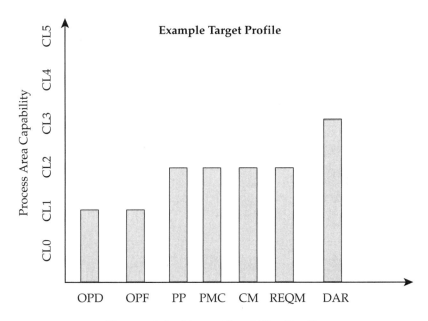

Figure 4-3: *Target Capability Profile*

It may not be obvious at first, but you can work with the two representations together, should you choose to do so. The way most organizations do this is to establish a baseline of their capability, using the continuous representation. This gives them a fair amount of detail on their strengths and weaknesses in different areas of the model. It especially helps them see something that is not apparent in a staged appraisal of a lower-maturity organization. In a staged appraisal, any Process Area that doesn't meet the goals for Capability Level 2 is automatically assigned to Maturity Level 1, with no further elaboration of its rating. In the continuous representation, a Specific Goal for Capability Level 1 drives you to implement the Specific Practices for each PA. If you meet those specific goals, that PA is at Capability Level 1, so you know that you're at least performing the expected practices of the PA in a basic fashion. If you do *not* meet the Specific Goals for a PA, that PA is rated as Capability Level 0—called the Incomplete Level, for obvious reasons! (Rich recommends referring to this level as "not yet Level 1," because no one likes to be a zero!) So the profile for a continuous appraisal gives you more rating detail than a staged appraisal.

That detail is really helpful for the team that is implementing CMMI. More than a dozen years of experience with these kinds of models, however, shows us that many senior executives (not to mention marketing departments) prefer the shorter expression of capability expressed by a Maturity Level, and for good reason. It's much easier to say, "Our widget organization achieved a Maturity Level 3 rating in our last appraisal" than to say, "Our widget organization is Capability Level 3 in the following Process Areas: Requirements Management, Requirements Development, Project Planning, Project Monitoring and Control, Product and Process Quality Assurance, Configuration Management, Measurement and Analysis, Organization Process Definition, Organization Process Focus, Risk Management, Decision Analysis and Resolution, Organization Training, Integrated Project Management, Technical Solution, Product Integration, Verification, and (have you taken a breath yet?) Validation." The first of these statements actually expresses the same content as the second, but in a much more concise way. And anyone who understands even the basics of the model will understand.

So when you complete an appraisal, if your Capability Profile is suspiciously close to that of a Maturity Level, communicating your achievement with a Maturity Level makes a great deal of sense. CMMI contains an explicit concept called *equivalent staging* that allows you to create a series of Capability Level profiles that are equivalent to each of the Maturity Levels represented in the staged representation, so this is completely feasible. While you're on your way to achieving one of those equivalent Maturity Levels, the Capability

Profile provided by the continuous representations allows your process improvement group to see current status and plan the next steps in a richer, more detailed fashion than by using just the Maturity Level information.

One "techie" way to think of the representations is as different report views from a single database. The database content is the same no matter which view you choose; each view shows you that content in a different way. Depending on your purpose at any time, one view may be more useful than another. It's the same with CMMI.

4.3.2 The alternative practices choice

This choice revolves around how rigorously you want to use the guidance at different abstraction levels within CMMI. From an appraisal viewpoint, the *required* content of the model includes the statements of the Specific and Generic Goals. This means that to get a particular capability rating for a Process Area, you *must* achieve the Specific Goals of the Process Area and the associated Generic Goal for the Capability Level.

Most organizations achieve those goals by implementing, in their own processes, the Specific Practices associated with the Specific Goals of the Process Area and the Generic Practices associated with the Generic Goal of the Capability Level being addressed. The Specific Practices and Generic Practices are designated as *expected* elements of the model. What this means is that an appraiser would expect to see implementations of the practices as the way that the organization achieves the associated goals. All the other material—front matter, purpose statements, subpractices, discipline amplifications, and so on—is designated as *informative*. If it helps you understand or implement the model, great! If it doesn't, don't use it. You will not be rated against informative material of the model scope you choose in an appraisal. The SEI appraisal method associated with CMMI is called SCAMPI (Standard CMMI Appraisal Method for Process Improvement).[†]

The designation of *expected* for specific practices can be a useful convention, particularly for organizations whose size, domain, or organizational focus makes the use of a particular Specific Practice to meet a goal inappropriate. In this case, the organization may choose to implement an *alternative*

[†] There is a bit of fun in the acronym SCAMPI even beyond the reference to culinary delights. When defining it, the developers were intent on making a point about how the method was used. If you don't use it for process improvement, thus removing the PI from the acronym, you're left with nothing more than a SCAM.

practice as the means for implementing the goal. Where, you may ask, will you find these alternative practices? You find them in your own organization's practices. There is no canonical set of published alternative practices.

We have observed two effects from this. First, many organizations are hesitant to use or document alternative practices because they're afraid that their alternatives will not be judged as acceptable by an appraisal team. This can lead to ineffective implementations of model practices, which in turn leads to a reduced return for your process improvement effort. The second effect is that appraisal teams sometimes are afraid to allow a particular alternative practice because they have no "official" reference for its acceptance.

Our recommendation is that initially, while you're still gaining confidence in your understanding of the model, implement the practices that obviously make sense for your organization. For those practices you aren't sure about, simply attempt a reasonable implementation. Why? Because often, you will find that you get unexpected benefit from a practice you didn't think would fit your organizational context. If, however, implementation of one of these practices turns into something unreasonable, either from an adoption-resistance viewpoint or a cost/effort viewpoint, we suggest two paths:

• If you're working with an authorized lead appraiser, try to get recommendations of alternative practices that may fit your situation or get an opinion on an alternative practice you're thinking of implementing.

• If you don't have access to a lead appraiser, document the difficulty that you encountered in your improvement notes for that Process Area, as well as the alternative practice you came up with and why you think it meets the intent of the goal it supports.

This may seem like a lot of trouble, but four or six or nine months from now when you engage in an appraisal, having those notes at hand will make things easier and faster for both you and the appraisal team.

4.3.3 The Generic Practices timing choice

The last of the choices we discuss in this section is the choice of when to introduce the Generic Goals and Practices into your implementation. If you're using the staged representation, and you're attempting to achieve Maturity Level 2, you'll be faced with implementing Specific Goals and Practices of six Process Areas, plus ten Generic Practices. The Generic Practices are called *generic* because they are expected to be applied against *every* Process Area within the scope of the Generic Goal they're associated with.

For example, Generic Practice 2.1, Establish an Organizational Policy, is expected to be applied to all six of the Process Areas of Maturity Level 2. Also, remember that as you increase Maturity Levels, the goals of the previous level are subsumed or included in the goals of the current level. So all the Maturity Level 2 Generic Practices would be expected to be implemented for all the Maturity Level 3 Process Areas, as well as those of Maturity Level 2. In the Maturity Level 2 case, for the topics of Project Planning, Project Monitoring and Control, Requirements Management, Measurement and Analysis, Process and Product Quality Assurance, and Configuration Management, an appraisal team would expect to see objective evidence that these topics are appropriately discussed in the organization's policies.

Note that you are *not* expected to generate a *separate* policy for each Process Area. That rarely makes sense. Many organizations would have one policy for Project Management that makes statements that apply to Project Planning and Project Monitoring and Control. They might also have a Corporate Quality policy that addresses some of the Measurement and Analysis coverage, as well as Product and Process Quality Assurance. And they may have another policy on Organizational Support for Projects that also applies to the rest of the Measurement and Analysis coverage, as well as coverage for Configuration Management. Coverage for the Requirements Management PA might be included in a policy called Engineering Management. On the other hand, the organization may have one policy called Project Support that covers all six Process Areas. (Obviously, there would be content in these policies besides statements related to CMMI.)

What does this discussion have to do with timing? Chances are that as you were reading it, if this is your first time dealing with CMMI, you were starting to think something like this: "Oh, no! Not only do I have to implement the practices in all these Process Areas, but I also have these other ten Generic Practices to implement across these six PAs! That's 10 x 6 = 60 implementations! Aargh! How will I ever get to Maturity Level 2?"

Your first reaction may be "Enough, already! I'll just start with the Maturity Level 2 Process Areas and worry about the Generic Practices later." That's a fairly common reaction. Understanding a little more about some of the inherent dependencies between the Process Areas and the Generic Practices, however, may help you time the addition of Generic Practices to your implementation a little more practically. Selected dependencies are elaborated in the front matter of the Chrissis, Conrad, and Shrum CMMI book.[3] There is also a very good presentation on GP/Process Area relationships by Sandra Cepeda from the 2004 NDIA CMMI User's Conference.[4]

The primary thing to note when looking at the relationship tables and elaborations in the CMMI book is that most of the Capability Level 2 Generic Practices are supported by, or are related to, a particular Process Area. The Configuration Management PA, for example, is related to Generic Practice 2.6, Manage Configurations. A practical way to approach Generic Practice implementation is to address a particular Generic Practice at the same time that you address its related Process Area. In the case of Configuration Management, when you start implementing practices related to version control, you would want to think about how you will address version control for the work products of your processes related to Project Planning, Project Monitoring and Control, and so on. When you've completed your overall implementation for Configuration Management, you will already have addressed the Generic Practice 2.6 implementation for your Maturity Level 2 PAs.

Although the dependencies between PAs and Generic Practices may seem complex at first, this is one of the unique elements of CMMI that, in our minds, makes it more powerful than other reference models we've used. When you've mastered the content of one of the PAs with a Generic Practice relationship, if you've thought explicitly about how it applies across the scope of PAs that you're implementing, you're already on your way to institutionalizing that set of practices. And that institutionalization aspect is what sets CMMI apart from most of the models available to support process improvement. Institutionalization is a concept that is thoroughly discussed in CMMI and in SEI materials. Fundamentally, it means that the level of adoption of a particular set of practices (in this case CMMI's practices) is deep enough, and broad enough, that their use would continue even through organizational and leadership changes. The generic practices are the primary mechanism used within CMMI to foster institutionalization.[†]

4.3.4 CMMI choices summary

That's probably as much CMMI detail as you want to know at this point in your journey. Check Chapter 15 for lots of useful references when you're ready for them.

If you find yourself unclear on some of the issues, don't worry—it happens to all of us. Most likely, you'll come back to this chapter after you've learned more about CMMI itself. (After you go a little farther and figure out more of

---

[†] Rich has always had problems with the use of *institutionalize* in referring to organizational process deployment. Where he grew up, this word meant the act of locking away a mentally ill person, and so he is confused as to the subject: processes or process improvers.

how the model really works, you'll reread this chapter and say, "Of course! Why didn't I see that the first time?")

None of the choices we talk about in this chapter is a "one time only" choice. If you make a choice and decide after more learning that a different choice is better, by all means change your choice, and go with the one that makes more sense! Remember, in the final analysis, George Box (a 20th-century mathematician) got it right when he said, "All models are wrong, but some models are useful." We want you to get the most utility from CMMI, even knowing that it cannot be completely right for any single organization. It is a model, after all.

4.4 Using CMMI to guide your improvement

At this point, we don't expect you to be able to interpret how CMMI supports typical process improvement tasks. So in Table 4-2, we've given you a starting point. As you're getting familiar with CMMI, you may want to refer to this table to think about how each of these tasks relates to what you're learning about CMMI. These are not the only tasks performed as part of an improvement effort, of course, but they are a good set to start with.

The tasks are organized around the challenges that we introduced in Chapter 3, and we've provided a reference for you to show where you can find additional information related to that task later in the book.

When you look at the list of tasks in the table, you may be thinking—"this is a lot to do!" and you're right—there are many tasks to do at different points in your improvement journey. The good news is, you don't have to do all of them at once. In the next chapter, we'll introduce you to a "lightweight" improvement life cycle that allows you to minimize your infrastructure while you're getting started with your improvement effort. And, as you get accustomed to the rhythm of your improvement cycle, you'll figure out which of the tasks you need to pay attention to at any one point.

In Parts 3 and 4, we'll introduce the tasks and techniques or approaches that we've used to support their accomplishment. Some of these approaches are more suited to larger contexts; in those cases, we try to give you some alternatives that are more suited to smaller settings. The biggest difference in how you approach the tasks is in the "Developing Infrastructure" and "Defining Processes" categories. How you approach tasks such as creating a measurement repository will depend on how big your organization is and what kind

Table 4-2: *Task/CMMI Cross Reference*

Summary Task	Process Group Task	Supporting PA(s)	For More Information
Developing and Sustaining Sponsorship	Communicating with and sustaining sponsorship	OPF, IPM	Chapter 8
Setting and Measuring Against Realistic Goals	Setting goals and success criteria aligned with sponsor objectives	IPM	Chapter 9
	Understanding the current state of the organization with relation to its business objectives	MA	Chapter 9
	Understanding risks related to PI and to CMMI implementation	RSKM, OID, CAR	Chapter 9
Managing an Appraisal Life Cycle	Understanding the current state of the organization with relation to CMMI	OPF	Chapter 10
Developing Infrastructure	Developing and sustaining skilled PI transition agents	OPD, OT	Chapter 11
	Developing and sustaining process group team members	OT, IT, OID, OPF	Chapter 11
	Establishing and maintaining a process asset library	OPD	Chapter 11

Table 4-2: *Task/CMMI Cross Reference* (Continued)

Summary Task	Process Group Task	Supporting PA(s)	For More Information
	Establishing and maintaining a measurement system to support long-term quantitative management	MA, OPP, CAR	Chapter 11
Defining Processes	Establishing and maintaining internal PI processes	OID, PP, PMC, PPQA, CM, DAR, REQM, OT, IPM	Chapter 12
	Establishing and maintaining appropriate CMMI transition mechanisms	RD, TS, PI, VER, VAL, OT, CM	Chapter 12
	Engineering solutions to identified process issues	RD, REQM, TS, PI, VER, VAL, DAR	Chapter 12
	Collecting/incorporating lessons learned from improvement activities	OPF, OID, OPD, CAR (QPM)	Chapter 12
Deploying Improved Processes	Finding and selecting pilots for CMMI implementation	OID, DAR, RSKM	Chapter 13
	Working with consultants	SAM, DAR	Chapter 13
	Deploying practices to the targeted organizational scope	OPD, OID, RSKM, DAR, PP, PMC, CM (QPM)	Chapter 13

(continued)

Table 4-2: *Task/CMMI Cross Reference* (Continued)

Summary Task	Process Group Task	Supporting PA(s)	For More Information
.	Monitoring improvement progress	PMC, PPQA, IPM (QPM)	Chapter 13
	Supporting and learning from implementation pilots	OT, PP, PMC, IPM, RSKM, OPF, OID, CAR	Chapter 13

of measurement infrastructure you already have in place. We'll highlight some of the different approaches we've seen as we go through them.

For a few of the tasks, we've gone into a fair bit of detail in relating the task to particular aspects of CMMI content. We've done this because we believe that the discussion may be helpful to you when you're making your own interpretations of CMMI.

Table 4-2 lists at least one supporting PA for each improvement task. We bring this up for two reasons. First, using CMMI to help you define your own improvement activities helps you learn the model. Second, and just as important, it allows you to model the behavior you would like your organization to exhibit—that is, to lead by example. This table can get you started down that path.

---

1. Garcia, Suzanne. "Standardization as an Adoption Enabler for Project Management Practice." In *IEEE Software*, vol. 22, no. 5, pp. 22–29.

2. Ahern, Dennis, Aaron Clouse, and Richard Turner. *CMMI Distilled: A Practical Introduction to Integrated Process Improvement.* 2d ed. (Boston: Addison-Wesley, 2004).

3. Chrissis, Mary Beth, Mike Conrad, and Sandy Shrum. *CMMI: Guidelines for Process Integration and Product Improvement.* (Boston: Addison-Wesley, 2003).

4. Cepeda, Sandra. "Generic Practices—What Do They Really Mean?" In *Proceedings of NDIA CMMI Technology & User Conference 2004,* www.nida.org (NDIA, 2004).

Chapter 5

A Decision-based Life Cycle for Improvement

You may wonder why, with all the various approaches to process improvement, we're adding another. Not surprisingly, we actually have different, but similar, reasons.

SuZ: I've always been a "try before you buy" consumer. Most process improvement life cycles I've used or read about make the assumption that you're ready to dive right in and "buy" both the concepts of the model they're using and their approach to dealing with the main issues we talked about in Part I. I don't believe that's always the best way to approach process improvement. So the life cycle presented here, called DLI, lightens the load on up-front investment in infrastructure so that you can try process improvement with your chosen model before you make a large commitment to infrastructure building, sponsorship, and appraisal.

Rich: I believe the agile software developers have the right idea when it comes to accomplishing a task and, as Martin Fowler says, "delighting the customer." Process improvement is like any other process or service in that it needs to meet the customers'—or, in our case, the sponsors'—needs. And like most customers, very few sponsors know exactly what they want right off. It's up to the PI team to anticipate, listen, and learn as they go. Most PI life cycles, although providing mechanisms for feedback, are rarely implemented that way because the feedback is not intentional within the process. I think DLI does a good job of balancing process and flexibility, and gives the organization the best opportunity to maximize the business value of PI.

In some ways, approaching PI is akin to trying to find the right map to use. Some maps provide one kind of information—a general lay of the land and some particular points of interest (Figure 5-1).

Others, as shown in Figure 5-2, provide different kinds of information—more of a navigational routing.

Still others provide specialty information of interest to a specific group: income demographics, as depicted in Figure 5-3.

What we've tried to do with our Decision-based Life Cycle for Improvement (DLI) is provide one of these "specialty maps," not as focused on the

Figure 5-1: *Points-of-interest view*

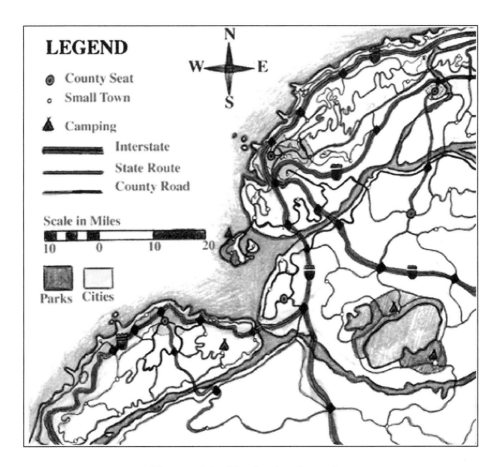

Figure 5-2: *Navigational routing*

navigational routings as on presenting the map from a specialty viewpoint: the viewpoint of what decisions you are likely to face as you engage in your improvement effort.

Most process improvement life cycles focus on the activities that need to be accomplished. What we've observed is that process improvement, especially at the beginning, is even more about making decisions than just performing activities.

DLI is a life cycle based on a decision-implementation model (Figure 5-4) that we've found useful for framing many kinds of technology choices, not just process improvement.

The bad news of this diagram is that to succeed in any technology adoption, you have to make the right decision about what you're adopting (in this case,

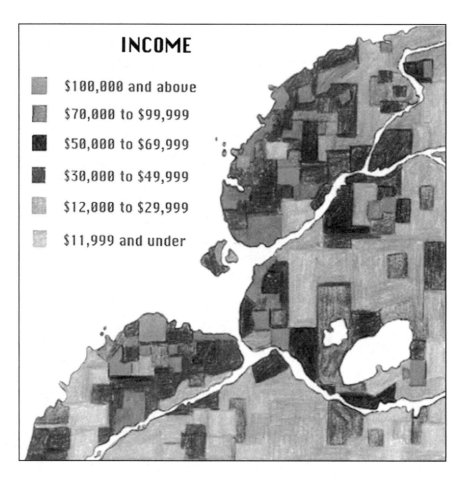

Figure 5-3: *Demographic view*

the approach to process improvement and the reference model you intend to use), *and* you have to implement that decision correctly. The good news of this diagram is that by treating these two actions separately, you can be a little more conscious in both your decision-making and your implementation, which we find leads to better outcomes.

The stages of DLI are illustrated in Figure 5-5 and defined in Table 5-1.

Besides the decision implementation model, the other basis for the DLI life cycle is the adoption commitment curve (Figure 5-6). It shows the stages that most individuals and groups go through when approaching adoption of a new set of practices or a new technology.

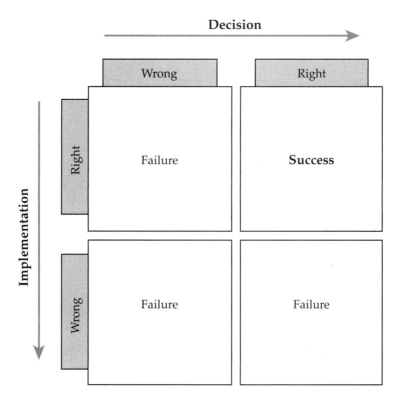

Figure 5-4: *Decision/Implementation and Failure/Success modes*

The first three stages—Contact, Awareness, and Understanding—are facilitated primarily via the support of communication mechanisms such as Web sites, conversations with people who have used the approach, seminars, workshops, and training events.

The remaining stages—Trial Use, Adoption, Institutionalization, and Internalization—are facilitated primarily via the support of implementation mechanisms. These include procedures, new measures and controls, policies, employee orientation programs, changes in the organization's reward system, and continuing communication mechanisms to ensure that those trying the new practices are encouraged that management intends for them to stick.

The focus of the Decide and Try stages of DLI are to get you through Contact, Awareness, Understanding, and Trial Use. Analyze, Commit, and Reflect also support Trial Use and are meant to move you into Adoption and Institutionalization for the particular set of practices you're working on in this cycle.

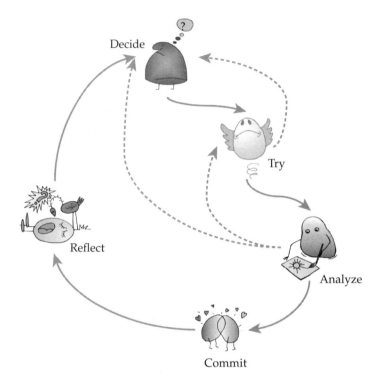

Figure 5-5: *DLI*

Table 5-1: DLI Stages

Decide	You have a set of choices to make: decisions about what, where, and when. We'll give you guidance on all these decisions.
Try	Having made the decisions to go forward, in this stage you try out the elements of CMMI or whatever model you've chosen as the basis for your improvement effort.
Analyze	Having done some actual improvement work, in this stage you make sure that you're getting the intended results, and if not, understand why and where you need to go from here.
Commit	For the changes that have been successful, you embed them into the day-to-day workings of the business. We call that Commitment. This is the point where you may transition to a more traditional IDEAL-based approach to improvement and start building a sustainable process improvement infrastructure.
Reflect	This stage is about looking at the process you used for your most recent improvement cycle and deciding what you want to or should change before you initiate another cycle.

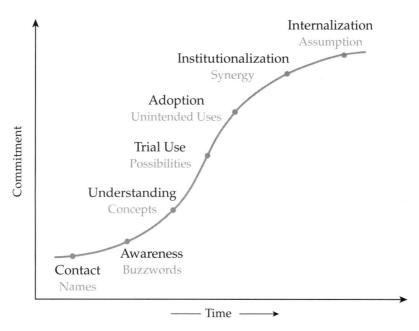

Adapted from Patterson & Conner, 1982 "Building Commitment to Organizational Change"

Figure 5-6: *Adoption commitment curve*

In this way, we hope to avoid the common problem of trying to move immediately to Adoption types of actions when some of the actions and elements that support getting through Contact, Awareness, Understanding, and Trial Use have been ignored.

5.1 Decide

The Decide stage asks you to think explicitly about and make different aspects of the decisions needed to implement process improvement successfully. You'll revisit this part of the life cycle each time you complete a cycle of improvement and want to go further.

5.1.1 Decision 1: Decide whether PI can help

Why am I thinking about this?

It is always good to list the reasons you want to pursue process improvement. In Part I, we talked about reasons we believe are appropriate. The main issue to understand as clearly as possible is how PI is going to impact your business positively. But beware complacency. As quality guru W. Edwards Deming said, "It is not necessary to change. Survival is not mandatory."

Business goals that make this worth thinking about

In *CMMI Distilled,*[1] the authors describe how CMMI supports several common business goals. Table 5-2 summarizes those points. You might use it as a starting place for your analysis.

Table 5-2: *CMMI Impacts on Business Goals*

Produce quality products or services.	CMMI evolved out of the Deming, Juran, and Crosby quality paradigm: Quality products are a result of quality processes. There is a strong focus on quality-related activities, including requirements management, quality assurance, verification, and validation.
Create value for the stockholders.	Mature organizations are more likely to make better cost and revenue estimates than those with less maturity and then to perform in line with those estimates. Quality products, predictable schedules, and effective measurement guard against project performance problems that could weaken the value of the organization in the eyes of investors.
Be an employer of choice for employees, maintaining an able, satisfied workforce.	Organizations with mature processes have far less turnover than immature organizations. Engineers in particular are more comfortable in an organization where there is a sense of cohesion and competence.
Enhance customer satisfaction.	CMMI focus on project management is key. Meeting cost and schedule targets with high-quality products that are validated against customer needs is a good formula for customer satisfaction.

Table 5-2: *CMMI Impacts on Business Goals* (Continued)

Increase market share.	Customers like to deal with suppliers that have a reputation for meeting their commitments and for high quality. CMMI improves estimation and lowers process variability to enable better, more accurate bids that are demonstrably achievable.
Implement cost savings and best practices.	CMMI encourages measurement as a managerial tool. By using the historical data collected to support schedule estimation, an organization can identify and widely deploy practices that work, and eliminate those that don't.
Gain an industrywide recognition for excellence.	The best way to develop a reputation for excellence is to perform well consistently on projects, delivering quality products and services within cost and schedule parameters. Many organizations proudly advertise their CMMI-defined Maturity Level rating alongside their ISO 9000 registration.

Adapted from *CMMI Distilled*, Ahern et al., Addison-Wesley, 2004.

Does it fit?

Every decision involves some risks, so it's important to identify those in your environment. In Chapter 9, we introduce the technique of Readiness and Fit Analysis (RFA). One of its main uses is to identify the non-technical risks associated with adopting a new technology or set of practices. Early in your decision making, you will want to perform a Readiness and Fit Analysis against CMMI (or the reference model you've chosen) to see how well it fits with your current organizational state and to identify the risks that you will have to mitigate and monitor as you go through your adoption.

Note that we've included only the Technology Assumptions Table—one of the elements of RFA—for CMMI. You'll have to create your own (usually with the help of someone who understands the reference model you're using *very* well) if you're using a different model, such as ISO 12207.

5.1.2 Decision 2: Decide to do it

When you've gotten an idea that process improvement may be a good fit for your organization (or if you're in the position of being mandated to use CMMI or another model), you need to make the decisions that will get you started on the path toward the next stage: Try.

You have to think about three questions, which we elaborate in the following sections.

Where do I start?

This question leads to more questions . . . more decisions!

Do I want to use a model to guide me?

Most people who have not done process improvement before decide that they would rather approach this with the help of some kind of process reference model (like the ones we talked about in Chapter 2), rather than use one of the techniques that depends on your analyzing your problems and coming up with unique solutions to them.

That's the assumption we're following in this book. So the question becomes "Which one?" For some readers, this choice has already been made for you: Your market or a parent organization has mandated the use of a particular model.

If you're not in that situation, you will have to choose a model to try. Use the information in Chapter 2 to help you decide which model makes the most sense for your situation, and use the references in Chapter 15 and the bibliography to get more information about the two or three models that seem most relevant to you.

A few things you need to know about the model you choose are

- What aspects of my organization's work are supported by the model?
- What kinds of skills does the model assume that I have available for implementation of its practices?
- What kinds of support (consulting, training, books, trade journals, and so on) are available for users of the model?
- What did organizations similar to mine experience when they used the model?

One book that does a nice job of laying out several possible models and comparing them for you is called *Systematic Process Improvement Using ISO 9001:2000 and CMMI*, by Boris Mutafelija and Harvey Stromberg.[2]

Although the title makes it seem that the book deals only with ISO 9001 and CMMI, it gives good coverage to other standards, including ISO 12207.

Which pieces should I try first?

For this section, we're assuming you've decided that CMMI is a reasonable fit for your organization to try as the basis for your process improvement effort. We make that assumption somewhat selfishly, because the technique we're going to introduce, model-based business analysis, needs an example to work from.

The purpose of model-based business analysis is to help you figure out which pieces of the model—in this case, CMMI—you want to try first. This decision is important for several reasons:

- All the reference models we mention in Part I are too big to take on all at once, especially if your organization is a small one, so you have to decide which pieces you'll try first.

- Presumably, your organization is not running perfectly, and there are things that you would like to improve. If you do a good job of matching model elements to the problems you're facing, you can potentially solve near-term problems at the same time that you're "trying on" the practices of the model you've chosen. In our experience, it's never a bad thing in business to meet two objectives with a single action!

- If you randomly pick elements of the model (particularly CMMI) to work on, you may miss some inherent dependencies that could offer you leverage if you chose more wisely.

You need three resources to conduct this analysis:

- A moderator/trainer who is knowledgeable about CMMI and connecting it to business issues

- The materials from the Huntsville CMMI pilots used to conduct this analysis: the CMMI overview presentation materials and the business analysis presentation materials (available from the SEI at www.sei.cmu.edu/ttp/publications/toolkit)

- Participants for the workshop who have a useful perspective on the activities and practices being used in the organization

There is a bit of the "chicken and egg" syndrome here. You probably won't know exactly which projects to involve until you've done this kind of business analysis. On the other hand, the people you choose to participate in the business analysis typically drive the set of issues to be ones that will solve their problems. So when you are selecting people to participate in the business analysis, pick those whom you think (1) will be willing to do something proactive to improve their project's situation and (2) will benefit, at least intuitively, from the kinds of topics covered in CMMI or the model you've chosen.

What you do in this analysis is combine some overview training on the contents of CMMI with some discussion of the typical kinds of problems that different clusters of CMMI practices (called Process Areas in the model) are expected to solve. Through this discussion, the group performing the analysis generally starts to recognize particular sets of issues that the model addresses and that currently are causing pain within the organization or within a subset of projects. The mapping of the organization's business problem with CMMI content allows you to do an initial filtering of the model from 22 potential Process Areas to 8 or 10 (usually; sometimes fewer, once in a while a couple more).

Then you look at that filtered set more closely, based on thinking about what the problems you're facing in each of those process areas actually are. This is where a knowledgeable consultant is *really* essential; he or she is the one who ensures that the problems are correctly mapped to the Process Areas and can explain model content that isn't as clear to you when you're trying to think about your problems in relation to the model. A consultant will also help you further prioritize your list of potential Process Areas based on some of the inherent dependencies in the model that you're not likely to be familiar with at this point, helping you leverage your initial efforts even more.

After you have filtered your list again down to four or five Process Areas, you start looking at some of the issues covered further on in DLI: which projects would be good candidates for testing new processes in the selected areas, and which projects are (or soon will be) at a point that is appropriate for one or more of the selected Process Areas. Again, an experienced process improvement facilitator is a great asset in this step; this person can listen to your project candidates and do a good job of asking questions that help you pick the one(s) most appropriate for your situation.

When you've completed the analysis, you can move on to your next decisions.

Although this analysis technique is not the only way to choose candidate model topics to address while you're thinking about model adoption, it's one that worked very well in pilot work on applying CMMI in small settings, and feedback we've gotten from people who have tried this approach in their own organizations has been very positive.

If you're not using CMMI . . .

If you are using some reference model other than CMMI, we recommend that you work with someone who knows that model well to build the same kind of translation of the model into business symptoms that we've demonstrated using CMMI (see the pilot kickoff materials referenced in the preceding section). You may be able to do this yourself just by looking at the contents of the model you're considering. Usually, however, because you are a new user of the model, you will miss nuances that could have impact on your decision about which pieces to try. You may also be able to find some of this information in presentations or articles written about the model you've chosen.

5.1.3 Decision 3: Decide where to try it

When you've decided which pieces of CMMI you plan to tackle first, you have to decide who will be involved in making the improvements.

This is one place where DLI differs from some other life cycles. At this point, we're *not* suggesting that you put together a whole group to do process improvement (often called an Engineering Process Group, or EPG). What we're suggesting is that you find the people who can make changes at the project level in the areas you've identified, so that you can see whether the model helps you (1) make appropriate changes productively and (2) fix the problem you think it will fix.

This means that you need to choose projects and team members who will be doing something about the topics covered in the Process Areas you've chosen in the near term. If you want to do something to improve Project Planning (one of the Process Areas of CMMI), for example, you need to have a project that's getting ready to go into planning. This sounds obvious, but you'd be surprised how many people pick a Process Area and then pick a project that can't do anything about that Process Area for months! Some Process Areas, such as Configuration Management, have something going on at almost any stage in a project, so they may be easier to fit to a project.

Table 5-3 generally associates Process Areas for Maturity Levels 2 and 3 with a typical product development life cycle.

Table 5-3: *General Association of PAs with Product Life Cycle*

If You're Starting This Life-Cycle Stage . . .	. . . Consider Implementing Improvements for This Process Area	Notes
Proposal/Initial Planning	Measurement & Analysis Project Planning Requirements Management	
Requirements Elicitation	Requirements Development Product Integration Verification Validation	For PI, VAL, and VER, focus on the goals associated with establishing your environments
Design	Technical Solution	
Implementation	Technical Solution	
Integration	Product Integration	
Product Testing/ Verification	Verification	
User Acceptance Testing/Release	Validation	
Throughout Life Cycle	Any of the Organizational Process Areas Decision Analysis and Resolution Project Monitoring and Control Product and Process QA Configuration Management Risk Management	

How many and which people should be involved depends fairly heavily on what you've decided to improve initially. Usually, the manager of the project and the key staff members who are involved in the processes being worked with would be the minimum set of people to include on an improvement team.

There are some other considerations in selecting projects and teams to work on process improvement. In particular, the amenability of the people involved to try new things and to be willing to be your "guinea pigs" is a key issue. One thing you can do to understand which projects or teams will be most likely to succeed is to do an adopter analysis. We cover this technique in Chapter 13.

Get team/project buy-in

In Chapter 11, we introduce a particularly effective model for analyzing and supporting teams: the Drexler-Sibbett Team Performance model. This is one of the many times you'll want to use it. When you start selecting the projects to work your improvements, you generally have a choice of more than one project for a particular improvement area. Spending some time working with the candidate project teams to determine which team is the best fit (yes, you can do a team-level RFA at this point, if you need to) for the improvement project is worthwhile. Going through the early stages of the Team Performance model is one way to see quickly how each project team would approach the improvement effort. *Especially* for your first pilot, a team that is committed to working with the new ideas to solve the identified problem is a huge step toward success. After the first pilot, teams that are less committed are more likely to adopt if the first one was successful.

5.1.4 Decision 4: Decide when to try it

Some of the issues about "when to try" are covered in the CMMI business analysis referenced in the preceding section. However, there are some additional things to think about beyond those covered in the business analysis.

How do the risks I've identified affect my ideas?

By the time you get through choosing a set of three or so Process Areas and the projects and people you think should be involved in them, you're at a good point to step back and compare the risks you identified through your Readiness and Fit Analysis with the PAs and projects you've chosen. If the projects you've selected reflect or exhibit the risks that you identified, you have a couple of choices:

- Avoid that project, and pick one that doesn't involve as many risks or less-severe risks.
- Work with that project, but include specific mitigation actions and monitoring to minimize the occurrence and/or effect of the identified risks.

If the risks you've identified make it clear that one of the PAs you've selected could be a problem, your choices are

- Pick another PA that may not solve as big a problem but reflects fewer risks.
- Work with that PA, but include specific mitigation actions and monitoring to minimize the occurrence and/or effect of the identified risks.

5.2 Try initial (additional) model elements

This is the real hands-on work of DLI. You'll need to plan carefully and communicate well so that you don't alienate the practitioners. Here's our checklist of things to do.

5.2.1 Baseline existing performance

Before you begin any process improvement initiative, get a baseline of how well the current way of doing things is performing. If you can't get actual measures (or even guesses from knowledgeable people), look into industry standards and benchmarks. You want to be able to measure yourself against something to show progress. Otherwise, any improvement can be discussed only anecdotally.

You should use whatever measures are available to you, especially in the first few cycles. A heavy measurement infrastructure may be the straw that breaks your supporter's back. Try to find measures that are already collected (defects, cycle time, customer responses, and so on).

5.2.2 Develop the guidance needed

This may be the first work you do that's visible to practitioners: creating and documenting the new or changed process. Information Mapping (described in Chapter 12) and technology adoption methods (described in Chapter 13) can be very useful in this work. Some other things to think about in developing guidance are:

- Make sure that you capture any rationale you want to communicate to the practitioners as you design the changes so that the changes don't get lost in the shuffle.

- Develop work aids to help practitioners execute the improved process, as well as some initial training material.

- Apply the adopter-analysis and value-network approaches in Chapter 13 to identify and include key stakeholders. This is extremely helpful in getting the process right, stating rationale, and enabling speedy adoption.

- Keep it lightweight. Taking a cue from the agilists, we believe that guidance should be the smallest amount possible of documentation (things practitioners have to read and understand) and ceremony (things that have to be done other than the task at hand). The only objective is to ensure understanding and compliance. Don't spend time writing novels (or even short stories). Write brief, concise descriptions, and use graphics (like swim-lane charts) to the best advantage.

- Keep your notes, and document your assumptions. Discussions always come up after the fact. Good notes are helpful in handling disputes about what was said when.

- Initially, use a trained facilitator, if at all possible. People with training in process capture and facilitation can save you a great deal of grief and usually save you considerably more money than they cost.

- Identify any risks that may result from the new process. Change always has some associated risk. Don't hide it. If possible, also identify ways to mitigate the risks, or build fail-safe steps into the process.

- Develop an implementation plan. As you document your new or improved processes, capture ideas for rolling it out, and get the practitioners to help you help them be successful. This isn't an Integrated Master Plan for an aircraft carrier; it's a time-ordered list of who's doing what by when. The planning process is more important than the documentation format and content.

- Identify the closure criteria. Make sure that you have a documented and agreed-upon way of determining when this specific phase is over. It usually is something like "The team is implementing the process correctly, and all necessary data has been collected."

5.2.3 Train users on the new guidance

You can't ask people to do something they don't understand how to do, and it's best that they know why and how it fits into the larger scheme of things.

You can do this through training. You have developed the process artifacts; now use them to train your people. Take the time to make sure that they understand clearly so that the improved process is implemented as you planned. Make sure that the practitioners know how they can suggest changes that they think would make the process even better for use in the next cycle. This is especially important if they haven't been involved at the beginning. The Satir change cycle's Integration and Practice stage (described in Chapter 13) can guide what kinds of things you include in your training experience.

5.2.4 Monitor deployment

Execute your plan. Use the list of risks produced as a tickler during the implementation. If you see the possibility that a risk is surfacing as a problem, act quickly. It may be necessary to delay some part of the implementation until the risk or problem can be resolved.

As you proceed, take notes on what is done each day and on any feedback or problems that arise. Simply keeping a blog or journal should suffice for this part. If there is a large implementation team, it may be useful to have team members contribute as well. A shared internal blog can be a productive way of facilitating this kind of informal communication.

5.2.5 Complete initial cycle

When you have accomplished the planned activities, and your closure criteria have been met, you can close out the phase. Be sure to gather any measures you've defined or to collect existing organizational measures that are relevant. Also collect any anecdotes from the practitioners, customers, and implementers for later review.

5.3 Analyze

You've finished the implementation and piloting of a process improvement increment. In this step you decide whether the result was good enough to deploy across a larger part of the organization. You might also decide that there need to be changes and another pilot run before committing to the deployment. To make this decision, you need to review the goals set, measures collected, and anecdotal evidence gathered, and then draw some conclusions. In some cases, this analysis phase is fairly cut and dried and you can see clearly whether the package as piloted was effective. In other cases, unforeseen problems or external events may have impacted the trial and need to be factored into the results, or the trial may need to be repeated. Where there are large numbers of participants, it may take some time to collect and check the data, and there may need to be a more formal analysis.

You should consider essentially four questions:

- What worked or didn't work?
- How well did we follow our plan?
- Do there need to be significant changes?
- What do the measures tell us?

5.3.1 What worked or didn't work?

There is always a certain level of intuitive processing in evaluating the effectiveness of some activity. Without resorting to measures per se, what do you feel went right in this process pilot? What went wrong? What part was inadequate?

This intuitive exercise is important because much of process improvement is about change management, and the success of change is essentially predicated on human perceptions. You need to know whether you (and the other participants) feel that this pilot was successful. You need to identify the places that could be improved, either for a retrial or for the next improvement cycle. In Chapter 15, we present another approach to understanding what worked or didn't work: the Chaos Cocktail Party. Many people find it a useful approach to looking at a great deal of evaluation data in a short period of time and getting an initial prioritization of the data.

5.3.2 How well did we follow our plan?

In evaluating the trial, you have to examine whether you did what you said you were going to do when you planned the activity. If you changed something that might have impacted the outcome, you need to understand why it was changed. Was the planned activity too difficult or unclear? Did an external event interfere? Was the planned activity ill advised or improper? All these factors have a bearing on whether you can declare the trial a success.

This is also where you take a look at the goals and measures you set up for the project initially, to determine how much progress you have made against them. See Chapters 9 and 15 for details on setting and measuring against your goals.

5.3.3 Are significant changes needed?

In analyzing the results, you look for anything that stands out as something to change for the next improvement cycle. At this point, the key things to change should be in the process package itself, although implementation changes could be considered. Was the guidance clear and concise, or does it need to be revised? Were the activities the right ones? Did the process as implemented do the job, or are there shortcomings that need to be addressed?

5.3.4 What do the measures tell us?

Finally, after you've evaluated all the other information, you look at the empirical data. Does it show that your new process was better than the old baseline (or benchmarks)? Is the change in performance sufficient to cover the cost to deploy? Are the measures you collected sufficient to determine any of the above? Do you need different measures or different collection strategies?

5.4 Commit

This is it. Now you have to decide if the new (or changed) process or artifact is ready to be used by a broader group in the organization. There are some differences in the decisions if this is the first time through the cycle.

5.4.1 First time through

After you've gone through a test or pilot of implementing CMMI-based practices, it's time to decide whether and how you will deploy these new practices into the rest of the organization in such a way that they will become institutionalized.

For a small organization, this could be relatively trivial; the whole organization may have been involved in trying the Process Areas you picked. But even in the case where the pilot *is* the organization, there are still deployment steps you need to take.

In particular, you need to figure out what transition mechanisms need to be added to your basic process description to help this new set of practices stick in the organization. You have two basic categories of transition mechanisms to think about:

- Communication mechanisms—things that make it easier to understand what the new processes are about and what the requirements for performance are

- Implementation support mechanisms—methods, tools, and techniques that are needed to make it easier to implement the practices

If you're working with the Measurement and Analysis PA, for example, you'll consider procedures for storage and handling of measurement data. A communication mechanism you may need is a template for providing synthesized management reports for the monthly company management meeting.

An example of a possible implementation support mechanism for this PA is the database needed to store the measurement data being collected.

This also may be the point at which you rewrite your initial process description related to the PAs you've been working on to reflect your initial experiences.

5.4.2 Subsequent cycles

After you've completed a few cycles of improvement, the Commit activities are likely to be related to embedding the new practices into your improvement infrastructure, as well as to establishing the transition mechanisms to ensure widespread deployment to the relevant practitioners.

Especially in a medium-size or larger organization, this phase involves planning the sequence and cycles of deployment that result in a robust implementation.

If you look back at the adoption commitment curve, you can think of Commit as the place where you're trying to move from Trial Use into Adoption, with all the transition mechanisms (especially implementation mechanisms) that are attendant to that stage. What this means is that your Commit stage is the place where you'll really be concentrating on building and deploying improvement infrastructure elements such as process asset libraries (PAL), Measurement Repositories, training courses, and job aids for particular processes. A good approach at this point is to go through the list of transition mechanisms described in Chapter 13 and reconsider some of the things in them that you rejected for your first improvement journey through DLI. You may find that now, when you're ready to commit to a larger improvement effort, some of them make more sense to develop or acquire.

5.5 Reflect

One of the most important characteristics of DLI is the Reflect stage. If process improvement is valuable, improving the improvement process is doubly valuable and requires the same careful attention as the other activities. Taking the time to look back at what you've accomplished and to learn from what you see is a rarely performed but fundamental step in your PI journey.

Reflect is about adding "double-loop learning" to your process. This is a well-known concept in organizational learning[3,4] that indicates a deeper learning than we typically engage in. *Single-loop learning* is when we see an error, make the correction needed, and then move on and don't think about that error anymore. *Double-loop learning*, on the other hand, is when we see an error, correct it, and then try to understand how it happened so we can prevent it in the future.

In the case of process improvement, you want to look at the process you used to get through the DLI cycle and think about what you could do next time to make it easier or more effective.

5.5.1 Perform project retrospective

Project retrospective techniques are very useful in supporting reflection. These techniques provide a set of areas or questions to think about to guide your reflection process. Some people call this process a *post-mortem*, although most of the time when they use that term, it's because the project has died. We agree with those who think that *project retrospective* is a more accurate and emotion-neutral label for this type of activity. For those times when you really do want to emphasize that something ended badly, and you need to process what happened, we have a technique that has proved to be useful, based on the "CSI" (Crime Scene Investigation) television series. SuZ learned this technique at a North American Simulation and Gaming Association (NASAGA) conference several years ago and has successfully adapted it for use in root-cause analysis.[5]

The basics of the CSI technique are to use masking or other tape to lay out a "body" shape (see Figure 5-7 for a variety of choices) and then put sticky notes with the "symptoms" of the death all over the body (in large print, so that it's readable when you're standing up!). Your participants write their ideas of the "cause of death" (the root cause) on index cards, and you can use different techniques from there to prioritize, discuss, and further process the root-cause ideas. SuZ's colleague and friend Shawn Presson created a series of archetypal "deaths" that he has given us permission to post on the Addison-Wesley Web site for you to use (or just chuckle at). The procedures for CSI and related techniques are included in Chapter 15.

A comprehensive resource for engaging in and facilitating project retrospectives is Norm Kerth's book *Project Retrospectives: A Handbook* for *Team Reviews*.[6] It not only provides tools and techniques for setting up and running retrospectives, but also provides help for staff members who want to justify holding a retrospective.

5.5.2 Repeat decision-making/implementation process until you achieve desired results

As in any improvement cycle, if you're serious about continually improving your performance, you have to go through the cycle multiple times

Figure 5-7: *Archetypal death cartoons*
(adapted from Garcia and Presson, "Beyond Death by Slides" tutorial)

as you learn more about how to improve and about what needs to be improved.

What is likely to happen in the beginning is that you will do the business analysis and figure out a couple of Process Areas (if you're using CMMI) that will help you solve current business problems. You will work on those areas and solve the identified problems. When these problems are out of the way, you will be able to see and pay attention to other problems that were not as obvious before.

So you go through your decision process again to determine, at this next point in time, what will be the most business-benefiting processes for you to work on next.

5.6 Summary of Part II

In Part II, we've presented our two favorite "maps" for getting you started on a successful process improvement effort: CMMI as your model map and DLI as your improvement life-cycle map. We've also recommended some other resources for learning more about CMMI. If you're a sponsor, you'll probably go only as far as to read something like *CMMI Distilled*, but if you're the person or group in charge of getting a sustainable improvement effort going, you'll need to go farther than that—probably to a formal class of some sort. At some point, you'll probably read the model itself. Let us remind you that *most* of the material in the 700-plus pages of the model is informative material, meant to help you understand the much smaller proportion of material that is normative. (These are terms used by ISO. *Normative* is the part of the standard against which an organization would be evaluated; *informative* is "just for your information; use it if you find it relevant" material.)

We expect DLI's emphasis on decisions to have two effects on an organization:

*   Helping organizations understand that they have many choices encourages them to understand that they are not meant to slavishly follow the "dogma of CMMI."
*   On the other hand, it also makes them realize that they probably need more information than they have to make those choices.

The good news about the latter effect is that it inspires the organization to take education events surrounding process improvement or CMMI more seriously, because they know why they need that particular education. The bad news is that if the organization is resource constrained, some of that information can seem to be out of reach. Although we won't claim that this book will address all your learning needs (we only scratch the CMMI surface), we do intend that it address some of the areas that are hard to find resources for in book form (such as determining adoption risk).

If you're a sponsor of a CMMI effort, this may be enough for you to feel ready to find a champion to take the effort forward. But we encourage you to read the next part as well. In it, we provide a fictional case study that might help you make the transition from "What is it?" to "How would it feel to do this?" And we provide some advice on survival that, although it will be more important to the champion of the effort, will probably have some utility (and maybe even some amusement) for you.

If you're the leader of a process improvement effort, your journey is just getting started, and the next section will help you preview what's ahead so that you won't be (as) surprised when you start seeing what's going on with improvement in your organization.

---

1. Ahern, Dennis, Aaron Clouse, and Richard Turner. *CMMI Distilled: A Practical Introduction to Integrated Process Improvement.* 2d ed. (Boston: Addison-Wesley, 2004).

2. Mutafelija, Boris and Harvey Stromberg, Harvey. *Systematic Process Improvement Using ISO 9001:2000 and CMMI.* (Boston: Artech House Publishing, 2003).

3. Argyris, C., and D. Schön. *Theory in Practice: Increasing Professional Effectiveness.* (San Francisco: Jossey-Bass, 1974).

4. Argyris, C., and D. Schön. *Organizational Learning: A Theory of Action Perspective.* (Reading, Mass.: Addison-Wesley, 1978).

5. Garcia, Suzanne, and Shawn Presson. "Active Learning Approaches for Process Improvement Training: An Interactive Workshop," presented at SEPG 2004. www.sei.cmu.edu/ttp/presentations/death-by-slides. (Pittsburgh: Carnegie Mellon University, 2004).

6. Kerth, Norm. *Project Retrospectives: A Handbook for Team Reviews.* (New York: Dorset House, 2001).

Illustration from *The Travels of Marco Polo*
by Witold Gordon (1885–1968)

Part III

Surviving the Passage

We never stop investigating. We are never satisfied that we know enough to get by. Every question we answer leads on to another question. This has become the greatest survival trick of our species.
Desmond Morris, *British anthropologist*

Observe almost any survival creature, you see the same. Jump, run, freeze. In the ability to flick like an eyelash, crack like a whip, vanish like steam, here this instant, gone the next—life teems the earth. In quickness is truth.
Ray Bradbury, *American author*

To live means to finesse the processes to which one is subjugated.
Bertolt Brecht, *German playwright and poet*

To survive there, you need the ambition of a Latin-American revolutionary, the ego of a grand opera tenor, and the physical stamina of a cow pony.
Billie Burke, *U.S. stage and screen actor*

Why, you ask, would we be talking about survival with respect to process improvement? Well, first, the title of this book includes the word *survival* (check the cover). Second, because no matter how well intentioned you and your stakeholders are, how good your plans are, or how much business value you look to receive from the initiative, it has to survive to be effective.

In the first two parts, we examined what it takes to get ready for a process improvement initiative in your organization. We talked about models, and tasks, and life cycles that are important to success. But can the trip be taken safely? What do we need to know to survive our journey?

In Part III, we pause for a moment to take a deep breath before the plunge. We consider what it will be like along the journey and identify ways to be prepared for the unforeseen rocks and shoals that lurk just under the surface in every business environment.

Because no one can predict the sorts of problems that will arise, we believe it's important to prepare ourselves and our team to handle the difficulties without losing ourselves or the process improvement benefits. In other words, we provide a real survival guide for process improvement teams.

But first, we provide a traveler's tale—a story to help you get a feel for the road ahead through the eyes of one who has gone before you. See what this person experienced and survived. Then we'll start on your personal survival training.

Chapter 6

A PI Case Study

Psychologists and knowledge management specialists tell us that people learn better and retain more when information is presented as stories. In this section, we put all the DLI phases in play and provide a narrative that describes how one (fictional) firm applied DLI to its particular problems.

This is the story of Vivian, a CEO at a small engineering-services house, who takes the plunge and implements a CMMI-based process improvement initiative.

6.1 Decide (Cycle 1: To do or not to do)

Vivian is not really surprised the first time she finds the term *CMMI* in a Request for Proposal. Her peers at other companies had mentioned the trend toward such requirements, so she guessed it wouldn't be the last. But what she has heard about CMMI from some of the other CEOs in town worries her. Although some suggested that it was helping their business, others openly confessed that they were using it only to be able to qualify to bid on certain contracts. Vivian isn't sure, but she has the impression that in the latter cases, CMMI wasn't such a good thing for the company.

So, not wanting to hypothesize her way into a problem that might or might not exist, Vivian calls Bruce—a friend who is, in her opinion, a pretty practical manager who had recently spoken about CMMI at a chamber of commerce Technology Council meeting.

Bruce gladly shares his experience and provided Vivian a few lessons learned. First, he warns Vivian that the experience of adopting CMMI is different for every company and that it is not a "process in a box" that you just buy and implement.

Initially, Vivian voices three concerns. First, is CMMI compatible with the ISO 9001 work her company was already doing, because it had been quite helpful in stabilizing her operational infrastructure? Second, is it flexible enough for her different customer and project size contexts? And third, can it really help with project management practices?

Responding to the last two concerns, Bruce tells her that CMMI covers a broad number of process areas, including project management, but that it is important to plan carefully and not try to do everything at once. She should choose the things that are most important to her to begin the improvement.

Bruce then recommends that she adopt CMMI because of her company's primary business: providing engineering services for large system integrators. He points out that with CMMI, she and her customers could speak the same project management language.

Vivian responds that it sounds to her as though CMMI has a set order in which you have to work on your improvements, without concern for the particular kind of business.

Somewhat sheepishly, Bruce responds that indeed, a set order was the traditional way of approaching CMMI, but his authority-averse organization used an alternative method that was based on a business analysis of its needs and where CMMI addressed them. As it turned out, those topics that seemed to have the greatest value for his company also turned up in the traditional list.

In response to Vivian's question on the cost of his initiative, Bruce offers to provide the data and encourages her to make sure her cost tracking is sufficient to capture the costs, because it was one of the first items his management wanted to see.

Vivian thanks Bruce, hangs up the phone, and considers what she heard:

1. CMMI seems flexible and has broad coverage.

2. CMMI would meet her need for improving project management.

3. She could estimate her cost by extrapolating from Bruce's data.

4. She could tie the improvement activities to business value.

5. CMMI is becoming more common within her customer base.

After reviewing Bruce's data and coming up with an initial cost estimate, Vivian decides to start a process improvement initiative using CMMI.

6.2 Decide (Cycle 2: What to do, where, and when)

Having decided to go forward, Vivian finds a local SPIN (Software Process Improvement Network) group and attends a meeting. Even though it started out primarily as a software-focused group, as CMMI has expanded its focus, so has the SPIN group. She is intrigued and heartened by what she hears at her first meeting, so she brings Lou, her vice president of engineer-

ing services, to the second one. His enthusiasm seems genuine, so she designates him the focal point for the improvement effort. A review on Amazon.com leads them to *A CMMI Survival Guide*. They both read it and, after discussing the pros and cons, decide to try DLI.

The next week at work, Vivian gets her direct reports together to discuss process improvement and their possibilities; she has purchased copies of both *CMMI Distilled* and *CMMI Survival Guide*

for them to read as an introduction to CMMI and process improvement knowledge.[†]

Concerned about his depth of understanding, Lou suggests bringing in one of the consultants they met at the local SPIN to do the business analysis and RFA (Readiness and Fit Analysis) suggested by our book. They call Judy, an independent consultant and SEI transition partner, who works with them to put together the right team and schedules two specific events.

The first event is similar to the kickoff described in the pilot toolkit referenced in *CMMI Survival Guide*. Pilot projects and improvement Process Areas are tentatively selected. Additionally, improvement goals and success criteria (mostly of the "solve this problem" variety) are established.

The second event brings in the project teams that would be involved in the pilot. The first project, led by Jim, has been dealing with unstable, changing requirements. Lynette, the team leader for Project 2, is facing a type of project the organization has never done before and so has no corporate experience to draw upon. At this second event, they do an RFA and confirm that these two projects are decent fits, but that there are obvious risks that need to be addressed. They create a top-ten risk list and identify preliminary strategies for monitoring and mitigating the risks. They agree to revisit the list weekly.

6.3 Try (Cycle 2: The first pilot)

The pilot begins! Judy works with each project to do a gap analysis using an informal SCAMPI C level assessment. Each team walks through the practices for the target Process Areas, and for each PA, the team lists both the things it does and the things it doesn't. The team members brainstorm about alternative practices but find only one or two that might really fit the requirement.

When the gaps are known, the teams use the one-hour process description technique to understand the gap between their current process and the PA requirements. Because it is unprecedented, Project 2 uses the "closest" projects it can find to talk about general project management practices and then extrapolates from those the areas where it believes new practices are needed. All use CMMI as a general guide, but Project 1 augments it with some techniques from agile methods that the team members believe can help them with the requirements volatility they have been experiencing.

[†] A very wise decision, at least as we authors see it. We do hope you will follow Vivian's good example.

Judy then works with each project to identify simple diffusion and level-of-use measures to use in the pilot. What she chooses is not a full-scale diffusion profile, but one tailored to the needs of the 20-person project teams.

As luck would have it, during the course of Project 2, Bette, the key engineer, wins the lottery and moves to the Caribbean to open a bicycling shop. The project is disrupted both by jealousy and by the arrival of the engineer's replacement, a fairly new employee named Mickey. Luckily, the work the team did in the two initial events and the gap analysis provides direct support for bringing Mickey up to speed. Having come from a company that had used CMMI before, Mickey is comfortable with the terminology and is able to contribute almost immediately. The change in staffing does slow the effort, however, and the project manager is worried that by the time new practices are defined, the project will be beyond the point of being able to use them. He brings up his concern to Lou at the biweekly meetings they have to discuss his project. They telecon with Judy to decide what, if any, changes they should make to their approach. Because the first area that they tackled was configuration management, Judy recommends that they continue with the improvement track, because much of the activity will occur in the testing phase of the project, which is still more than two months away.

Both projects have periodic meetings focused on the process improvement goals and status. Project 2 has also added PI progress and issues to its daily standup meetings. From these meetings, several issues arise, including difficulty in understanding the new processes by those who had not attended the one-hour workshop.

6.4 Analyze (Cycle 2: The first pilot)

About halfway through the life cycle of each project, Judy gets the teams together with the management sponsors to talk about what's working and what's needed.

One thing that comes up is that there are no templates for helping the teams do any of the things Judy is asking them to do. In response, Lou charters a sub-team to work on this with Judy. Keeping in mind that they are also thinking about ISO 9000 registration, he charges them to make sure that whatever they do is compatible with the ISO standard. Unfortunately, Judy doesn't work much with ISO 9000, but she recommends someone with both CMMI and 9000 experience who can help them set up a PAL (process asset library).

The process asset team sends one of its members, Athena, to a class on information mapping for proce-dures. She comes back with a bunch of templates to use for Web pages that appear to be applicable in Project 1.

As the teams continue, the process asset subteam takes the work done so far and converts it, using meth-ods from the "developing useful process guidance" section of the *Survival Guide* book and the information-mapping knowledge that Athena has gained from her class.

At the second progress meeting, the adoption progress measures are reviewed, and two more transition mechanism gaps are identified. After some initial investigation, it's decided that the teams should solve these indi-vidually. The management team, now calling itself the PI Steering Group, authorizes the expenditures needed. At this point, both teams are able to pro-vide some qualitative benefits.

6.5 Commit (Cycle 2: The first pilot)

By the third progress meeting, the PI Steering Group and the projects are feel-ing that this is worth taking farther. They look at how much money they've spent so far on consulting and in-house effort (that's the one thing that Judy got them to track on spreadsheets, because their internal effort-tracking sys-tem wasn't set up to handle detailed effort allocations) and figure that they can afford about twice that amount per year as their PI budget.

Lou is set up as head of the steering group, and Vivian agrees to sponsor and resource the broader institutionalization of the assets developed in the pilots.

6.6 Reflect (Cycle 2: The first pilot)

Judy runs project retrospectives with each of the projects. For the top five problems identified, the teams use the CSI technique from the *Survival Guide* to get a better idea of possible root causes of the problems and some possible changes that could prevent them next time.

One of the main things teams talk about is the need for a repository of artifacts and lessons learned. This would initially serve the people involved in the improvement projects but would ultimately support the projects using the new processes. The subteam that worked on process documentation standards volunteers to work on a PAL project. They again look to the *Survival Guide* to help them understand the requirements they need to establish before looking for a solution.

Lou suggests that the steering group also conduct a retrospective to think about what worked and didn't work from the group's perspective. They decide that an internal staff focal point for improvement would be useful, and they ask Athena, one of the most respected systems engineers (who went to the info-mapping class), to take the job.

She agrees, but with the caveat that she can have access to some of the company's organizational development staff, because she's primarily a "geek," in her words, and doesn't understand how to do all the change management

stuff that Judy always talks about. Although she's read many of the books that were recommended in the *Survival Guide*, she doesn't feel comfortable attempting the activities without some experienced help. Lou agrees and adds Sue, an HR person, as a permanent consultant to the team in charge of internal professional development. Sue is ecstatic. She has a strong background in OD and has complained about not getting to use much of that background in her current role.

The other request Athena has is to add Sean to the team, at least part time. He's the IT/finance guy who is responsible for all their accounting and effort-recording systems. Athena has some ideas about making those systems friendlier to measurement and wants Sean to have a good understanding and commitment to what's needed. Lou agrees to this as well. The minutes from the reflection meetings are reviewed, agreed to, and slated to be added to the PAL when it is available.

6.7 Decide (Cycle 3: What's next)

Judy helps the projects figure out how much they can expect to get done, based on the kinds of issues identified in their original business analysis. Vivian decides that most of the identified problems fit with CMMI Maturity Level 2 (ML2), so she tentatively sets achieving that as the first model-based goal. She also commits to lead by example and solve their problems related to CMMI with CMMI wherever possible.

Judy and Lou set up another CMMI-based Business Analysis with a broader set of the engineering and management staff. They use it to validate the first analysis and to see whether any different priorities come out. Sure enough, a few things they hadn't known about need more attention than they thought, although they're still primarily ML2 issues.

New pilot teams are selected, and one person from each previous team is included to help with the transfer of learning from one project to the next.

Lou recommends that they go forward with establishing some kind of PAL; the team is chartered to initially organize what's been done so far. As soon as that's finished, they are authorized to look for an external solution that will serve the business as it grows in terms of improvement activity and staffing.

Vivian decides to review progress every quarter in general and in six months with Judy to see how close they are to being ready for an external appraisal. She admits to Judy that although the improvement is the foremost goal, she thinks attaining ML2 will be beneficial for the corporate image.

Vivian sees Bruce at one of the chamber of commerce meetings several months after their first conversation. He asks about what she's done with CMMI and how it's working for her. She admits that it was slow going at first, but that momentum has picked up, and the teams that are working in CMMI-enabled projects seem to be working more effectively than the ones that don't have access to the assets they've been building. She's most worried about the cost of consulting and the cost of the external appraisal she wants to do in the new year, if they're ready. Bruce agrees that funding to get

external expertise is one of his biggest continuing challenges, although he also says that as people inside the company get more understanding of the model, the reliance on external consulting does go down.

After the meeting, Vivian reflects on how different a conversation she had with Bruce this time in comparison to the first time they talked about CMMI. She can only hope that the next "new thing" to come along in their world is as fruitful as CMMI has been so far!

Chapter 7

SURVIVAL and PI

As we have stated already, there are significant risks to any process improvement effort that vary according to the environment. So it makes sense to provide some general comments on how you can react to and overcome risks that turn into problems.

Perhaps surprisingly, we turn to the U.S. Army's survival handbook to help us with a framework for our discussion.[1] As shown in Figure 7-1, the handbook uses the word *survival* as an acronym for a set of principles. The remainder of this chapter describes how each of these principles applies to you and your PI initiative. Unlike in DLI, you should keep these principles in mind no matter where you are in your improvement journey. For each element, we'll start with the army's version and then follow it with our interpretation for process improvement.[2] You are free to interpret and extrapolate for yourself as well, of course. For each of the elements of SURVIVAL, we will list relevant techniques discussed in this book or provide additional references.[†]

[†] Thanks to Chuck Myers for coming up with the idea of using the *U.S. Army Survival Manual* in the referenced "Process Improvement Insurgency" tutorial several years ago. This is one of those metaphors that just keeps working!

S ize up the situation

U ndue haste makes waste

R emember where you are

V anquish fear and panic

I mprovise

V alue living

A ct like the natives

L ive by your wits, learn basic skills

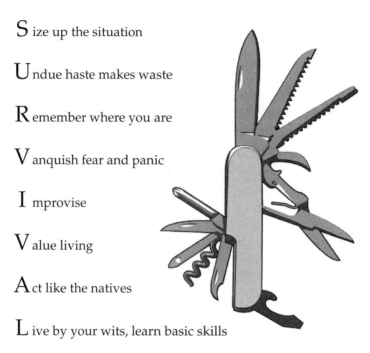

Figure 7-1: *SURVIVAL*

7.1 Size up the situation

The *U.S. Army Survival Manual* says:

> Size up your environment, physical condition, and equipment.
>
> - **Environment**—Learn the rhythms of the area you are in.
>
> - **Personal condition**—Take stock of any injuries from battle.
>
> - **Equipment**—Take stock of the condition of your weapons.

The first thing you need to do when confronted with a survival situation is to take a good, long look at the environment: where you are, what you're doing, and what might be impacting your progress. To do this, you can expand the notion of environment to include all the parts of the PI initiative and all the internal and external forces that impact it. Note that this is essentially what the process-influence triangle in Chapter 1 describes. This must include political and social factors. Have these factors changed since you began? In what way does the change affect your activities? Are there immediately obvious threats or protections? If you don't take time to look around and assess the situation, you may respond in a way that could jeopardize the PI effort's chances of surviving.

Sizing up your personal condition includes looking at how you and other members of the PI team are handling the stress that always comes with change. Are you asking more of yourselves and your stakeholders than you can effectively provide? Do you have the right skills and capabilities? Are there issues within the team that need to be resolved before dealing with the immediate problem? Checking the health of the people involved ensures that there are no other problems. As a friend from England once said, "You may be applying plaster after plaster to the wound you see, all the while bleeding to death from the wound you don't see!"

Taking stock of tools and weapons involves looking at your approaches, your people, your infrastructure, and even the target organization. Are the approaches and methods you are using effective and showing results? Is the network of people you need for information and support still viable? Do you need to look for a new tool or tactic? It's important that you know the tools that are working and those that aren't so that your recovery plan doesn't depend on a faulty premise.

Techniques that support *Size up the situation:*

- Readiness/fit analysis
- Satir change model

7.2 Undue haste makes waste

The manual says:

```
You may make a wrong move when you react quickly
without thinking or planning, and that move may
result in your capture or death. Don't move just
for the sake of taking action. Consider all aspects
of your situation (size up your situation) before
you make a decision and a move. If you act in
haste, you may forget or lose some of your equip-
```

```
ment, and you may become disoriented so that you
don't know which way to go. Plan your moves so that
you are prepared to move out quickly without endan-
gering yourself if the enemy is near you.
```

One of the most important reasons for sizing up the situation is to prevent taking action that ultimately could be harmful. Much of the scouting and planning we describe in the first two parts of the book is useful even during the execution of your project. A common pitfall for change efforts is charging ahead before sufficient commitment for the effort has been made by the relevant management team.

There are several possible ways to make sure you take the appropriate amount of time. Using the Reflect phase of the DLI life cycle as a "haste" monitor can keep you from jumping from success headlong into a major barrier. If you treat organizational change as a project with the relevant product development standards being applied, you can slow down before moving into unknown territory and identify the risks that are likely to occur. By having thought through your activities during planning, you'll also be less likely to become disoriented or distracted from your goals.

Techniques that support *Undue haste makes waste:*

- Technology adoption measurement
- Project retrospectives
- Readiness and fit analysis

7.3 Remember where you are

The manual says:

```
Pay close attention to where you are and to where
you are going. Do not rely on others present to keep
track of the route. Constantly orient yourself.
You should always try to determine, as a minimum,
how your location relates to:
```

- The location of enemy units and controlled areas.

- The location of friendly units and controlled areas.

- The location of local water sources (this is especially important in the desert).

- Areas that will provide good cover and conceal-
  ment.

Although true for every kind of project, it is especially critical that PI initiatives maintain orientation and track effort and benefits. One of the best tools for survival is the ability to show benefit from your effort. That will never happen if you aren't vigilant in monitoring your progress.

Maintaining communications with both supporters and the opposition (friendly and enemy units) is important to knowing where to expect pushback and where you can depend on support. Without this understanding, you may find yourself without the support you expected or miss an opportunity to turn an enemy into a friend.

Knowing safe territory and where to find scarce resources can help you through the inevitable lean times. Paying attention to your successes over time can provide you a stock of good will and champions when they are most needed. Having several sponsors and funding sources is ideal, although admittedly rare.

Not relying on others to determine your status keeps your opposition from hijacking your project and framing the numbers to put you in the worst possible light. Always be ready to defend your position and status. One of the key parts of your infrastructure should be a measurement framework to measure your progress toward your established goals. Measurement can't be left to chance; it has to be embedded in almost everything you do, but without a lot of overhead. A well-designed, lightweight measurement framework can help—especially one that tracks progress toward adoption of the new practices you're trying to implement.

Techniques that support *Remember where you are:*

- Satir change model
- Communications planning
- Technology adoption measurement (diffusion and infusion)

7.4 Vanquish fear and panic

The manual says:

> The greatest enemies in a combat survival/evasion
> situation are fear and panic. If uncontrolled,
> they can destroy your ability to make an intelligent

```
decision. They may cause you to react to your feel-
ings and imagination rather than to your situation.
They can drain your energy and thereby cause other
negative emotions. Previous survival/evasion train-
ing and self-confidence will enable you to vanquish
fear and panic.
```

Although generally not expressed by running and screaming, fear and panic often occur in process improvement or other change efforts. Both the change agent and the changed are vulnerable. Actual or perceived actions or conditions can trigger the panic response. Recognition and preparation can mitigate this risk by providing time to adapt and negating the impact of surprise.

Often, fear and panic are caused by a chain reaction of poor communication, active imaginations, and preconceived notions that result in imagined conclusions. Perception is all-important. Maintaining a clear understanding of where you are includes honestly and intentionally testing the perceptions of those involved. In the same vein, don't succumb to reacting to rumors. Track down the truth to the best of your ability, and use it to break the panic cycle as soon as possible.

Communication and training are also prophylactic activities for preventing fear and panic. Taking time to have the team role-play some common scenarios may seem to be overkill, but if the organization is likely to resist your activities strongly, role-playing may be useful.

People are often fearful when they first approach a model like CMMI. It looks so big and seems so complicated, and you hear all kinds of stories about it (both good and bad). Which stories should you believe? As with many scary things, the reality is often less than the image. When you're looking at the size of CMMI, for example, it is worth noting that the required and expected elements of the model take up fewer than 50 pages of the 600-pages-plus CMMI book.[3] The other pages contain informative material intended to help you understand the use of the model and multiple contexts for its use. Often, giving new users that piece of data alone reduces the fear level by a significant amount!

Techniques that support *Vanquish fear and panic:*

- Satir change model
- Communications planning

7.5 Improvise

The manual says:

> This easy-to-come easy-to-replace culture of ours
> makes it unnecessary for us to improvise. This
> inexperience in improvisation can be one of the
> greatest enemies in a survival situation. Learn to
> improvise. Take a tool designed for a specific pur-
> pose and see how many other uses you can make of
> it. Learn to use natural things around you for dif-
> ferent needs. An example is using a rock for a
> hammer. No matter how complete a survival kit you
> have with you, it will run out or wear out after
> awhile. But your imagination will not. Use it.

Imagination and creativity can be some of the most effective competencies to bring to bear on process improvement tasks. Agility depends on using the things at hand to solve problems. Being able to see new uses for existing objects is the best way to keep costs down and react quickly to problems.

Existing objects can be structures, communication paths, tools, reports, data, processes, practices, or gatherings. Piggyback on existing meetings or reports so as to lower overhead. Can you use the corporate dashboard to show improvement progress along with other project data? Use existing planning or requirements tools for your improvement project. Approaches from other disciplines—Total Quality Management (TQM), lean manufacturing (Toyota), Business Process Reengineering, software, systems, or other types of engineering—may be just the thing for you to get through to those difficult individuals or groups. Could a TQM force-field diagram help you determine the best way to approach a difficult audience? If you see something you think could be useful, follow SuZ's process improvement guerilla battle cry: "Reuse with pride! (But don't forget to credit your source.)"

Techniques that support *Improvise:*

- Crime Scene Investigation exercise
- Developing useful process guidance
- TBA-IPI and the IBMM

7.6 Value living

The manual says:

> All of us were born kicking and fighting to live. But we have become used to the soft life. We have become creatures of comfort. We dislike inconveniences and discomforts. So, what happens when we are faced with a survival situation with its stresses, inconveniences, and discomforts? This is when the will to live—placing a high value on living—is vital. The experience and knowledge you have gained through life and through your Army training have bearing on your will to live. Stubbornness, a refusal to give in to problems and obstacles that face you, will give you the mental and physical strength to endure.

This is one that's a bit tough to interpret at first, because we usually don't think of our organizational interactions as being "life or death"—but the change effort may mean the difference between retaining in-house software development capability and outsourcing that part of a product.

You may not need much physical strength to endure the organizational environment, but most change agents would agree that you need significant mental *and* emotional strength to endure. Certainly, key factors in success are the perseverance and stamina of the process improvement lead. There will be times when it will be easier to quit than go forward. The ability to overcome the temptation to quit for the wrong reasons is another important characteristic of PI leaders. There are some valid reasons to quit or radically change a PI effort, of course, and the strength to accept those is just as important.

One way to interpret *Value living* is to think of it as *Value living in this organization*. Essentially, one of the things you will want to review at various times in your improvement effort is whether you're still content being a citizen of the organization you're working in. If you reach a point where the answer is "No," you have ceased *Value living* in your organization, and it's probably time to think about alternatives.

We don't have particular techniques in Part 3 to address this (SuZ is fond of saying, "I don't do organizational therapy"). However, here are a couple of useful external resources we've used to help understand our own role in an organization and how we are dealing with it:

- *Please Understand Me,* by David Keirsey and Marilyn Bates, a book on using a popular personality typing technique, the Myers-Briggs Type Indicator, to understand some of your own and your fellow team members' preferences in several dimensions.[4]

- *Emotional Intelligence,* by Daniel Goldman, a book that postulates an Emotional Quotient similar to the more familiar Intelligence Quotient (IQ).[5]

7.7 Act like the natives

The manual says:

> The natives and animals of a region have adapted to their environment. To get a feel of the area, watch how the people go about their daily routine. When and what do they eat? When, where, and how do they get their food? When and where do they go for water? What time do they usually go to bed and get up? These things are important to you as an evader.

To some extent, we all adapt to the cultural environment of our organization. Learning to identify what adaptations people need to make to be effective in their organization can indicate areas where improvements would be welcomed.

You need to understand the "as is" organization and how decisions are reached in the current environment in the same way that you understand an "as is" process—perhaps not to the same level of detail, but well enough to realize how products get from "here to there" and into their next important transformation.

Observing the people affected by process change is also important. Try to adjust your communications and acceptance-building to the rhythm and structure of their activities. Easing into the flow will help you be less intrusive and perhaps seen as less of a threat to the status quo.

Communicating new or changed processes is difficult, particularly in large organizations. Central repositories are essential, but access must be easy, and incentives must be provided for use; otherwise, the electronic (or physical) dust will grow deep. Team-building and understanding the human dimensions of change can help speed acceptance and generate new change agents.

Techniques that support *Act like the natives:*

- Satir change model
- Developing useful process guidance

7.8 Live by your wits, learn basic skills

The manual says:

> Without training in basic skills for surviving and
> evading on the battlefield, your chances of living
> through a combat survival/evasion situation are
> slight. The time to learn these basic skills is
> *now*—not when you are headed for or are in the bat-
> tle. How you decide to equip yourself prior to
> deployment will impact on whether or not you sur-
> vive. You need to know about the environment to
> which you are going, and you must practice basic
> skills geared to that environment. For instance,
> if you are going to a desert, you need to know how
> to get water in the desert.

It takes time to adapt your behaviors to a "hostile situation." Thinking ahead and practicing early will make the transition easier. Understand your tools and techniques, and be efficient in using them. Wasting people's time trying to get a new appraisal spreadsheet to work doesn't endear you to the busy people you are hoping to help.

As stated in Part I, you should scout out the environment so that there are as few surprises as possible. The skills you need to manage change in different organizational contexts are quite different in some areas. Make sure you have the right skill set for the context. Do good planning, but don't be locked into the plan if the territory changes.

Developing and sustaining the mechanisms to perform the various process improvement activities and to manage the initiative over time is difficult and fraught with peril. If too little effort is spent, the initiative may be mired in a swamp full of tasks that never seem to be assigned to anyone. On the other hand, too much effort can kill any chance of a positive ROI, as well as give rise to the dreaded "process police" syndrome.

Part of the purpose of this book is to introduce you to some of the skills that we have seen as being crucial to starting and sustaining an improvement effort. Getting the right training for your improvement participants earlier rather than later (although not so early that they'll forget what to do in between training and applying!) is usually a good investment, especially if you're at a place where you know you need to do something but don't really understand what.

Techniques that support *Live by your wits, learn basic skills:*

- Everything!

7.9 Summary of Part III

In this part, we paused to take a breath before going forward with our process improvement journey and to provide some tools that will help you see things differently as you move forward. Our fictional case study has given you a picture of success in terms of what a relatively smooth initial improvement effort would look like. Your story will be different—smoother in some areas and rougher in others—but we encourage you to record your own story as you go along, for two reasons:

- The act of recording your story is one of the ways to reflect on your experience, which we strongly believe is one of the success factors in improvement.
- The SEI, as a community repository of industry data, often solicits case-study information, and contributing what you can is one of the ways that you can help advance the state of the practice in process improvement.

We also provided you with a literal survival-manual excerpt that has an amazing amount of wisdom for those who are working "in the trenches" of process improvement. We're sure that the U.S. Army never thought about this particular use of the wisdom that has gotten generations of soldiers through physically perilous situations. But the people we know in the army would be glad that even us "desk jockeys" have found something worthy in their doctrine. SuZ has given out many copies of a slide with the SURVIVAL acronym spelled out to people she's consulted or worked with. Even without the material in Part III, just having a discussion with someone about what this means can be enlightening.

Break's over, and it's time to get back to the tasks at hand: getting your improvement effort started and keeping it on track. If you're a sponsor of improvement, you may want to dip into Chapter 8, where we talk explicitly about obtaining and sustaining sponsorship for improvement, and Chapter 9, where we talk about setting and measuring against goals. Beyond that, you may not be as interested in the tools and techniques that we'll be presenting, although we'll be pleased if you decide that they are worth your time.

If you're the process improvement champion or leader, this is the heart of the book and the heart of the activities you'll be involved in. If you've already been through your own improvement effort, this may be where you start reading to find approaches that you missed on your first pass. At minimum, we expect that we'll be able to explain some of the things that may have puzzled you as you worked your way through your first cycle.

1. U.S. Army. *FM 21-76: U.S. Army Survival Manual.* (New York: Dorset Press, 1999).

2. Garcia, Suzanne, and Charles Meyers. "Out from Dependency: Thriving as a Process Insurgent in a Sometimes Hostile Environment." In *Proceedings of SEPG 2003.* (Pittsburgh: Carnegie Mellon University, 2003).

3. Chrissis, Mary Beth, Mike Conrad, and Sandy Shrum. *CMMI: Guidelines for Process Integration and Product Improvement.* (Boston: Addison-Wesley, 2003).

4. Keirsey, David and Marilyn Bates. *Please Understand Me II: Temperament, Character, Intelligence.* (Del Mar, CA: Prometheus Nemesis Books, 1998).

5. Goldman, Daniel. *Emotional Intelligence: Why It Can Matter More Than IQ.* (New York: Bantam Books, 1995).

Illustration from *The Travels of Marco Polo*
by Witold Gordon (1885–1968)

Part IV

Experiencing the Journey

> *I cannot rest from travel: I will drink*
> *Life to the lees: all times I have enjoy'd*
> *Greatly, have suffer'd greatly . . . that which we are, we are;*
> *One equal-temper of heroic hearts,*
> *Made weak by time and fate, but strong in will*
> *To strive, to seek, to find, and not to yield.*
> **Alfred, Lord Tennyson in** *"Ulysses"*

> *It's a dangerous business, Frodo, going out your door. You step into the Road, and*
> *if you don't keep your feet, there is no knowing where you might be swept off to.*
> **Gandalf the Wizard in J.R.R. Tolkien's** *Lord of the Rings*

> *You must travel a long and difficult road—a road fraught with peril, uh-huh,*
> *and pregnant with adventure. You shall see things wonderful to tell. . . . I cannot*
> *say how long this road shall be. But fear not the obstacles in your path, for*
> *Fate has vouchsafed your reward. And though the road may wind, and yea, your*
> *hearts grow weary, still shall ye foller the way, even unto your salvation.*
> **An old blind man on a flatcar in** *O Brother, Where Art Thou?*
> *by Ethan and Joel Coen*

> *Remember; no matter where you go, there you are.*
> **Buckaroo Banzai**

You've scouted, planned, imagined and prepared. It is time to launch your
initiative. Part IV provides you a journeybook describing the path you'll be

following through the observations of those who have gone before. It is your sailing log handed down from those who went before, warning of dangerous shoals and reefs, reminding you of how the winds blow, and describing the locations of the safe harbors. It is also your practical manual, providing you advice and tools to help along the way.

If, while reading this part, you sense an underlying structure, you will be absolutely right. We all know folks who never take the medicine they prescribe. To avoid being accused of such a fault, this part applies CMMI to the development and implementation of a process improvement program. We've referred to this approach elsewhere as "leading by example." In this case, it means that our toolkit, although arranged around the specific process improvement tasking from Chapter 3, is also based on the goals and practices of the CMMI Process Areas. We hope that this will provide you with a double benefit: presenting tools and ideas to help in your initiative and also showing how the model can be used creatively to support a variety of tasks.

One thing you will notice as you go through this material is that not *all* chapters go into equal depth in connecting CMMI Specific Practices to the improvement tasks. To highlight the connections, we've chosen a couple that are fairly obvious and a couple that are often problematic. Our experience is that after you've gotten into thinking this way and have seen some illustrations and examples that help you see typical ways to make the interpretations, you'll be fine with just the Process Area hints that we've provided in the table and sidebar.

Chapter 8

Developing and Sustaining Sponsorship

For many organizations, developing and sustaining sponsorship are difficult, nebulous tasks. The questions we often hear from champions of process improvement who are not part of the organization's leadership include

- How do I get sponsors to provide the right resources (both type and amount) for our improvement effort?
- How do I help them set realistic goals?
- How do I help them change their behaviors to be more consistent with the goals we've agreed on?
- How do I sustain my sponsors' interest in improvement, especially when results come slower than anticipated?
- How do I sustain sponsorship when the leadership of the organization changes? (This could be through merger, acquisition, personnel changes, and so on.)

For champions of process improvement who are already part of the organization's leadership, some of the questions are easier to deal with. We'll be focusing this section on champions who are trying to develop sponsorship and are not part of the organization's formal leadership.

As you can see from the previous questions, much of the focus of developing and sustaining sponsorship involves goal setting, goal alignment, and communication. Especially where process improvement champions come primarily from an engineering background, these may be skills that have not been exercised very deeply up to this point.

8.1 Communicating with and sustaining sponsorship of organizational leadership

> CMMI content related to this topic:
>
> - Organization Process Focus
> - Integrated Project Management
> - Generic Practice 2.10 Review with Higher Level Management

It's hard work to obtain effective sponsorship for your improvement effort. Equally important is sustaining that sponsorship. Each organization is different in terms of the exact mechanisms that will be needed to sustain your leadership's involvement in and sponsorship of the improvement effort, but we've never run into an organization where communication wasn't a key to those sustainment mechanisms.

What do sponsors want to hear about? In our experience, they mostly want assurance that (1) they've made the right decision to sponsor the improvement effort, (2) visible progress is being made toward the objectives that have been established for the improvement effort, and (3) The progress being made is consistent with the business goals of the organization.

CMMI has two Process Areas that specifically address these issues: Organizational Process Focus and Integrated Project Management. There is also at least one Generic Practice supporting the communication process that we'll mention.

Organizational Process Focus's goals are about the overall improvement effort: setting goals, appraising the state of the organization against those goals, and planning/implementing improvement actions in accordance with the organization's current state and the goals. Consider the following appraisal practice:

SP 1.2 APPRAISE THE ORGANIZATION'S PROCESSES

Appraise the organization's processes periodically and as needed to maintain an understanding of their strengths and weaknesses.[1]

This practice is a key to providing sponsors confidence that their investment is on its way to reaping the benefits that led to the decision to invest. Surprisingly, this practice is not just about formal activities that result in auditable results, such as an ISO 9001 certification audit or a SCAMPI A appraisal. The main point of this practice is to encourage you to think about and implement ways to understand the progress of your improvement effort so that you can provide all the stakeholders—including the sponsors of the improvement effort—information on progress.

A more subtle interpretation of this practice involves evaluating the process improvement practices of the organization. Appraising the internal processes used for improvement is a good way to understand better how to conduct appraisal activities and also helps those working in process improvement understand the work they have to do on their own processes to meet their objectives.

Communication per se is covered in Integrated Project Management. Again, this is a goal-level issue:

SG 2 COORDINATE AND COLLABORATE WITH RELEVANT STAKEHOLDERS

Coordination and collaboration of the project with relevant stakeholders is conducted.

The "project" we're talking about here is the improvement project. When we think about the relevant stakeholders we need to collaborate and communicate with, sponsors are pretty high, if not at the top of the list. So here's a case where we can directly use practices within the project management category of CMMI to apply to our own process improvement "projects."

There's also a Generic Practice, one of the practices that can be applied to any Process Area of the model, that explicitly calls for communication with sponsors:

GP 2.10 REVIEW STATUS WITH HIGHER-LEVEL MANAGEMENT

Review the activities, status, and results of the PA process with higher level management and resolve issues.

This Generic Practice doesn't define who "higher-level management" is in terms of exact roles. Instead, it encourages you to define which roles in your project/organization need to track status and then engage in review activities with them.

As you read the model, you will find other places that call for some specific communication about a particular topic.

8.2 Seeking sponsors: Applying sales concepts to building and sustaining support

One of the most interesting experiences SuZ had when working as the deployments manager for a small software company in the '90s was attending a "high-tech sales" seminar. This was one of those free, all-day awareness-building seminars meant to get you interested in taking a longer course. The topic of the seminar was Solution Selling, and the seminar was supported by a book of the same name.[2] There she was with all those entrepreneurs and sales professionals, and after about the first hour, all SuZ could think about was how the concepts the instructor was talking about applied beautifully to process improvement. The concepts and techniques provided insights on why some of her most frustrating PI moments occurred. She started looking at sales techniques from the viewpoint of *persuasion techniques*: persuading sponsors to part with financial resources and political capital.

When you look at sales concepts and techniques as persuasion techniques, their fit in process improvement efforts becomes obvious. First, you have to persuade potential sponsors that it's worth their time and effort to sanction the effort. Then you have to persuade key staff to participate in improvement activities. And then you have to persuade the group to actually adopt the new processes and practices that have been developed. That's a lot of persuading going on! And if you've been educated as an engineer, you've most likely been taught that the primary tool for persuasion is your data set. The data set for engineering decisions is a good bit different from the data set for organizational improvement decisions. And often, the most persuasive data isn't available until *after* improvement activities have taken place. So the alternative is a priori persuasion, which relies on analogy and anecdote.

Solution Selling techniques provide a nice series of understandable models to aid building and sustaining sponsorship. We'll introduce a few of the concepts here but strongly suggest that you add the Solution Selling book to your reading list if you're going to be one of the people trying to persuade your leadership to begin an improvement effort.

Key concepts from the Solution Selling seminar include

- *Sales strategies are problem-solving strategies.* The same kinds of issues that come up in facilitating a buyer's acquiring a product come up in facilitating the introduction ("sale") of a new technology into an organization.
- *Pain-Impact-Vision Cycle.* The things you need to do to be successful in sales are similar to those you need to do in building sponsorship:
  - ➤ Understand the buyer's/sponsor's need—the "pain" they are trying to overcome.
  - ➤ Help the buyer/sponsor move from a "feeling" of pain to an understanding of the business impacts of the pain.
  - ➤ Help the buyer/sponsor create a vision of "what could be different" if the new practices were adopted.
- *Buyer's Risk Cycle.* This cycle explains that understanding what's important to buyers at different points in their buying cycle is very insightful when you're looking at sponsorship decision cycle.

8.2.1 The Pain-Impact-Vision Cycle (PIV)

This cycle, shown in Figure 8-1, is what any buyer/sponsor navigates to get to a point where they can actually implement a complex solution. Solution Selling was invented to address the needs of high-tech sales professionals who are selling complex or advanced technical concepts to business-oriented decision makers. So the first step is to try to identify the "pain points" in the organization that relate to your solution and bring them to the forefront of the sponsor's mind. At this stage, it is likely that those pain points are latent; they have become part of the background of the organization that is always there, and you really notice them only if the condition goes away. Those of you who have chronic back problems can relate easily to this. You don't really realize how much pain you were in until you wake up one day (usually after medication and exercises and proper application of ice and heat . . .) and the pain is gone. What makes you decide to take the meds, do the exercises, and so on? For most of us, it's the increase of pain beyond its chronic state into an acute state. Up until then, it's just something we live with.

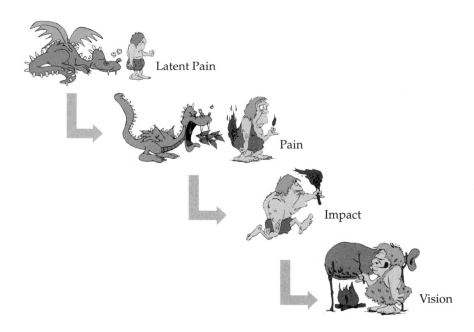

Figure 8-1: *Solution Selling's* Pain-Impact-Vision Cycle

Solution Selling's approach to moving a sponsor from latent pain to acute pain (pain uncomfortable enough to take action to change) is to focus on *anxiety* questions. These are usually open-ended questions that allow the sponsor to describe and elevate the awareness of areas of pain within the organization. So for identifying process improvement–related pain, you might use questions like "Tell me about your experiences with project completion in this organization" or "What is it like to manage projects when your organization goes through a hypergrowth spurt?" This allows them to talk about problems (and successes) and bring them to the forefront of their awareness.

When some areas of pain are identified, you help the sponsor understand the business impact of the pain areas. So here, you would ask *capability* questions, such as "How does not having enough people impact your ability to estimate projects accurately?" or "How much time do you think is lost in one-on-one training of new people in proper configuration management practices?" These questions are meant to connect some aspect of pain (shortage of resources, inefficient use of scarce resources) to a concrete business impact (cost and schedule overruns, quality). Especially at the beginning of an improvement cycle, this is a crucial aspect of getting buy-in, because you typically don't have the kind of measurements going on within the organization that would allow the calculation of a "real" Return on Investment. If you have strong connections between pain areas and the business impact of the problems, solving them automatically provides a strong benefit to the organization. Clearly articulating these connections can act as a surrogate for ROI until you get more standard measures in place.

Moving a sponsor from business-impact realization to Vision involves connecting the solution (in this case, process improvement) to the Pain and the Impact. Often, this is done with *control* or *confirming* types of questions, such as "So you're saying that if you had a way to include formal estimation in each project, you think your project performance would be better?" or "Would having a standard set of procedures for creating baselines help with your configuration management training problem?" Embedded in these questions is actually a piece of a solution.

The CMMI Business Analysis, covered in Chapter 12, is one technique for helping identify acute pain areas in relation to CMMI within an organization and understand their business impact. One of its purposes, by design, is to help move the organization through the PIV cycle.

Becoming familiar with this cycle and techniques to navigate it will help you get a potential sponsor's attention and turn that attention into action. Interpreting the answers you get from the questions, however, can be more complicated than you might guess. This is because there are sets of conflicting issues that a buyer/sponsor is typically dealing with when going through this cycle. That's where understanding the Buyer's Risk Cycle comes into play.

8.2.2 The Buyer's Risk Cycle

The four issues sponsors are juggling in their heads when provided a proposal for process improvement are

1. What are my needs related to process improvement?
2. How would this initiative fit my needs?
3. What is the cost/price of the initiative?
4. What are the risks if I say yes?

As Figure 8-2 illustrates, the amount of attention and concern that each of these elicits changes over time. Needs and cost issues are paramount to defining the sponsor's pain and impact. As the sponsor moves toward Vision, the solution and price of the solution come into play, and at the very end of the cycle (when everything seems to be going swimmingly from your

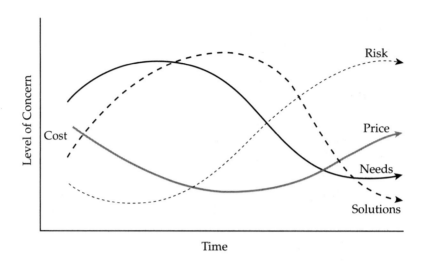

Figure 8-2: *Buyer's Risk Cycle*

viewpoint as the champion), risk becomes the dominant issue. Understanding that this is a natural cycle will probably save you a few sleepless nights and help you understand the kind of information that's needed, particularly at the end of the cycle.

SuZ relates the following story as an example:

When I was implementing process improvement in my home organization in the late 1980s, one of the practices I proposed was formal inspections—a technique that had tons of data behind it in terms of its ability to reduce the number of defects fielded in a complex system. It has some particular organizational needs, so I thought one of our more advanced projects would be most likely to succeed with it. I presented it to the project's management, who liked the idea and had me present it to the technical staff. Up until the technical-staff presentation, everything looked like the project manager would approve.

At the presentation to the technical staff, there was a general reaction that "our projected defects are low enough at this point that we don't see much benefit in a rigorous technique like this." In other words, they weren't feeling any pain (yet!). The project manager knew they were starting to slip schedules, but he didn't see the connection between rework due to defects and schedule slips. So the negative tech-staff reaction raised the risk of reducing productivity by adopting a new technique. Two days later, he canceled the inspections initiative. His pain wasn't acute enough to accept the risk of alienating his staff, who couldn't even consider any pain. So I went to another project that was not nearly as "advanced" but had a tremendous number of defects. Their schedule couldn't tolerate the rework from the defect injection level they were experiencing. Their pain was acute, and its business impact was clear to both the team and management. Formal inspections were a visibly perfect match to their situation.

Not surprisingly, after the first delivery on the "advanced" project, their technical lead came to me asking if I could teach them formal inspections; their delivered defects versus projected defects were not even close, and they were experiencing the pain of customer complaints in a big way. Their latent pain had indeed become acute!

8.3 Being a sponsor: Welcome to the "foreign element"

So you're in a position of leadership within an organization, and you've decided to think about adopting some model for process improvement. You've probably made changes happen in your organization before, but you may not have thought about what was happening in your organization while the change was taking place. We've found that understanding some of the dynamics of how people react to change (after all, it's *people* we're asking to change their behavior) is helpful both to sponsors and to those asked to change.

There are several ways of representing the cycle of responses human beings make to change. The most useful one that we have found is called the Satir Change Model, after its author, Virginia Satir. It is useful both because it is descriptive (it does a pretty decent job of explaining the symptoms that we often see in organizations going through a change) and because it is somewhat prescriptive (it provides some ideas of what you can do to make it easier for people to navigate the cycle of change). Our interpretation of the Satir model relies most heavily on Gerald Weinberg's explanation of it in his book *Quality Software Management Volume 4: Anticipating Change.*[3]

Figure 8-3 presents a graphic summary of the Satir Change Model. The individual or group starts out at some level of performance, represented as the Old Status Quo. The introduction of a change intended to improve the individual or group's performance is treated by the group as a "foreign element." The group will have different reactions to the foreign element. Some of the possibilities include

- Trying to ignore the foreign element
- Trying to find a way to accommodate the foreign element within their own current way of doing things
- Trying to explicitly reject the foreign element

The energy that goes into these reactions causes swings in the performance of the group that can be dramatic, depending on the character and size of the change being introduced. At some point, if the foreign element doesn't go away, most groups will find what Satir calls the "transforming idea" that will allow the group to integrate the change into their way of doing things and will allow them to move on. When the group has found and accepted a transforming idea, it proceeds to integrate the new behavior into its routines by practicing the new behavior. During this time, the group's performance starts to improve; however, this increased performance can occur only if there is opportunity for practice of the new behavior. After the new behavior is integrated into the group's behavior, it becomes the new status quo, and whatever performance increases have been achieved are likely to continue at this point.

We'll discuss particular aspects and implications of the Satir Change Model at various points in our journey. One of the most important aspects of the Satir model in relation to building and sustaining sponsorship is to recognize that the timing of the cycle is different for different individuals and groups within the organization. In particular, what often happens in an organization

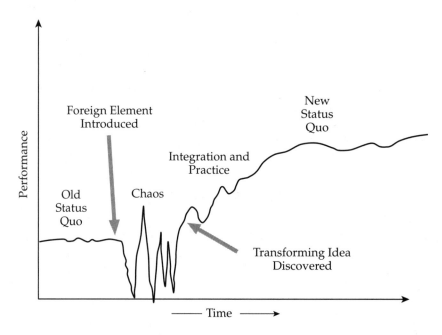

Adapted from G. Weinberg, *Quality Software Management, Volume 4: Anticipating Change*

Figure 8-3: *Graphical summary of the Satir Change Model*

is that the members of the leadership group get exposed to a foreign element, go through their own phase of chaos, figure out the transforming idea and integrate it into their own thinking, and then are ready to have the organization adopt it. When you, as the sponsor of the change, propose it or announce it to your subordinates, you've gone through your change cycle, but they haven't yet, so what you're introducing to them is *their* foreign element. They still have their own change cycle to go through. This lack of synchronization between the change cycles of different groups within an organization (one group has already integrated the change, another is in the middle of trying to find its transforming idea, and still another hasn't even seen the foreign element yet) is one of the greatest challenges for sponsors, especially when the sponsor has already completed the change cycle and has a vision of how he or she wants the organization's performance to be enhanced.

1. Chrissis, Mary Beth, et al. *CMMI: Guidelines for Process Integration and Product Improvement.* 2d ed. (Boston: Addison-Wesley, 2006). All references to CMMI components in this chapter are from this source.

2. Bosworth, Michael, et al. *Solution Selling: Creating Buyers in Difficult Selling Markets.* (Scarborough, Ont.: Irwin Professional Publishing, 1995).

3. Weinberg, Gerald. *Quality Software Management Volume 4: Anticipating Change.* (New York: Dorset House Publishing, 1997).

Chapter 9

Setting and Measuring Against Realistic Goals

Even if you're just trying to improve one or two small processes, being clear about your goals and having an explicit plan for how you will measure progress against those goals will improve your overall chances of success. In this chapter, we'll talk about various aspects of setting goals and some aspects of measuring against them that you may not have seen before. Note that here and elsewhere in the book, when we talk about goals, we're talking about the general notion of goals as something that you are striving to achieve. In CMMI, goals are actually a model contruct—there are Specific Goals and Generic Goals. When we are using the CMMI notion of goals, we'll capitalize them as you see here to distinguish them from the common usage.

9.1 Setting goals and success criteria aligned with sponsor objectives

CMMI content related to this topic:

- Organizational Process Focus
- Integrated Project Management
- Measurement and Analysis
- Organizational Innovation and Deployment
- Causal Analysis and Resolution

There is some direct guidance related to this task in three Process Areas of CMMI: Organizational Process Focus (OPF) (through the IPPD-related goals), Integrated Project Management (IPM), and Measurement and Analysis (M&A). In addition, when thinking about sources of goals, two other Process Areas—Organizational Innovation and Deployment (OID) and Causal Analysis and Resolution (CAR)—may be useful.

It may seem strange for us to mention two Process Areas that, from a Maturity Level viewpoint, are high maturity Process Areas (OID and CAR are both Maturity Level 5 Process Areas). It is true the greatest benefit from both of these comes when you have a quantitative basis for making the decisions called for in their practices. However, we see organizations making good use of the practices in these Process Areas even at the beginning of their improvement journey.

In relation to setting and measuring goals, both CAR and OID have practices related to selecting improvements to try in the organization. In CAR, the decision is based on analyzing past defects and problems to see how to prevent them in the future. In OID, the decision is based on analyzing what's going on in the overall organization as well as outside the organizational boundaries to find potential innovations and improvements. Both of these are good sources of candidate improvement goals. Both also talk about evaluating the results from the improvements you make, which relates to measuring against your goals. In the following discussion we look at the primary process areas that directly address sources of improvement goals and measuring against them.

Organizational Process Focus emphasizes creating and following a process improvement plan that is based on the sponsor's objectives.

In IPM, one of the specific practices is

SP 3.1 Establish the Project's Shared Vision.[1]

Establish and maintain a shared vision for the project.

Creating a shared vision of the improvement project is one of the ways to understand whether you have correctly understood and aligned this initiative with your sponsor's objectives. The term *shared vision* is defined in the CMMI glossary as "a common understanding of guiding principles including mission, objectives, expected behavior, values, and final outcomes, which are developed and used by a group, such as an organization, project, or team. Creating a shared vision requires that all people in the group have an opportunity to speak and be heard about what really matters to them."

This is one of the places where the model uses its practices as a way to help organizations and projects (and remember, your process improvement effort is in many ways a project) understand the values upon which the model is based. This practice is at least as much about the value of open communication as it is about the mechanics of creating a shared vision.

Alignment with the organization is what is particularly called for in IPM. Organizational goals need to actually affect the behavior of the people who create organizational value or they aren't very useful. In addition, projects are tied to the *process* objectives of the organization via IPM's tailoring practices; these practices expect that your project's process will be explicitly derived from the organization's set of standard processes. In an organization that has invested in creating process guidance that reflects the organization's goals, constraints, and values, this is another way to support alignment of projects with the organization.

Finally, in Measurement and Analysis, a Specific Goal focuses on establishing goals that are aligned with the organization's objectives:

SG 1: Align Measurement and Analysis Activities

Measurement objectives and activities are aligned with identified information needs and objectives.

When you look at the Specific Practices under this Goal, you will see the focus on aligning measurement activities with the appropriate objectives and the information needed to accurately provide a perspective on whether those have been met.

9.1.1 Setting useful goals

As you can see from the preceding discussion, the goals that you set have a significant effect on what activities you undertake, how you decide to measure them, and what kinds of attitudes and behaviors you incentivize and discourage. So setting useful goals is something you should be willing to spend an appropriate amount of time and effort on with the leaders within your organization.

What is a useful goal? We like the model of SMART[2] goals:

- *Specific.* It's something whereby successful completion can clearly be determined.

- *Measurable.* The measure could be a specific value (average 500 widgets/day over 3 months), binary (yes/no), or scaled (10 percent versus 50 percent), but the measure must be appropriate for the goal.

- *Achievable/Attainable.* It's something you can actually do something about.

- *Realistic/Relevant.* Even though it may be a stretch, it's something you truly believe is within the capabilities of your staff and the constraints of your environment, and is something whose achievement will be beneficial to you.

- *Time-based/Tangible.* For some goals, a time factor is necessary; otherwise, the goal is OBE (overcome by events). Goals that are not time-based should be tangible and observable, so that an objective evaluation of their satisfaction is feasible.

Ideally, your improvement goals will be based on your business goals. There are lots of resources on business goals if you feel that you need to work on this before you get too involved in improvement activities. We often find that organizations haven't spent enough effort thinking about their business goals to be able to tell what improvement goals would be most useful to them. If you don't find something specifically on that topic, look in Strategic Planning references (we like the ones from www.grove.com). In particular, you might look for information on the Balanced Scorecard concept.[3]

The Balanced Scorecard concept is one that is used in many industries, and it provides a way of segmenting your goals so that no single aspect of your business gets exclusive focus. The scorecard is usually presented as a four-quadrant matrix, with typical headings including

- *Financial.* Goals related to the financial health of the organization.

- *Customer.* Goals related to the market segments and customer focus of the organization.

- *Operations.* Goals related to the processes, facilities, and other aspects of the organization. (This is where you most often see the initial alignment between business and improvement goals.)

- *Learning and innovation.* Goals related to improving the distinctive competencies of the organization and making it more responsive to the relevant changes in its technical and market environment.

Different authors use different specific labels, but these are the ones we find most useful.

In Chapter 15, we include an example of setting SMART process improvement goals for you to think about when developing your own goals.

9.1.2 A word about Maturity Level goals

In a book dealing with CMMI or any other model with associated achievement stepping stones, we really have to say something about a common improvement goal that we see in many organizations: *the Maturity Level goal.* This goal usually takes the form *"Achieve Maturity Level <n> by <date y>."* The parts of SMART that this kind of goal usually violates are: A—it is often not achievable with the current staff capabilities, and R—the date time frame is often not Realistic, and the Relevance of this goal may be visible only to the managers who set it.

There's one other problem with this goal, if you're the person who agreed to be responsible: *you* can't achieve it without successful adoption of the new practices in parts of the organization that you're not responsible for. (Note that this goal doesn't even talk about the organizational scope for this achievement—another problem.) This is *not* a goal that you should accept as "your" goal. It may be appropriate for the sponsor of the effort to accept, provided that he or she has explored the derivative goals that would need to be accepted by you and the parts of the organization that will be implementing the new practices.

More reasonable goals for the process improvement group (depending on where you are in your improvement effort) might be

- Facilitate at least two improvement teams that successfully implement new practices for the XYZ Process by implementing practices of the necessary CMMI Process Areas by <desired date>.

- Establish the measurement repository and procedures that will be needed to operate at Level <n> by <desired date>.
- Create and deploy end-user process description standards that are approved by the Steering Group by <desired date>.
- Ensure that role-based training for roles X, Y, and Z in processes A, B, and C are available for delivery by <desired date>.

Establishing (and negotiating) SMART goals for your improvement effort is challenging but necessary for an ongoing improvement effort.

9.1.3 SMART goals for your first DLI cycle

You may decide to adopt some simpler goals before investing in a huge amount of effort to align your organizational business goals with a set of organizational improvement goals. These are what we call "solve the problem" goals. They are usually much more constrained in scope and effort but are still valid SMART goals, and they are the kind of goals that often make the most difference in your organization's willingness to go forward with an ongoing improvement effort. These are goals such as:

- By <desired date>, establish a mutually agreed-upon project-status meeting agenda to be used every month by the project team and the customer.
- By <desired date>, establish and use a procedure for approving changes to previously released products that is agreed to by all of the following roles: <list the stakeholders for this procedure>.

How do you find goals like these and determine whether achieving them is worth the effort invested? Sometimes it's easy; just look at the minutes of your last few management meetings, and see what problems or issues keep coming up multiple times. Sometimes you need to spend a little time explicitly investigating where your staff are experiencing problems. Our technique for doing this includes the bonus of connecting typical business problems to areas of CMMI. (Someone familiar with another model could do something similar for that model.) It's called CMMI-based Business Analysis, and step-by-step instructions for performing one are provided in Chapter 15.

9.2 Understanding the current state of the organization: Readiness and Fit Analysis for CMMI

When deciding on your readiness to start a model-based improvement effort, we believe it's best to go into it with your eyes wide open. One of the implications of this philosophy is that, as part of approaching process improvement, you should look at the "fit" of your organization's conditions with the assumptions that are built into whichever model you're planning to use. For the discussion of this technique, we'll use CMMI as the model we're comparing to.

A prerequisite to this technique is that you understand the assumptions of the model (or product; this technique is also useful for evaluating the fit of a particular support product to your organization). SuZ has developed analyses for several technologies and products that she has worked with. In general, anyone who is familiar with how a particular model is implemented should be able to look at one of our sample tables and derive a similar table for that model.

The organizational factors that are covered in this technique involve non-technical factors that have historically affected (positively or negatively) adoption of practices/technologies similar to the one being contemplated. Several of these factors are derived from Paul Adler's work related to updating a company's technology base, and they are supplemented by SEI research related to managing technological change in organizations.[4] Areas considered in the technique include

- *Business Strategy.* How well aligned is the model being contemplated with the overall business strategy of the organization?
- *Reward System.* How well has the organization constructed reward systems that encourage use of the new practices and discourage continuation of old practices?
- *Sponsorship.* How well does sponsoring management for new practice adoption "walk the talk" by recognizing and reinforcing use of the new practices?
- *Work Practices.* How easily does the organization historically implement work practice changes related to adoption of the model? (Note that the primary method of assessing this with a model like CMMI is to do some kind of practice-based gap analysis.)

- *Values.* How well does the organization match its own company values to the values implied by practices it has adopted in the past?
- *Skills.* Does the organization traditionally ensure that employees have relevant technical experience and/or project management experience related to adopting new practices?
- *Structure.* How well has the organization historically recognized the (potential) need for new roles and responsibilities when new practices were implemented?
- *History.* What lessons has the organization internalized (for good or ill!) related to past history of new practice adoption?

Understanding your organization's historical pattern in these nontechnical risk areas can help you avoid choosing an improvement model as the basis for your improvement effort that is likely to play to your organization's weaknesses versus its strengths.[5]

9.2.1 What does a Readiness and Fit Analysis (RFA) look like?

There are two elements of a RFA: a summary profile and a list of risks to be mitigated as part of the improvement planning activities. The summary profile can be represented either as a histogram (bar chart) or Kiviat diagram (also called a radar chart).

Figure 9-1 shows a bar-chart version of a RFA, and Figure 9-2 shows the same data depicted in a radar chart.

The bar chart helps you understand the variation in responses from the individuals who did the scoring; the radar chart helps you see where there are strengths and weaknesses related to the factors. In this example, the greatest strength is that CMMI fits well with the organization's business strategy, but the rest of the factors are not differentiated dramatically. The two lowest are Reward System and Sponsorship (2.3 average rating each), so those would be the areas where we would expect to see the most significant risks come up in the risk-identification part of the RFA.

The second, and more important, part of the analysis is the identification of conditions or risks that led the people involved in the scoring to make that particular judgment. Here is a sample list of conditions that were identified during the running of several RFA workshops. Note that they take different language forms, depending on the way each organization talks about risks. These types of statements tend to be highly contextual to the organization that generates them, so they may be difficult for outsiders to understand.

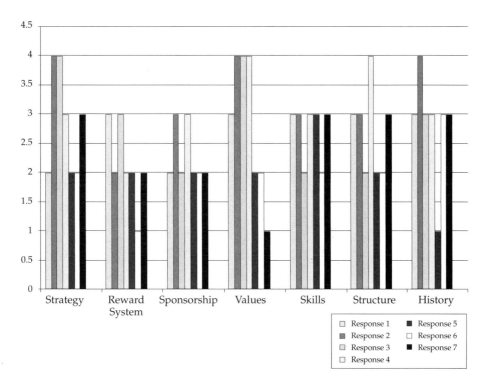

Figure 9-1: *RFA bar chart showing individual response variations*

Strategy-related:

- Given new business and regenerated growth, resources will be fully utilized in this quest rather than improving performance.
- A higher force than process improvement here is customer management.
- The focus is toward winning business versus improvement.

Sponsorship-related:

- Rotation of top management is frequent, and consistency of sponsorship is not maintained.
- Given that we built a fear culture at the senior management review, there is a possibility that we will drive a fear-based culture throughout the organization.
- Top-management time may not be sufficient to support full rollout.

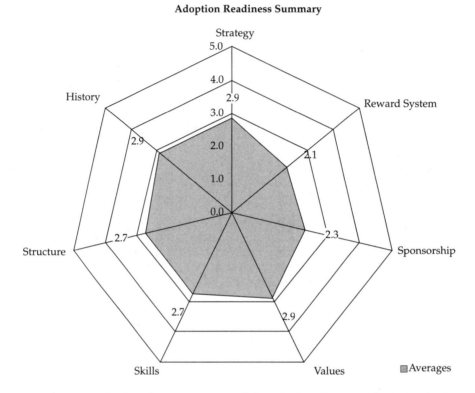

Figure 9-2: *Radar-chart summary of CMMI Readiness and Fit Analysis*

Reward System-related:

- Given that past projects have missed the overall cost when a single part of the organization benefits, there is a possibility that we will deploy processes that don't lead to overall benefit.
- Given that each business area is measured on financial goals, there is a possibility that we have a very stovepiped approach.

Values-related:

- History suggests that we still reward firefighting above all other things; we have more qualified firefighters than any other discipline.
- High-level management is interested in metrics for driving improvements, but history means many people are suspicious of their intent and think punishment may follow.

Skills-related:

- Some skill areas will find CMMI too much because they are still learning other skills.
- Structured training programs are not available and clear career development paths are not defined.

Structure-related:

- Values are not adopted at all levels; neither are they refreshed often enough.
- There are too many hats per person.
- Generally, we have the structure in place for management of projects, but there are risks with interfaces and definition of responsibilities and accountabilities.

History-related:

- Experience of past change: There is a possibility that we may not be aligned moving forward.
- Given that we are by nature a constantly changing organization, there is a possibility that new ways may, after CMMI is started, be seen as initiative.

When a set of conditions or risks has been generated that is specific to the organization, it can be used to plan (1) prioritization of model-based improvement activities and (2) specific mitigation strategies to improve the fit of the model to the organization.

9.2.2 A nominal assumptions table for CMMI†

Table 9-1 is the assumptions table we've used with organizations to help them understand some of the nontechnical assumptions that are inherent in CMMI.

The characteristics listed in Table 9-1 provide a picture of the "ideal" organization implementing CMMI. You could argue that if all these elements were present, you wouldn't need CMMI, which could be true. We've encountered very few organizations that exhibit all these characteristics and that don't use a model or set of practices or principles similar to CMMI to guide them and keep them on track.

---

† Note that if you find other references to this technique, you'll see the assumptions table referred to as a *technology* assumptions table. Those of us in the technology transition research field think of CMMI and similar models as process technologies. However, for many people, using this terminology proves problematic, so we've simplified the term for use in this example.

Table 9-1: *CMMI Assumptions Table*

Fit Dimension	CMMI Assumptions
Strategy	Improving organizational effectiveness is a priority. Improving effectiveness of processes to achieve better performance is an accepted approach.
Work Practices	Because the whole model is work practices, this factor is addressed in detail through a model-based gap analysis. *Note: This factor was initially intended to consider work practices associated with the adoption of a commercial software product. In the examples provided, which are CMMI-centric, we don't include the Work Practices dimension in the summary profiles.*
Reward System	The organization rewards participation in overall efficiency over individual department efficiency. The organization rewards improvement in skills related to process management and support. The organization rewards fire prevention more than firefighting. The Reward System will support incentives for high-performance teams (if IPPD is to be implemented).
Sponsorship	The organization's leadership exhibits strong, consistent support for improving old practices or implementing new ones. Penalties for avoiding the new practices are applied consistently. Sponsorship is sufficiently broad to include all processes and activities to be improved.
Values	Measurements are used to improve the organization's performance, not to punish individuals. Participative management is encouraged. Mistakes are tolerated, as long as they lead to improved processes/performance. Long-term improvement is worth short-term effort, even if ROI is obtained later.

Table 9-1: *CMMI Assumptions Table* (Continued)

Fit Dimension	CMMI Assumptions
Skills	Project planning and management skills (enough to manage a process improvement project) are available.
	Organization-change management skills are available.
Structure	Clear definition of roles/responsibilities/authorities exists.
	Management is a role that is responsible for the effectiveness of the processes in use within the organization, not a performing role, in terms of delivering products and services.
	Activities can be rationalized and organized around the concept of projects.
History	Helpful if other practice-based technologies have been successfully adopted with this management/leadership team.

One quick way you can use this table is to look at the assumptions and decide whether the things mentioned there are things you would like to see in your organization. If the traits shown are of no interest to you, you may find that another set of practices would be more useful (but be sure to check its assumptions also). If you're in the situation of being "mandated" to use CMMI, you won't be using these assumptions as much to check the desirability of using CMMI as you will to mitigate the risks of adopting CMMI into your organization.

For most potential sponsors of improvement, risk analysis is the primary use of RFA. Whether you have to use CMMI or think you want to use CMMI, knowing where the assumptions built into CMMI practices clash with your organization's current characteristics helps you understand areas that you'll have to spend more effort on in your change-management activities. In some cases, you may decide (if you have the choice) that your organization needs to work on some of these areas before formally adopting CMMI.

9.2.3 How do the risks I've identified affect my ideas?

By the time you get through choosing a set of three or so Process Areas and the projects and people you think should be involved in them, you're at a good point to step back and compare the risks you identified through your Readiness and Fit Analysis with the PAs and projects you've chosen. If the projects you've selected reflect or exhibit the risks that you identified, you have a couple of choices:

1. Avoid that project, and pick one that doesn't involve as many risks or risks as severe.
2. Work with that project, but include specific mitigation actions and monitoring to try to minimize the occurrence and/or effect of the identified risks.

If the risks you've identified make it clear that one of the PAs you've selected could be a problem, your choices are

1. Pick another PA that may not solve as big a problem but reflects fewer risks.
2. Work with that PA, but include specific mitigation actions and monitoring to try to minimize the occurrence and/or effect of the identified risks.

Chapter 15 provides more detailed instructions on performing Readiness and Fit Analysis.

9.3 How do you tell if you've succeeded?

> CMMI content related to this section:
>
> - Measurement and Analysis
> - Organization Innovation and Deployment

In section 9.1, we highlighted the importance of establishing useful, achievable goals and identifying clear measures to record progress. In this section, we'll look at measurement issues more closely, discuss some of the issues we've seen, and identify some approaches that can help you avoid or at least mitigate them.

The task is to define, and then measure progress against, realistic and measurable goals for your improvement effort. Most organizations that undertake model-based improvement have a mix of different goals in mind. There are usually some very well-defined goals, like "Reduce defects by some percentage in delivered products" or "Decrease time to market by some percentage." Then there are always the somewhat squishy goals, like "Improve organizational communication."

The well-defined goals are usually easy to measure, and ROI for the sponsors can be calculated in a straightforward manner. The squishy goals are harder to measure. How do you know if the organization is communicating better: because project performance has improved or because more people attend staff meetings? And what is it worth to have the organization communicating better? Trying to establish ROI here is on very shaky grounds, so to sell your sponsor, you may need to discover indirect measures that can help show the benefit. Squishy goals are also often difficult to accomplish. They may require a big enough improvement effort that you probably need to consider whether you have the money, and want to spend the money, on achieving them.

To be clear, though, measurable doesn't always mean quantitative. Especially in the beginning, a goal that solves a specific problem is often the type that gives you immediate relief from some organizational pain, and the measurable improvement is "no more pain." That's a binary, qualitative measure, but it still could have powerful business value, depending on how the painful problem is actually affecting your business.

9.3.1 Return on Investment (ROI)

ROI is a thorny issue. The primary reason for this is that it involves business rather than technical measures. ROI is so highly dependent on how you define costs and benefits that it acts more as a sponsorship rationale than as a truly useful measure.

ROI is essentially the net benefits received less the expenditures made, divided by the net benefits. Defining costs is fairly straightforward. Labor hours, facilitation and meeting costs, and possibly lost productivity are all manageable and countable. It is the pesky benefits side of the equation that generally is the most difficult to pin down. One issue is causality. Process improvement rarely happens in a vacuum. There are always external factors that come into play. Did the defect rate improve because of process improvement or because of the new engineer we hired? Are we quicker to market because of leaner processes or because of the new Web-based development support environment? Generally, arguing causality is wasted effort. It becomes a matter of perception rather than fact. What you can do is compromise and claim some percentage of the specific benefit, although allocation can also be contentious.

Much can be gained by establishing your ROI measurement efforts with the idea of presenting the results to management firmly in mind. Don Reifer, a longtime engineering and process consultant, has wrestled with the ROI problem and how to present it to executive sponsors for many years. He offers some tips on packaging ROI numbers that we think are worthwhile, so (with his permission) we provide them here:

- When developing ROI numbers, use a multiyear timeframe. This approach makes the investment strategic and buys you several years to accumulate what management thinks is an acceptable return or payback.
- When pursuing reductions in cost, emphasize cost avoidance instead of cost savings, because management views the latter as reductions in staff, not expenses.
- Quantify cost avoidance simply by showing how costs on the organization's highest-priority project (the "cash cow") can be reduced through the use of existing process resources.
- Use cost models (such as COCOMO II for software) to show the cost, productivity, and time-to-market impacts of process improvement programs, both organizationally and for large and important projects. By varying model parameters such as Process Maturity (PMAT) in COCOMO II, you can show parametrically how effort and duration vary as a function of maturity level.
- If you can get competitor performance data from public sources, use it to show how process improvement will help you improve the organization's competitive position. If not, use industry benchmarks. Reducing perceived or actual gaps with competition is the most compelling case you can develop when justifying expenditures.
- Use public sources of data to validate the numbers. Also, compare cost, productivity, and quality norms against those that are used in the organization. These are the rules of thumb your executives use to validate the numbers that come before them. If your numbers are different, you will have to explain why. Be prepared even when the organization's numbers are either fantasy or folklore.
- Enlist the support of staff organizations (finance and accounting, legal, marketing, and so on), when they exist, to package the numbers in acceptable ways. They can help you put the right executive spin on the numbers.

Although Don recommends that low-maturity organizations use cost and productivity to justify their numbers, he switches to quality measures as the primary basis for benefits for high-maturity groups. It is interesting to note that his research confirms that quality improvement yields the biggest gains when the process is institutionalized.[6]

9.3.2 Hawthorne effects

As you establish measures, it is probably wise not to forget that human psychology is a key ingredient in processes that involve critical thinking and creativity. You should probably consider the *Hawthorne effect*—a well-supported premise from group psychology that any kind of change often (but not always) results in some kind of measurable improvement, because just paying attention to people often creates motivation.[7,8] And when people know they are being studied/measured, they will often try to optimize their performance around the variable they *perceive* is being measured, completely unrelated to what is actually being measured.

Here's an example from the software world of measuring something and getting something different from what you wanted. If you measure productivity in terms of Lines of Code per hour (LOC is a typical size measure in the software industry), and people are rewarded for having higher productivity numbers (for example, more LOC per hour), you will start to see some anomalous behaviors. People may start writing code that is inefficient but verbose or adding lots of comment lines with nothing in them, so that when the code is counted, they show lots of LOC. Now if you change the measure to *Source* Lines of Code (comment lines don't count), you'll see a big reduction in the amount of commenting (not necessarily a good thing), but you'll still see choices being made that favor verbose code versus efficient code. This might be exactly what you want if you think that the verbose code is easier to understand than the more efficient code (often, this is the case). If you really need very efficient code to meet the software's performance goals, verbose code is *not* likely to be what you want. But the measure that you're using incentivizes verbose over efficient code. If you want to get efficient code, you'll have to change the measure for productivity.

Many organizations have moved away from lines of code as a size measure because of problems like this. A popular alternative, that focuses more on the amount of functionality delivered per time unit, is called function points. There is an international organization that sets standards for and provides support for function points as a size/complexity measure for software. Go to www.ifpug.org for more information on function points and related measures.†

9.3.3 Measuring progress through diffusion and infusion measures

One thing that should be clear from reading the section on goals and business value is that you can't measure many of the results until you've actually done something differently. And for some goals (such as Return on Investment for a particular change), you may have to go through an entire project life cycle before you can see the effects of the change. If your projects are short (<6 months' duration) or you use an incremental life cycle with short (<6 months) increments, this may be just fine. But if you're involved in longer-term increments or projects, you probably don't want to wait 12 or 18 months to find out whether what you've done is having the effect you want. So progress measures become important in this case.

Progress measures are usually a surrogate for the measures of business value that you really want from an improvement activity. There are three types of surrogate measures you will want to pay attention to: project measures, diffusion measures, and infusion measures. As in any project, you can measure things like milestones achieved and resources consumed. You can get information on those types of measures from most of the models themselves (certainly, you can within CMMI) or from project management guides (such as the Project Management Institute's *Guide to the Project Management Body of Knowledge*[9]). We won't go into those here. The ones you won't find in those kinds of sources are measures for *diffusion*—how broadly a new practice has reached within the organization—and *infusion*—how deeply a new practice has penetrated into the intended audience for the practice.[10, 11]

Chapter 15 provides guidance on how diffusion and infusion measurement can be used to help you determine the adoption progress of your new practices. Both *depth* and *breadth* of adoption progress need to be measured if you hope to know when you're ready to measure Return on Investment. Infusion measures help you establish some of the transition mechanisms needed to achieve your Level of Use goals. Diffusion measures help you establish some of the rationale behind the transition mechanisms you have chosen to achieve your infusion goals.

---

† An irony is that much discussion and research has gone into how to convert function points to lines of code and back again—*c'est la guerre*, eh?

1. Chrissis, Mary Beth, et al. *CMMI: Guidelines for Process Integration and Product Improvement.* 2d ed. (Boston: Addison-Wesley, 2006). All references to CMMI components in this chapter are from this source.

2. Rouillard, Larrie. *Goals and Goal Setting: Achieving Measured Objectives.* 3d ed. (Boston: Thomson Learning, 2003). This is only one of many sources for this acronym.

3. Kaplan, David, and Norton, Robert. *The Strategy-Focused Organization* (Cambridge, Mass.: Harvard Business School Press, 2000).

4. Adler, Paul. "Adapting Your Technological Base: The Organizational Challenge." In *Sloan Management Review,* Fall 1990, pp. 25–37.

5. Garcia, Suzanne. "Managed Technology Adoption Risk: A Way to Realize Better Return from COTS Investments." In *Proceedings of International Conference on COTS- Based Systems 2004* (New York: Springer-Verlag, 2004), pp. 74–83.

6. Reifer, Donald J. *Making the Software Business Case: Improvement by the Numbers.* (Boston: Addison-Wesley, 2002).

7. Mayo, E. *The Human Problems of an Industrial Civilization.* Chapter 3. (New York: Macmillan, 1933).

8. Roethlisberger, F. J., and W. J. Dickson. *Management and the Worker.* (Cambridge, Mass.: Harvard University Press, 1939).

9. Project Management Institute. *Guide to the Project Management Body of Knowledge.* (Newton Square, Penn.: Project Management Institute, 2000).

10. Zmud, R., and L. E. Apple. "Measuring Technology Incorporation/Infusion." In *Journal of Product Innovation Management* 9:148–155.

11. Leonard-Barton, D. "Implementation as Mutual Adaptation of Technology and Organization." In *Research Policy* 17(5):251–2.

Chapter 10

Managing an Appraisal Life Cycle

When you start working with almost any model, the topic of appraisal—or assessment, or evaluation, or gap analysis; there are many similar terms—comes up. That's because any model that can be used for a guide to improve practices can, just about automatically, be used to evaluate practice conformance. The attractiveness of this is that you can use the same (usually public) model for both guiding your improvement and understanding achievements in relation to it.

In this chapter, we'll talk in general about decisions related to appraisal and a small amount on CMMI-specific appraisal. You will not get an in-depth understanding of how to prepare for and conduct an appraisal from this section. If you want or need that—at least for SCAMPI, the appraisal method that accompanies CMMI—we recommend the book *SCAMPI Distilled*, by Dennis Ahern et al.[1] It will give you a good understanding of the mechanics of these types of appraisals and how to prepare for them. Another good source on appraisal philosophy is Tim Kasse's *Action-Focused Assessment* book.[2]

> CMMI content related to this topic:
>
> - Organizational Process Focus

10.1 To appraise or not to appraise: Is that really the question?

Some people think that you can have a successful improvement effort without ever doing an appraisal. If what they mean is that you never do a formal, externally validated appraisal, we can agree with that statement, as long as you don't need to publicize some achievement against your model of choice. As soon as publicity becomes a requirement, you really need to do some kind of external, validated appraisal before you publicize your achievements.

Aside from external appraisals such as SCAMPIs, there are lots of appraisal activities beneficial to an improvement effort that, in our minds, should not be skipped. For example, the Process Change Management method that is taught in the SEI's Mastering Process Improvement course emphasizes an "Organizational Scan." This is a type of appraisal that explicitly seeks projects with best practices to leverage in the improvement effort. So, from our viewpoint, "to appraise or not to appraise" is not the question; the question is, "when and how should you appraise?" Appraisals are one of the best ways to get the information you need to understand whether you have achieved your improvement goals.

The flip side of the organization that "never" appraises is the organization that never stops appraising. This type of organization sees the entire improvement effort as one big "getting ready for the next appraisal" activity. In this type of organization, continuous appraisal is seen as equivalent to continuous improvement. We don't agree with that perspective either. The reason we consider this approach problematic is that focusing everyone's attention on appraisal and conformance to the practices is likely to cause what we term "foolish compliance"—that is, compliance without thinking about the contribution of the practices to meeting your business goals. Any time that link is lost, you stand the risk of your improvement effort's becoming a model-compliance effort, and our experience, as well as what's seen in the improvement literature, argues that a model-compliance effort does not result in long-term (or even short term) improvement in the business.

10.2 Different appraisal philosophies

So what are your choices in terms of using appraisals effectively? There are several philosophies related to when and how you should appraise. Table 10-1 summarizes our perspective on the ones we've had experience with. Note that this is a general summary, more or less neutral as to technique or model. The promoters of individual models usually have more specific guidance on their Web sites as to how and when to appraise, and how to select qualified appraisers for their model. Go to www.sei.cmu .edu/cmmi/appraisals for the home page for SCAMPI (Standard CMMI Appraisal Method for Process Improvement), the SEI's appraisal method for CMMI. There, you can find links to authorized lead appraisers, and look at appraisal results posted for companies that have undergone a SCAMPI Class A appraisal and have permitted publication of their results.

Table 10-1: *Appraisal Approaches*

Appraisal Approach	Main Features	Pros/Cons/Notes
(1) Formal appraisal against defined model scope at beginning of effort and at scheduled times throughout the effort	An extensive gap analysis between the organization's practices and the chosen model is performed, usually by externally trained experts (often with participation of organization members) as an input to the planning of the improvement effort. Externally performed, validated appraisals are scheduled at specific time periods. (The range is generally between 9 months and 2 years.)	**Note:** Formal appraisal at specified periods is one of the requirements for ISO 9001 registration; however, many organizations don't start their ISO 9001 effort with a certification-level appraisal/evaluation. **Pros:** You have a pretty accurate picture of how far your practices vary from your chosen model, and having known dates for future appraisals makes clear the sponsors' commitment to pursue the improvement effort proactively. *(continued)*

Table 10-1: *Appraisal Approaches* (Continued)

Appraisal Approach	Main Features	Pros/Cons/Notes
		Cons: Starting the improvement effort with a large (in terms of organizational resources) appraisal effort can make the effort seem more about appraisal results than about actual business results. The same can happen with prescheduled dates. If the dates don't synchronize well with the actual progress of the effort, they will be seen as artificial, and momentum toward actual improvements can be lost.
(2) Informal appraisal against defined model scope at beginning of effort, followed by formal appraisal "when ready" to show achievement	A less formal appraisal (often, one that does not result in explicit ratings against the chosen model) is conducted to get an idea of where the major gaps in relation to the chosen model exist. This may or may not be conducted by externally trained individuals. For the first appraisal, however, most organizations will use someone externally trained to get an objective, well-informed perspective. In fact, it may be as simple as a roundtable walkthrough of the reference	**Note:** Almost any model has a variety of informal appraisal methods that have been developed by consultants supporting organizations using the model for improvement. These are usually much less expensive, though less detailed in terms of results, than the more formal appraisals that result in an externally validated rating. **Pros:** These almost always cost less both in terms of monetary and labor resources. Using the formal appraisal as a validation of achievement can provide a significant morale boost to

Table 10-1: *Appraisal Approaches* (Continued)

Appraisal Approach	Main Features	Pros/Cons/Notes
	model to identify obvious strengths and weaknesses. When improvements have been implemented, a formal, externally validated appraisal is conducted to validate achievements.	organizations, especially to those that have been active in the improvement activities. **Cons:** There is more risk in this approach that the results of the informal appraisal do not actually reflect the state of the organization. If the choice of timing for the formal appraisal is left as a judgment as to when "we're ready," there may never be an appraisal. Without an external forcing function, the people involved in the improvement effort may never think that they're ready. Putting the formal appraisal off too long can also imply the effort isn't that important to the sponsors.
(3) Formal appraisal against defined model scope followed by "incremental" informal appraisals that verify only that identified gaps have been closed.	This approach may be used at the beginning of an effort or at any point that a formal appraisal results in findings indicating gaps the organization would like to see closed. After the formal appraisal is conducted, follow-up events are planned that deal with	**Pros:** If an organization does not achieve its desired state, this is a less expensive way to confirm that actions taken after the appraisal have resulted in improvement. **Cons:** Because only one issue at a time is being addressed by the incremental appraisal activities, there is a risk that other behaviors

(continued)

Table 10-1: *Appraisal Approaches* (Continued)

Appraisal Approach	Main Features	Pros/Cons/Notes
	specific issues or findings brought up in the original appraisal. When all the follow-up events are closed, the achievement is declared as though another full appraisal were completed.	will have slipped in the meantime, especially if there is significant time between the end of the formal appraisal and the completion of all the incremental appraisal activities.

10.3 Managing the resources needed to plan and conduct appraisal activities

You will need to manage several classes of resources when you decide to plan and conduct an appraisal. How much of what you will need depends on the type of appraisal you are planning to conduct. The resource classes are

- *External labor.* Consultants and/or appraisal team staff to help you prepare for and conduct the appraisal planning and execution.

- *Internal labor.* Appraisal team members, process improvement team members, interview candidates, and logistics support staff to help prepare for and conduct the appraisal planning and execution.

- *Appraisal support materials.* Depending on the type of appraisal, special forms to record evidence (for CMMI, these are called PIIDS, or Process Implementation Indicator Documents), electronic documents that point appraisal team members to process assets, appraisal recording tools (both commercial and shareware tools are available), measurement reports, and so on.

- *Appraisal team support materials.* Flip charts, markers, sticky notes, meeting rooms, laptops, catering, and other materials needed to keep the appraisal running smoothly.

Rather than duplicate the very useful information in appraisal method descriptions and books like *SCAMPI Distilled*, in this section we'll point out a couple of the ways that organizations often cause themselves more pain in conducting appraisals than is needed.

10.3.1 Preparing evidence for appraisals

One of the potentially time-consuming and seemingly wasteful activities that is necessary for many types of appraisals, particularly those in which some kind of compliance rating will be given, is preparing evidence. Evidence is usually collected in the form of artifacts that verify certain types of activities have taken place, or artifacts that document some aspect of guidance for a process. And to minimize the time for the appraisal team to process that evidence, some sort of mapping between the evidence and the reference model you're appraising against (for example, CMMI) is usually recommended. That is generally the time-consuming part. Doing this kind of mapping requires a decent knowledge of your process implementation *and* your reference model.

A job aid produced by the SEI to support recording evidence is a document called a PIID. This document is organized by Process Area and Specific Practice, and provides fields for recording different types of evidence. Microsoft Word and Microsoft Excel versions of the PIIDs are available from various Web sites (do a Google search for *PIID templates,* and you'll get plenty of hits, some of which contain free downloadable templates), and processable versions of them are the basis for several of the commercial appraisal tools that are available.

If you know you will be conducting an appraisal as one of your improvement activities, you will want to make the process of evidence recording as painless as possible. This generally means collecting and recording evidence as you actually perform a process. The trick is that to make this efficient, whoever is recording the evidence should know enough about the model to map the artifacts to the reference model of interest. This is one of the reasons that some organizations go overboard (in our opinion) in training everyone in the organization in the model; they think that by getting everyone trained in the model-ese, they'll be better at helping with the evidence collection/recording. And some of them will be, but unless you're in a very small organization where the staff working in improvement are also the staff doing most of the management and engineering, you probably will have many people who, despite model training, won't be very good at recognizing how their activities and artifacts map onto the model of interest.

This is one of the places where having some skilled model support is helpful; whether it's a person from inside or outside your organization, having access to someone who knows both the processes you're implementing and the model you're referencing can speed this task along tremendously. In smaller organizations, having one person who takes the artifacts from projects and your process descriptions and maps them into the evidence library, whatever approach you're using, will improve consistency of the mappings and provide a focal point for appraisal team questions. You can use a device as simple as a project notebook (electronic or paper) with a list of the artifacts that should be collected as a way of minimizing impact on project staff while making it feasible for the evidence mapper to collect and record efficiently.

The biggest mistake we see people make in their evidence collection, especially when they're getting started, is to wait until just before the appraisal to gather all the evidence. You'd be amazed by how difficult and time-consuming it can be to find something ("I know I have it here somewhere") that is just the right piece of evidence to support an aspect of the appraisal. Of course, there is also the disruption of people's work to find something that could easily have been provided at the time it was generated without interrupting the project.

So how do you know what things to collect? Actually, that's one of the benefits of using the PIIDs mentioned earlier; they have taken the "typical work products" section from CMMI and transcribed it into this form. That's not to say that you *must* have the work product mentioned; the work product suggestions that are provided, however, will probably give you ideas for work products that might serve the same function on your own project. Some of the downloadable PIIDs contain additional instructional example material to help you.

10.3.2 Composing appraisal teams

Another problematic area, especially for small organizations, is composing a useful but efficient appraisal team. For certain types of appraisals, such as a SCAMPI A appraisal that results in Capability Level or Maturity Level ratings, there is a minimum number of appraisal team members (four) who have all been through "official" Introduction to CMMI training, and one of those team members must be an authorized SCAMPI A Lead Appraiser.[3] Chances are that if you're just starting out, you won't have a lead appraiser in your organization, and you may not even want to dedicate three of your own staff members to an appraisal activity for several days.

Here are a few things to consider when putting together an appraisal team:

- Having one team member from inside the organization who knows both the process implementation and something about the model you're using as your basis is almost always a good idea. The money you spend training that person and the time he or she spends preparing for and participating in the appraisal will generally be made up for easily in terms of the time you save for the external members of the team, for whom you're probably paying a daily rate.

- The lead appraiser is probably going to be your highest-cost external labor item. Choose one who knows your type of business and has some experience with your context. Hiring a lead appraiser who has done appraisals only in a large-organization context could cause some interpretation problems if your company is very small.

- If you decide not to staff the rest of the team with internal team members, you may want to look around for people in your area who are "candidate" lead appraisers needing appraisal team experience. One of the requirements to become a lead appraiser is that you must participate in two SCAMPI A appraisals as a team member. There are often candidates looking for opportunities to participate in a team to complete their prerequisites for taking the next step toward authorization. Often, they are willing to discount their labor/travel fees as a way to make it attractive for you to allow them to participate in your appraisal. Make sure that you coordinate all your team-member candidates with your lead appraiser.

There are many other things to consider in preparing for an appraisal, and as we've said, several books on the subject cover the necessary elements to consider in planning and conduct. We recommend that you obtain one of them before getting involved with selecting a lead appraiser and your appraisal team.

---

1. Ahern, Dennis, et al. *CMMI SCAMPI Distilled: Appraisals for Process Improvement.* (Boston: Addison-Wesley, 2004).

2. Kasse, Tim. *Action-Focused Assessment.* (Boston: Artech House, 2001).

3. Assessment Methods Team. *Standard CMMI Appraisal Method for Process Improvement (SCAMPI), Version 1.1: Method Definition Document.* CMU/SEI-2001-HB-001. (Pittsburgh: Carnegie Mellon University, 2001).

Chapter 11

Developing Process Improvement Infrastructure

At some point in your process improvement effort, although probably not at the beginning, you will want to have some stable infrastructure for this effort, just like you would for any other continuing operation. When you're ready to approach this, you need to engage in several tasks to ensure you create a sustainable infrastructure.

First of all, you need to find people willing to work on process improvement tasks, and form one or more teams to execute the tasks that we're laying out in this chapter.

Then you need to decide how to organize the people performing improvement tasks. In CMMI circles, you'll most often hear this talked about as forming an EPG (Engineering Process Group). However, there are many ways to organize for improvement, and a permanent structure may not be where you start.

Depending on the type of structure you implement, you'll need infrastructure—budget, support resources, space, and so on—to support it.

The bulk of the work done at first will be around defining project and organizational processes—we cover these in the next chapter. But there will be other things that your improvement teams will also have to deal with. For example, figuring out how/where to securely store measurement data.

Defining new/revised processes does the organization no good unless you actually deploy/implement them into the projects of the organization. This takes you out of the infrastructure realm into the "real world." These tasks are covered in Chapter 13.

The last task we'll talk about is collecting and incorporating lessons learned—from building/sustaining sponsorship, building/sustaining infrastructure, and deploying improved processes—back into the practices and assets of the organization.

When you look at the set of things needed just in the infrastructure tasks, you can understand why many organizations create a permanent group to coordinate and facilitate these activities. But if you're just starting out, your team may be you and a couple of other members of your project; your infrastructure may be an agenda item on project review meetings and an action-item list, along with a shared Web space where you keep PI work products. And the "lessons learned" activities may be the project retrospective and pizza lunches once a month that actually (sometimes?) result in some notes.

SuZ once worked in an organization where most of the improvement work was done on Friday afternoons. The company had a policy that staff were not to work on their daily tasks on Friday afternoon; that time was dedicated to learning something new or working on some kind of organizational improvement task. There was no "formal" improvement infrastructure beyond this and a staff member who had an assigned quality assurance role. With only ten development staff, this "infrastructure" generally worked well.

11.1 Developing and sustaining process improvement team members

> CMMI content related to this topic:
>
> - Integrated Project Management
> - Organizational Process Focus
> - Organizational Training

As you've probably already discovered if you're new to process improvement, the skills and tasks needed to be successful in process improvement are not entirely the same as those needed for traditional engineering. Unfortunately, that is the home ground for many of the people working in process improvement. So it's natural that investment in training and mechanisms to help people adjust to their role will be needed.

What types of skills will be needed? A good place to look is the "O" process areas of CMMI. You'll need people who can implement the practices in Organizational Process Focus, Organizational Process Definition, Organizational Training, Organizational Innovation and Deployment, and (eventually) Organizational Process Performance. You'll certainly need people with project management and project support skills, because you will be implementing improvement projects. You'll also need access to specialists in several different aspects of product engineering and organizational support.

If you don't already have access to staff with the requisite skills, you'll need to find people willing to acquire them. You can look at this book as a primer on some of the skills/techniques you'll need to have mastered; lots of training courses offered by SEI partners and others will address the skills that you need. One of the questions we frequently get asked is "How do I choose training and trainers that will be right for my situation?" That's a more complicated question to answer now than before CMMI, because the widespread adoption of CMMI has led to an explosion of consultants and trainers offering services.

There are two things we would recommend when searching for training services:

- Take advantage of the SEI Partner Network, presuming that you're using CMMI as your base model. The members of the Partner Network have gone through extensive training in the model and its application in appraisal to achieve authorization as either an Introduction to CMMI trainer or a SCAMPI Lead Appraiser. They are authorized to deliver authentic SEI services, and part of their authorization requires that they stay current with advances in the model and in the improvement arena in general. The SEI maintains a Web site with lists of the individuals and companies that are partners. In the absence of other preferences, find several that operate in your region, and check their Web sites to get a feel for them.

- When you've found several candidates to think about, we recommend going to both the SEIR (Software Engineering Information Repository) and the NDIA (National Defense Industrial Association) Events Web site (www.ndia.org) to find presentations or tutorials that your candidates may have offered. The SEIR collects many of the presentations from the System/Software Engineering Process Group conference. The NDIA sponsors a CMMI Technology and User's conference annually, and publish its proceedings for free on the Events section of their Web site. Reviewing presentations gives you a better idea of the philosophy and approach of different trainers/consultants. Keep in mind, however, that not all trainers/consultants will present every year, and we certainly wouldn't recommend hiring someone *just* from his or her presentation materials. But it is a way to start if you don't have recommendations from people in other organizations whom you trust.

Developing and acquiring the skills is part of the task. The other part is forming the groups that will be working together into effective teams. In the next section, we'll discuss our favorite team life cycle management model. CMMI doesn't specify any particular team model, but in IPM it does call for the creation and sustainment of teams that implement an integrated project's plans and provides a basic set of practices that we would expect to see supported in any team life cycle model.

11.2 Developing a team

There are many contexts within an improvement effort where working together as a team is both necessary and beneficial. Generally, the people who are facilitating the improvement effort will be an explicit team of full-time people permanent in that role while others may be part time and temporary. Those working on a specific improvement issue will be working together as a team. Hopefully the management sponsors of the improvement effort will also be working as a team.

So team development and sustainment is a critical knowledge-and-skill area for your toolkit. As with most of the techniques we describe, there are multiple choices for the approach you take to team development. The two we've worked the most with are the Joiner and Associates high-performance team approach[1] and the Drexler-Sibbett Team Performance Model.[†] We'll give a brief overview of the Drexler-Sibbett model because, in our experience, it has the richest set of support tools and is both the most explanatory and most diagnostic of the approaches we've used. Table 11-1 shows the stages of the Drexler-Sibbett model and the key questions that are answered at each stage of the model.

[†] Team Performanc Model is a trademark of Grove Consultants International.

The model is supported by a set of books and tools that are all available from Grove, the publisher of the model, at www.grove.com. We consider this model useful for both planning team engagements and for diagnosing team issues. In addition to providing a description of the model, Grove provides diagnostic aids that describe symptoms you may see if particular stages of the model are not successfully traversed and suggest activities/approaches for solving them. Although Grove also offers training, should you need it, it is also a useful resource for trained team facilitators, because most of the knowledge needed to effectively use its models are captured in a set of guidebooks and job aids available directly from the Web site at a reasonable price.

In Table 11-1, we provide a short overview of the stages and what we think each stage contributes to team performance. If you look at it, one thing you may notice is that the "work" of the team—what are we doing, and how will we do it—is not the first thing the model deals with. We think that this is one of its strengths. When overlooked, understanding why you're here as an individual and the level of trust needed and available to perform the task of the team often causes problems when figuring out team operations. That's not to say that you have to spend tons of time in each of these stages. We often work with groups that complete Stages 1 and 2 within the first hour of a one-day planning session and spend most of their time on Stages 3 and 4. If the task is small enough, they might even work some of Stage 5.

Table 11-1: *Drexler-Sibbett Team Performance Model Summary*[2]

TPM Stage	Key Question	Contribution to Team Performance
1. Orientation	"Why am I here?"	Understanding the purpose and meaning provides a core for all subsequent activities.
2. Trust Building	"Who are you?" Do you have mutual regard, forthrightness, and spontaneous interaction?	Concern with trust occurs in direct proportion to the need for interdependence within the team. The lower the interdependence, the lower the need for trust. It deepens through repeated interaction and will be most visible in later stages of the team's cycle.

(continued)

Table 11-1: *Drexler-Sibbett Team Performance Model Summary* (Continued)

TPM Stage	Key Question	Contribution to Team Performance
3. Goal and Role Clarification	"What are we doing?"	Specific goals, objectives, and a clear understanding of roles are necessary to move forward effectively. Clarity is often a challenge, because people vary widely in their understanding and use of language.
4. Commitment	"How will we do it?"	When goals and roles are clear, teams automatically begin to ask how to get into action. The creative tension between the vision of the goals and the constraints of resources and operational decision-making is prevalent in this stage.
5. Implementation	"Who does what, when, and where?"	Scheduling and sequencing activities is necessary to create coordinated action.
6. High Performance	"Do we have flexibility, intuitive communication, and synergy?"	When working in a state of flexibility, intuitive communication, and synergy, the team is likely to produce results beyond expectations. You may be a successful team if you navigate the Implementation stage successfully, but you'll be a high-performing team only when these attributes come into play.
7. Renewal	"(Why) should we continue?"	The obvious time to ask this question is when the team has achieved its objective; however, there can be other major changes that would imply a need for renewal, including policy shifts, organizational changes, or taking on new members.

The main book we use from the Grove Web site, the *Team Leader's Guide*, contains detailed descriptions of the types of tasks to include in each phase, as well as symptoms and solutions for problems. The guide also address the different needs of different types of teams. The senior leadership team, which is a team that persists over a long period of time, probably needs different kinds of support than a process improvement task force chartered to solve a specific problem in the course of one or two months). One of the SEI courses in process improvement, *Mastering Process Improvement*, explores the Team Performance Model in its activities. There are also members of the SEI Partner Network who include the Team Performance Model in their training/consulting.

11.3 Establishing improvement infrastructure to support and sustain CMMI implementation

CMMI content related to this topic:

- Organizational Process Focus
- Organizational Process Definition
- Organizational Training
- Organizational Innovation and Deployment
- Fundamental Support Process Areas

This is the set of tasks that will see the most variation, depending on (1) the size of your organization and improvement effort and (2) where you are in terms of your commitment to CMMI (or other reference models). Most of the topics discussed here won't be ones you'll address fully until you have committed to your improvement approach and are ready to build a sustainable infrastructure suitable for your size and context. We cover choices for both larger and smaller organizations in the discussions that follow.

11.4 Staffing and organization

One of the reasons we call DLI a "light" life cycle is that we try to minimize the staffing requirements for process improvement, at least while you're trying it for the first time. One of our experiences in working with organizations is that they decide to do process improvement and then spend six months to a year (sometimes even more!) putting together a process improvement group and a management steering group to provide oversight. During that time, the improvement group is usually doing useful things in terms of building your improvement infrastructure, but they're not solving any of the immediate problems of the organization—those things that led you to decide to work on improvement to begin with. This can create a serious problem with sponsorship and with the members of the organization to whom you're intending to deploy new practices.

When you've decided to commit to a long-term improvement effort, you will need to staff some kind of ongoing group within your organization to perform the kinds of tasks you saw in Table 4-2, The Task/CMMI Cross Reference, which relates process improvement tasks to CMMI. There are many approaches for doing this. We'll cover and comment on a few of the common ones that we've worked with.

11.4.1 No ongoing improvement team infrastructure

Yup, we've seen this one. It can work for a while. How long is "a while"? This staffing model breaks down when you want to start leveraging the process assets you've developed and are successfully using in some projects by deploying them into your new projects. The projects that have participated in improvement activities get benefit from them, but the other projects don't. If your company is very small, with only a couple of projects, this could work for quite a while. The small company SuZ worked for in the '90s managed with this model for almost two years, although both the CEO and SuZ were expert enough in improvement to be able to provide some guidance on a very limited effort basis.

11.4.2 Single focal point for improvement, others part time, designated senior-management sponsor

This is the model that is common for many small to medium-size enterprises. When a commitment to ongoing improvement is made, one staff member is assigned at least half time, if not full time, to this effort. That person organizes the infrastructure and the improvement projects with part-time staff and possibly external consultants for specialty tasks, such as appraisals.

This model works best if you can hire someone into this role who already has improvement background, skills, and experience. It also helps if the designated senior management sponsor has experience in successfully sponsoring an improvement effort. (We know we're asking for a lot!) If you can manage that, this can be a very effective model while you're small. With sufficient resources for external consultants, even midsize companies can use it.

The risk with this approach is that you have a single point of failure. If your focal point gets tired of the work or decides to leave the position or your company, you've got a big hole to fill. This is especially true if he or she leaves in the middle of your effort—and when you get going in your improvement effort, you're almost always in the middle of something!

11.4.3 Internal focal point, designated senior-management sponsor or steering group, external consultants for most of the work

In this model, the primary role of the internal focal point is to coordinate with the external consultants to make sure they get access to the internal folks they need, and to report status back to the senior management sponsor or steering group. It can be a useful model if you *don't* have anyone internal with process improvement background and skills, but you do have someone who knows the ins/outs of the organization and is willing and ready to learn those skills.

This model works best if you focus the external consultants on teaching the internal staff, not just doing the improvement work for them. There are two advantages to this:

- If the consultants are teaching PI skills, you're building internal capability that you can take forward into future cycles and have less dependence on outside staffing.

- You will get a lot more buy-in from your staff if they have participated in generating the new assets rather than just watching them get built and being responsible for using them.

11.4.4 Internal PI group, senior-management steering group, external consultants for training/specialty work, internal part-time improvement teams for improvement projects

This is the classic EPG (Engineering Process Group) model. It is the model taught in SEI training courses like Mastering Process Improvement (MPI) and many SEPG conference tutorials and was covered in the first publication on process improvement organization that the SEI published, called *Software Engineering Process Group Guide*.[3] If you decide to read this report, understand that it was written when the software CMM (the predecessor of

CMMI) had not even been released. Some of the advice is sketchy, because the base of experience wasn't nearly as broad as it is today. Other process improvement textbooks also go into a good bit of detail on how to organize and staff this kind of structure.

The relevant elements of this model are that a group of full-time staff—usually supplemented by rotating part-time staff—is responsible for the improvement infrastructure, improvement-related training development and delivery, managing appraisal consultants and/or developing internal appraisal capability, and deploying improvements throughout their designated scope. The guidance from their efforts comes from a Management Steering Group that is usually composed of some subset of the organization's senior management. This group has sufficient resource authority to enable the EPG to get what it needs, and it holds the EPG accountable for the resources spent and the results achieved. These two structures are supplemented by improvement teams from the organization at large. These teams are temporary and staffed by subject-matter experts in the activity being worked on. Usually, one of the EPG staff will either lead or facilitate each of these groups.

The advantage of this structure is that if you have sufficient numbers to warrant it, you can get a lot of progress from a small number of full-time people, and you can sustain management sponsorship if you have the right kinds of communication going on. You also end up with an organic, sustainable capability in PI methods and techniques that can support you through a number of improvement cycles.

The risk with this model is that you can end up putting too much resource into building and sustaining your infrastructure. There's always more to do, and the more resource you put into it, the more you can do, but you have to weigh that against what you should do to improve your business outcomes. Aligning your improvement goals with your business goals is a critical mitigation for this risk.

11.5   Creating and evolving a PAL (Process Asset Library)

CMMI content related to this topic:

- Organizational Process Definition

A working definition of process asset library (PAL) that works for us in teaching about developing and using process guidance is

an organized, well-indexed, searchable repository of process assets that is easily accessible by anyone who needs process guidance information like examples, data, templates, or other process support materials.

Please note that this definition says *nothing* about the technology base used to create or deploy the PAL. From a strict CMMI viewpoint, the PAL is a technology-independent concept. However, from a practical viewpoint, this is a high-payback area to invest in technology to support a process improvement effort.

The term *process asset* may need explanation. CMMI defines a process asset as "anything that the organization considers useful in attaining the goals of a process area."[4] We tend to go beyond this definition.

In our experience, a process asset is

any process guidance, in whatever form, that an organization believes will provide sufficient return on investment to commit the resources necessary to store and evolve the asset.

Even if CMMI is not being used as the basis for improvement, identifying process assets and making them accessible are worthwhile investments for a business.

The purposes of a PAL include but are not limited to the following:

- Provide a central knowledge base for acquiring, defining, and disseminating guidance about processes related to the organization's tasks (usually, product or service development, management, and improvement).

- Reduce unnecessary duplication of process assets in the organization and the work that goes into re-creating assets.

- Provide mechanisms for sharing knowledge about the organization's process assets and how they are used.

- Support an effective learning environment for new employees expected to use the organization's processes.

- Provide a basis for making decisions about evolving and tailoring the organization's processes.

- Support maintaining version and configuration management of key assets such as your set of standard processes and your organizational policies.

- Improve the consistency of content and application of process guidance throughout the organization.

Why would an organization invest in designing and deploying a PAL? For a small organization, a PAL is a key infrastructure element that reduces training time that can be ill afforded during growth spurts, and that helps lead to a process-focused culture that provides a backbone of discipline for the organization. In addition, an effective PAL is a key element in supporting reduction in time needed for planning new projects—a typical area where both small and large projects are challenged. The ability to rapidly deploy and use processes to serve the needs of the marketplace is a critical attribute of an organization experiencing hypergrowth.

For a large organization, a PAL provides one of the infrastructure elements required to support movement from one set of behaviors to another, by making public the "new rules" that the organization intends to live by. A well-designed and deployed PAL also reduces planning, implementation, and training time, especially for processes that are performed only intermittently. In these processes in particular, having access to relevant guidance to "refresh" even competent practitioners can prove a potent accelerator of confidence, and as a follow on, speed of execution.

Depending on the other process characteristics of the organization, other business benefits may accrue. These include

- increasing the adherence to the preferred processes in the organization by making the process guidance in the PAL the auditing basis for process compliance audits;
- increasing the participation of staff in making suggestions for changes to process assets, if responses are reasonably and visibly responded to; and
- reducing the cost of project startup, both from the perspective of less training time required to get staff up to speed on the processes to be used and from the perspective of active, planned reuse of existing assets where appropriate.

To accrue any of the benefits cited above, a PAL must be well designed and effectively deployed. The attributes of the PAL itself influence its ability to support the purposes and achieve the potential business impacts cited above. Table 11-2 describes several attributes of a PAL that we look for when evaluating its design and implementation. These attributes are not necessarily ranked in order of importance; the ones that are more important tend to vary in terms of overall organizational culture and other factors that are outside the design of the PAL itself.

Table 11-2: *Critical Attributes of a Process Asset Library*

PAL Attribute	Why It's Important
Easy navigation	User Interface studies indicate that requiring users to navigate more than three layers adds significant frustration and unwillingness to continue interacting with the system (AOL internal study). If users won't use the PAL, they won't be able to use the process assets, no matter how wonderful they are!
Reinforces useful process definition concepts	There are many ways to approach process definition; some are very rigorous and precise but are not hugely useful for communicating the intent and information needed to effectively transition a new process into practice in a project or organization. Trying to get staff to use rigorous and precise process definitions that are not useful for them to learn what to do and how to do it is usually unsuccessful.
Easy searching, including rule-based searches	The easier it is for staff to find the information they need to guide their process, the more likely they are to actually use the guidance provided. Rule-based searching allows staff to easily find guidance that is related to their primary need so that they have a complete picture of the guidance that is available.
High degree of relevance for information organized together	When individuals are looking for process assets to guide tasks, finding irrelevant information is not only a distraction, but also can reduce the motivation for continuing the search for the relevant guidance.
Multiple views of information based on multiple criteria, including user-defined criteria (for example, views by role)	The reasons for coming to the PAL to search varies based on many factors, including role in the organization, purpose (to find guidance, to make change requests, to evolve assets), level of familiarity with the library, and so on. Multiple views that are keyed in ways that relate to typical usage make it faster to find the relevant information the user is seeking.

(continued)

Table 11-2: *Critical Attributes of a Process Asset Library* (Continued)

PAL Attribute	Why It's Important
Secure tracking of document status	The high level of investment in reviewing and gaining consensus on process guidance makes it important to be able to protect the investment in comments and document status. In addition, if adherence to some external standards is desired (for example, ISO 9001), protection of this information is required.
Supports management of change requests against process assets from multiple sources	Process assets are not, and should not be, static. They evolve to reflect changes in the organization's structure, product lines, technology, and other business factors. These changes must be accommodated appropriately if the guidance is to continue being used.
Allows multiple versions to be stored together while making clear the status of all the assets	As time evolves, some guidance evolves, but the "old" version still has to be used by older projects due to contract or other similar requirements. The status of documents in use needs to be clearly understood so that commitments related to the particular asset are made appropriately.
Widespread read access; appropriately restrictive write/ delete access	The significant investment in creating and maintaining assets makes it important to protect the contents of the organization's assets. On the other hand, this investment also means that organizations usually want many more people to have access to read the guidance and use it to correctly perform the processes included in the guidance.
Encourages use of process assets, not just their creation and maintenance	The ultimate purpose of the guidance included in a PAL is to enable correct execution of the processes for which guidance is being provided and to collect feedback on where the process guidance is incorrect or needs improvement to be more useful.
Transparent tracking of document use	To avoid the case of the PAL's becoming a "depository" rather than a "repository," tracking of the actual retrieval of and commenting on documents in the PAL is necessary to be able to keep the content fresh and relevant. Assets that are not being used may have content problems, awareness/communication issues, or other issues that prevent their use. Understanding the patterns of use makes it more likely that these issues will be dealt with.

We're sure you won't be surprised to learn that there are challenges in effectively designing and deploying a PAL. A few of the typical ones we've encountered are

- *Lack of participation.* Problems can arise with insufficient participation and buy-in from opinion leaders among the staff expected to use the PAL.
- *Allocating too much resource to PAL design.* It's easy to end up spending too much of your improvement resources on creating the software and infrastructure needed to support the PAL, rather than spending that effort/money on actually improving your work practices.
- *Insufficient/inappropriate training.* Understanding how the information is to be used and training users in how to access the correct information for their purpose increases the utility of the PAL greatly. Not providing training, on the other hand, makes it more likely that guidance will be misused and/or ignored.
- *Moving from print-focused documents.* Moving from documentation that is designed for use in print to documentation in a PAL that is designed to be used via the computer desktop is one of the often-overlooked issues in creating and deploying a PAL.

11.6 Measurement system/repository

CMMI content related to this topic:
- Organizational Process Definition
- Measurement and Analysis
- Organizational Process Performance
- Quantitative Project Management

Many of the same issues that are relevant to building and sustaining a process asset library apply to developing and sustaining a measurement system. By *measurement system,* we mean all the tools, repositories, and procedures related to collecting, storing, analyzing, and reporting on measurement data for the organization.

Although the repository issues are similar to the PAL's, there are some particular requirements for a measurement repository that you should pay attention to:

- *Security requirements.* Measurement data, like some "lessons learned" data, can be sensitive from the viewpoint that it could be used inappropriately. So things like keeping names of data contributors out of reports are something that you will have to think about for your measurement repository.

- *Filtering and synthesis requirements.* The amount of data that is likely to be stored in a measurement repository for almost any organization will grow large and difficult to navigate very quickly if it isn't designed carefully. Be sure that you keep only the minimum data required for your processes and that short-lived data expires in a reasonable time and can be purged.

Beyond the repository itself, the data collection procedures and tools are an issue for the measurement system. Understanding how the data is collected (from a process audit by a third party? from the person who generated the work product? from a tool set?) can be important for most kinds of data. And tooling is one of the things that can make or break a measurement system. We have worked with several organizations that lost a lot of ground in their measurement program because the data they were asking people to collect

- had to be collected manually; and/or
- was work added on to the process they were performing, not a natural result of it.

These may seem like trivial barriers, but they are frequently cited in presentations and workshops as the two things that have the greatest negative impact on data collection.

The third issue for most people asked to collect data is that they don't know or trust how the data they are providing will be used. If they perceive that the measurement will be used against them, they are likely to provide data that they believe protects them most. For an interesting discussion of the effects of asking for the wrong data from people, read Donald Wheeler's *Understanding Variation.*[5] It's a great book on the management uses of statistical process control and is probably the shortest measurement book you'll ever be asked to read.

All the details of developing a measurement infrastructure are outside the bounds of this book, but you can find excellent guidance in the Practical System and Software Measurement (PSM) materials available at www. psmsc.com.[6] PSM is sponsored by the U.S. Department of Defense and provides reference guides, books, and courses that take you step by step through the measurement process. PSM's approach is also compatible with the ISO/IEC 15939 standard, Software Measurement Process. Other resources include the Software Engineering Laboratory at NASA (www.sel.gsfc.nasa. gov for Goal-Question-Metric) and the SEI Web site (www.sei.cmu.edu for Goal-Question-Indicator-Metric), as well as several SEI Series books on measurement.[7]

1. Scholtes, Peter R. *The Team Handbook: How to Use Teams to Improve Quality.* (Madison, Wis.: Joiner and Associates, 1988).

2. Adapted from Grove *Team Leader's Guide,* www.grove.com. Accessed July 2006.

3. Fowler, Priscilla, and Stan Rifkin. *Software Engineering Process Group Guide,* CMU/SEI-90-TR-024. (Pittsburgh: Carnegie Mellon University, 1990).

4. From the glossary in Chrissis, Mary Beth, et al. *CMMI: Guidelines for Process Integration and Product Improvement.* (Boston: Addison-Wesley, 2003).

5. Wheeler, Donald. *Understanding Variation: The Key to Managing Chaos.* 2d ed. (Knoxville, Tenn.: SPC Press, 1999).

6. Card, David, et al. *Practical Software Measurement: Objective Information for Decision Makers.* (Boston: Addison-Wesley, 2001).

7. Paulk, Mark, and Mary Beth Chrissis. *2001 High Maturity Practices Workshop.* CMU/SEI-2001-SR-014. (Pittsburgh: Carnegie Mellon University, 2002).

Chapter 12

Defining Processes

As you might guess, this chapter focuses primarily on the building of process solutions to your organization's process-related problems. Remember, as Figure 12-1 shows, developing processes is analogous to developing products. We start with a technique to help you choose which processes will be most useful for you to (re)define at any given time and then discuss some techniques that have been successful at getting a set of useful process guidance in a minimal amount of time. Notice, however, that minimal is not "no time." If these are the processes that your business depends on for producing the products that make the profits that keep everyone employed, it's a good bet that they are worth careful thought, consideration, and review by those who will be asked to use them.

12.1 CMMI Business Analysis as a source of requirements

CMMI content related to this topic:

- Requirements Development
- Requirements Management
- Technical Solution
- Product Integration
- Verification
- Validation
- Decision Analysis and Resolution

The CMMI-based Business Analysis, as described in Chapter 15, is meant to help a group that is contemplating using CMMI to understand how its current business problems might be addressed by various parts of the model and prioritize the many Process Areas the group could start with.

As you have learned up to this point, you have requirements besides just the process requirements to think about in engineering your process solutions. You have time and cost constraints; you have skill and knowledge requirements; and you have communication and sponsorship requirements, to name just a few. All these requirements need to be taken into account when you design process solutions for your organization.

Product Development Phases	Inception	Elaboration	Construction	Transition
Common Goals	Identity needs	Determine how to meet needs (prototype)	Build and test the solution	Deliver capability to user
Process Development Phases	Requirements	Design	Implementation/ Validation	Deployment

Figure 12-1: *Product versus process development phases*

From the perspective of thinking about engineering your process solutions, the CMMI Business Analysis is one way for you to elicit requirements for the processes you want to work on. You're using your business goals as the customer needs, and your gap analysis against CMMI is helping you narrow those needs down to a set of "product" requirements—that is, which Process Areas are most useful for you to define and improve at this time.

After you've used CMMI-based Business Analysis to select the Process Areas you want to use as guidance for your improvement, our next section will help you create process guidance that provides utility to your stakeholders.

12.2 Developing useful process guidance

CMMI content related to this topic:

- Technical Solution
- Product Integration
- Verification
- Validation

A critical aspect of supporting a process improvement effort is developing and deploying useful guidance on performing the important processes of the organization. The purpose of process documentation or guidance is to capture how to do something for future reference. This may be for your own use, in case details/agreements you've made are forgotten, or it may be for use by someone else who may not have performed that part of the process before. When you capture the expectations for what will happen when common activities are performed, you typically shorten the training time for new people performing the process. You can also use process documentation to capture expectations that will help develop time estimates for activities; if you generally go through the same set of steps to perform an activity, over time you can get a sense of what it takes to nominally perform that activity. Finally, you can use process documentation to compare actual results of an activity to expected results. Through checklists and adding specific instrumentation into process guidance, it is clearer whether an anomalous result is due to the process itself or to some outside influence.

One of the most challenging aspects of this task is figuring out "how much is enough" when it comes to writing this kind of guidance. In working with groups trying to write process guidance, one of the guidelines we suggest is that different kinds of process guidance be written for different roles and different skill levels within the organization. What this means is that *one size does not fit all* when it comes to guiding people through performing processes. A common mistake we see when looking at process guidance written by organizations that are just starting their improvement effort is that they write very detailed guidance about processes that they know very well, and they write very sparse guidance for processes that they don't understand very well.[†]

Some other typical problems in the process guidance we've reviewed include

- Too many different types of guidance (information types) included in one document
- Inconsistency in the types and levels of guidance that are provided (very detailed in one procedure, followed by something very sketchy in the next)
- Difficulty in finding the information needed by a particular role in the process
- Lack of a shared mental model of how the information should be organized

One of the techniques that we've found useful in overcoming the first three of these problems is Information Mapping, described in our next section. The fourth—lack of a shared mental model of how information should be organized—relates to the concept of a *process architecture*. A process architecture is an explicit description of the boundaries of the set of process guidance and how the various processes relate to each other. We describe the basics of establishing a nominal process architecture in Section 15.4.2, when we talk about the "One Hour Process Description Method."

12.2.1 Information Mapping

A set of useful principles and practices for developing process guidance that solves these and other typical problems comes from a technique called Information Mapping (IM). Information Mapping is essentially an engineering approach to writing that was developed back in the 1950s and has been evolving since then. It uses a structured set of information types and has a set

---

[†] Succumbing to this pitfall makes process consultants look like magicians when we come in, review representative process documents, and (presto!) immediately produce a profile of the organization's problematic processes.

of representation rules that provide a useful set of heuristics for setting up different types of process guidance. There are separate IM guidelines on developing print-based and electronic information. We find that the IM definitions for information types are useful for developing good process guidance, even without using IM representational conventions.

Table 12-1 illustrates the information types and some suggestions for making them easily distinguishable in your writing.

Table 12-1: *Information Mapping Information Types*[1]

Information Type	Typical Contents	Guidance
Principle	Includes things like policies, rules, constraints, and strong guidelines	Use strong, active language. Use a label that clearly indicates the intended use of the information in the document/section. Often include "why" information to motivate acceptance of the principles.
Procedure	"How to" information on completing steps in a task or process element, including defining the different decision points; usually very action focused.	Begin each step with an action (verb). Make sure steps are distinct. Make decision points/resolutions clear. Make tables and flowcharts in typical formats. Avoid "lists" of steps; although common, these are less effective.

(continued)

Table 12-1: *Information Mapping Information Types* (Continued)

Information Type	Typical Contents	Guidance
Process	Description of what needs to happen that focuses on characterizing the vision for getting to a goal, as well as the relationships among roles and controls and measures	Use third-person language and active voice. Make cause/effect relationships clear. "Flow" should move forward over time. Stay away from "how to." Use diagrams to provide overview. Tables are often useful for grouping information.
Structure	Includes elements of a topic and their relationships, and (if appropriate) architectural and/or reference information	Diagrams are a good way to communicate high-level and detailed relationships. "Parts/function" tables provide links between definitional and structural information.
Concept	Includes definitions, examples, nonexamples, and critical attributes of a topic	Illustrate the critical attributes in a definition with an example and, where feasible, a nonexample. Identify relationship of the concept to the larger topic it supports.
Fact	Includes data relevant to understanding a concept, construct, and/or structure of a subject	Clearly label the information as to its relationship to the relevant aspects of the topic that are covered in other areas of the document.

Table 12-1: *Information Mapping Information Types* (Continued)

Information Type	Typical Contents	Guidance
Classification	Includes list, hierarchies, and other schemes for organizing the topics	Introduce your lists with context information. Place most important sorting factor on the left. Use "parallel language" throughout the list (same type of grammar/language for each level in the hierarchy).

Other typical technical-writing concepts (also emphasized in Information Mapping) that are worth paying attention to include

- *Chunking.* Visually distinguish related chunks of material so readers can find what they're interested in.
- *Relevance.* Keep together things that are needed to meet the purpose of the document, and use an appropriate representation for each information type.
- *Hierarchy.* Break the information into chunks in a way that allows readers to move from general to specific.
- *Labeling.* Label the information in a way that tells the reader what to expect.

When you look at the writing process recommended by Information Mapping, you can see parallels between this process and the typical engineering development process:

- Analyze the audience and its use of the information.
- Define the types of information needed to meet the audience's needs.
- Define the organization of the information to optimize reader navigation, based on the reader's defined needs.
- Plan the elicitation of the information for the document from relevant subject-matter experts.
- Execute the information-elicitation plan.
- Test the document design with pilots.
- Complete the document and/or publish it.

The best way to learn about Information Mapping is to take one of the Information Mapping, Inc., courses. (See www.infomap.com for more information.) They are offered all over the United States, as well as outside North America, and come in a variety of formats.

Another approach to structured process guidance that we've seen used very successfully is the scripting technique associated with the Team Software Process (TSP). The Addison-Wesley Web site for the Team Software Process books (www.awprofessional.com/title/020147719X) contains examples of process scripts that are used to guide the project management and other team processes supported by TSP implementation.[2]

12.2.2 Process diagramming techniques

In a process improvement effort, the elicitation of the information to be put in process guidance is usually done via some kind of process definition activity. Again, there are many approaches to process definition, from very formal graphical constructs (such as IDEF—Integrated DEFinition method) to informal prose documents, and many techniques in between. In our experience, the more formal static definition techniques are useful to process engineers and analysts who understand the formalisms, but they are not typically meaningful for the users of the process guidance—the managers and practitioners who are expected to follow it. An intermediate technique that is easy to support with nominal tools (Microsoft Word tables and Microsoft Visio diagrams) is called "swim lane" diagrams or, more properly, Rummler-Brache diagrams, after the authors who originated the technique.[3] The relevant characteristic of a swim-lane diagram is that it provides a row or "lane" for each major role that participates in the process and uses a fairly basic flow-charting technique for identifying the tasks and intermediate work products and decisions that are part of the process. The technique is easy to do with sticky notes and mural paper or flip charts posted together. In a customer pilot of CMMI for small-business settings, this technique was considered to be the most significant new technique that the improvement team learned. Its swim-lane mural became a working document that team members used extensively to communicate about the projects they were working with, and to refine their understanding of the new process expectations. Figure 12-2 is an example swim-lane chart drawn using Visio, a drawing product that has lots of templates for different types of diagrams, including swim lanes.

One of the implications of "one size does not fit all" is that you will initially generate multiple versions of the same basic process that reflect how different projects or groups accomplish that process. It's tempting to move straight

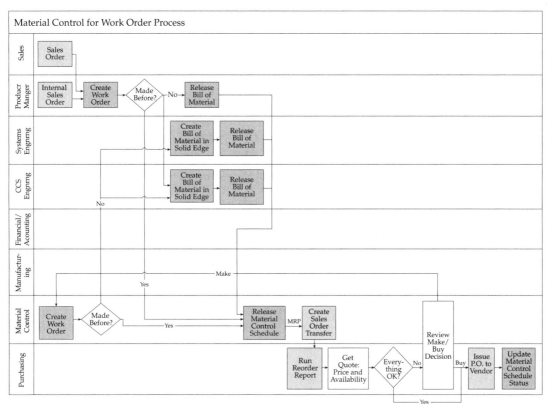

Figure 12-2: *Example swim lane diagram*

to a "standard" process that *everyone* will follow. That is rarely a successful strategy, for several reasons. First, gathering "the way we do it now" from the different groups that perform a similar process (for example, estimation) gives you a sense of the variation that already exists in the ways that people within your organization communicate about processes and what they think is important to record. Second, defining a standard process without the inputs of the current process could lead you to define something that is infeasible in one or more of the contexts that your organization works in. And third, when you develop a process without reference to the processes that are already being performed within the organization, you're really increasing the chance that the new process will be seen as a foreign element, rather than just as an improvement on what's already happening.

Even when you get to the point of synthesizing a standard process for your organization, you will find that you really need a *set* of standard processes. In most organizations of any size, there are sufficient differences in the context in which the process is performed that having multiple processes to start from is usually beneficial. First, the more the standard process looks like the one the group or project is accustomed to using, the more likely it is to be accepted. Second, having a few standard processes that have to be tailored (adapted) minimally for each use gives you better data for measuring process performance than having one standard process that has to be tailored extensively each time.

As you can see from the preceding discussion, there are many things to consider when developing useful process guidance. In general, stay as simple as you can, and always keep in mind that the practitioner or manager is the end user of the guidance, *not* the improvement consultant or the process improvement team. You will probably need to learn some new ways of writing that will be awkward at first, but they will get easier with time. Techniques like swim-lane diagrams and Information Mapping can help, but don't expect this to be a simple task. One common mistake we've seen is for an organization to download a Web site full of process documents written for some other organization and try to use them with minimal adaptation. The language, jargon, and approach are usually just the beginning of the problems. And after the organization figures out that it needs to seriously rewrite the material it has purchased or gotten free, it wonders whether starting with its own, even poorly written documentation would have been easier. In Chapter 15, we describe the one-hour process description method—our favorite method for eliciting the process information that will eventually become useful process guidance.

12.3 Collecting/incorporating lessons learned from improvement activities

CMMI content related to this topic:

- Generic Practice 3.2
- Integrated Project Management
- Organizational Process Definition

There are many ways to learn from your improvement activities. You can learn from both successes and failures. In both cases, learning can occur only if you reflect on what you have experienced and integrate that understanding back into your approaches and methods. Sadly, by the time we've finished an improvement activity, the team usually has very little energy left for the reflection and integration activities that lead to the deepest learnings. This is especially true in the smaller settings, where there are so many competing demands for mind-share that taking the time out for lessons-learned activities ends up at the bottom of the to-do list.

A very simple technique for collecting lessons learned as you go is to use a small amount of meeting time to perform in-process evaluations. Ask participants to think about the event they're involved in right now and to answer two questions:

1. If we were to do this again, what would you want to *keep* from the approaches and techniques we've used?
2. If we were to do this again, what would you want to *change* in terms of the approaches and techniques we've used?

We usually collect these on—you guessed it—sticky notes and post them on two flip charts; one says "keep," and the other says "change."

After the meeting, transcribe the items into a spreadsheet or other document, along with an identifier as to what phase the project was in when you collected the data. At the end of the pilot or project, ask the team members to review the list and suggest any changes that they would like to make. The reason for this is that sometimes in the middle of a process/method, you realize there are additional activities or information required to obtain the intended benefit from the technique. Most people find the "review the list" activity much easier to do than generating a list for the entire project time span.

We also use this basic approach for gathering evaluation data for workshops, courses, and other events, and generally get consistently useful information from participants.

Another layer to add to this approach is to have a specific area in your process asset library (PAL) for lessons learned. An interesting and fruitful activity for your improvement staff to do is to look across a cross-section of events to see whether there are common threads in the keep/change lists. This could be one of the inputs to a causal analysis activity, if warranted.

---

1. Adapted from *Developing Procedures Handbook,* IMI, Inc., 1993.

2. Humphrey, W. *TSP—Coaching Development Teams.* (Boston: Addison-Wesley, 2006) and Humphrey, W. *TSP—Leading a Development Team.* (Boston: Addison-Wesley, 2006).

3. Rummler, Geary A., and Brache, Alan P. *Improving Performance: How to Manage the White Space in the Organization Chart.* (San Francisco: Jossey Bass Business & Management Series, 1995).

Chapter 13

Deploying Improved Processes

In this chapter, we discuss the challenging task of deploying the processes that you have defined or evolved. There are many different aspects to deployment, but most have to do with people. You will most likely face staffing issues, the necessity of using outside resources, and the critical need to convince practitioners that the new process is in fact better than their current one.

When you're ready to try a new or improved process, except in the smallest of settings, it's usually a good idea to pilot the new process on one project before deploying it to its intended scope. In some cases, it may even be worth doing multiple pilots.

13.1 Finding/selecting pilots for CMMI implementation

CMMI content related to this topic:

- Organizational Innovation and Deployment
- Risk Management

There are many advantages and few disadvantages to using pilots in your improvement effort. This is actually one of the explicit practices in the Organization Innovation and Deployment process area:

SP 1.3-1 PILOT IMPROVEMENT

Pilot process and technology improvements to select which ones to implement.[1]

When thinking about pilots, we classify them into two categories: *technical feasibility* pilots and *adoptability* pilots.

Technical feasibility pilots are useful if you are uncertain as to the soundness of the new process that you've developed. For this type of pilot, you want a project that is probably not on your organization's critical path, and preferably one that contains people who would be considered innovators or early adopters (see the next section on adopter analysis for an explanation of these classifications). Essentially, technical feasibility pilots' determine the technical feasibility of the new process. Adoptability pilots, on the other hand, are done when you're confident of the soundness of the new process, but you're not sure whether the things you've developed to support it—checklists, training, procedures—will work well with your mainstream organizational population. In this case, you're generally looking for a project that contains people who are representative of the general population that you intend to deploy the new process to. They may not be the people who are the fastest to take up a new technology. For an adoptability pilot, you don't really want the innovators; you want the pragmatists, who have to have a reason to try something new. If the adoptability pilot works with them, chances are that the support products you've built will work with the rest of your organization.

13.1.1 Understanding your adoption population: Adopter analysis

Adopter analysis is a technique that comes from technology adoption. The idea is that individuals have some predisposition toward adopting a new technology or set of practices based on lots of different factors. The factors themselves aren't that important, because most of the time, if you describe the "thing" to be adopted and the characteristics of several preformulated adoption categories, most people can tell you where they would fit in relation to whatever technology/practice you want them to adopt.

The categories come from Everett Rogers's work on technology adoption[2] but are actually easier to understand based on their popularization in Geoffrey Moore's book *Crossing the Chasm*.[3]

Table 13-1 gives brief descriptions of the adopter categories used by Rogers and Moore.

Table 13-1: *Rogers/Moore Adopter Categories and Characteristics*

Adopter Category	Distinguishing Characteristics	Notes
Innovator	Gatekeepers for any new technology Appreciate technology for its own sake Appreciate architecture of technology Will spend hours trying to get technology to work Very forgiving of poor documentation, slow performance, incomplete functionality, and so on Helpful critics	These folks are useful for co-developing new processes/technologies.
Early Adopter	Dominated by a dream or vision Focus on business goals Usually have close ties with techie innovators Match emerging technologies to strategic opportunities Look for breakthrough Thrive on high-visibility, high-risk projects Have charisma to generate buy-in for projects Do not have credibility with early majority	These folks are useful for doing early technical feasibility pilots, but not for adoptability pilots.

(continued)

Table 13-1: *Rogers/Moore Adopter Categories and Characteristics* (Continued)

Adopter Category	Distinguishing Characteristics	Notes
Early Majority	Do not want to be pioneers (prudent souls) Control majority of budget Want percentage improvement (incremental, measurable, predictable progress) Not risk averse, but want to manage it carefully Hard to win over but are loyal once won	These are the folks to use for adoptability pilots—with them you can test whether or not the practices are packaged in a useful, pragmatic way.
Late Majority	Avoid discontinuous improvement (revolution) Adopt only to stay on par with the rest of the world Somewhat fearful of new technologies Like preassembled packages with everything bundled	These folks will *not* be volunteers for your improvement projects and will wait, if possible, until there are lots of job aids/tools available to make their implementation easier.
Laggard	Naysayers Adopt only after technology is not recognizable as separate entity Constantly point at discrepancies between what was promised and what is delivered	These folks will avoid the improvements until they have no other choice; however, they are often very good at pointing out flaws in packaging.

Adopter analysis is something you can do to identify individuals or groups that will be helpful to you with different aspects of the improvement task. Innovators and Early Adopters are likely to volunteer for your process improvement teams in areas that affect them. However, they will probably be satisfied with a partial solution that will *not* satisfy other adopter types. So for an adoption feasibility pilot, you probably want to find some Early Majority participants. If you want to know what kind of transition mechanisms (things that help with the communication or implementation of the new practices) need to be built over the longer term, you would want to talk with some Late Majority or Laggard types.

One of the things to note about different adopter types is that they typically move through change cycles (for example, the Satir cycle we discussed earlier) at different speeds, so you may run into a situation where some of the people in a group are enthusiastically embracing a new set of practices and others are clearly dragging their feet.

Adopter type is not the only characteristic that is useful to you in choosing people to participate in different aspects of the improvement effort. Another thing to look at is where they fit in your value network, one of the topics covered later in this chapter.

13.1.2 Staffing your first improvement pilot

Our recommendation for your first improvement project is to first find the people who have some passion around making improvements in the organization, then put them to work *doing* improvement activities within their projects. This will require some oversight so that appropriate resources are expended, and so on. But again, that doesn't have to be the entire management team; it could just be one senior manager who has a stake in the improvement effort. It's especially useful if that person has successful experience with improvement projects.

And yes, what you're doing is really a project. It probably delivers a different kind of product from the other projects in your organization, depending on your business domain. A process improvement project delivers

- a set of assets upon which to base new practices;
- the experience of using those assets by the pilot project that develops them;
- experience and skill-building to enable further improvement projects.

One of the Catch-22s of process improvement is that project management skills and practices are among the things you'll need to use first and effectively for the improvement activities to be successful, but that's probably one of the areas of organizational weakness that led you to model-based improvement to begin with! We have witnessed the dawning of this conundrum countless times, and our answer is generally twofold:

- There are probably people in the organization who *are* good at project management, they just haven't had a chance to use those skills in your environment. Find and recruit them!

- This conundrum gives your first improvement team a chance to get into the details of the chosen model, because their first use of the model, for almost all the models you would think about using, can be to apply project management practices to their own improvement project!

Depending on the skills/abilities of the staff you have available internally, you may want to consider a process improvement consultant familiar with the model you're using to help get you started. If you want someone to follow the kinds of principles and practices we're writing about here, you may actually have to do a little more work on your own to get them to understand your requirements for the project, because some of them will want to spend their initial time with you working on infrastructure, training, and appraisal rather than getting improvement projects started off quickly. And in truth, for some of the larger organizations we have worked with, this was exactly the right approach. In those kinds of organizations, the process deployment task was very large (often involving hundreds, if not thousands, of people) and having a bunch of little improvement efforts going on all over the place proved too chaotic. The lack of an infrastructure to bring their results together and provide unified training for the staff was sub-optimal at best.

To give you an example, the consulting provided for using CMMI in a small company in Huntsville, Alabama, was about four days of training/mini-appraisal effort, followed by one day of on-site consulting per month, and less than one day of offsite work per month until the company started preparing for a SCAMPI A appraisal. At that point, the effort increased a bit. This was a company, however, that already had been registered with ISO 9000, and it already had some of the infrastructure we talk about in Chapter 11 in place. So, just like with automobiles, your mileage may (and probably will) vary. Also, we were working with only three projects and three Process Areas, so the scope of this effort in comparison to yours may be a good bit smaller. If you want more information on how this project was accomplished, go to www.sei.cmu.edu/ttp/publications/toolkit, and you can look at the description of the whole process, as well as download the materials we used. Some of them are included in this book as well, and there are some things we've added to the book that were not done with this pilot. (We try to learn from our experiences, too.)

13.2 Working with consultants

> CMMI content related to this topic:
>
> • Supplier Agreement Management
> • Integrated Project Management
> • Organizational Training

Chances are that sooner or later in your process improvement journey you'll hire one or more process improvement consultants to help you with your process implementation. The guidance in the Supplier Agreement Management Process Area is good advice when selecting and managing the relationship with your consultant(s). As in any field, there are many competent consultants to choose among, and many of the differences come down to personal style or preference, and experience working in a particular context or domain. A few things to ask your candidates to help get a better fit might be:

- Are you a member of the SEI Partner Network? These are individuals who are authorized to deliver authentic SEI services. Depending on their authorization, they may be able to provide SCAMPI lead appraiser/team leader services and/or Introduction to CMMI training, as well as other process improvement–related technologies.

- What is your experience working in our business domain? Ask for customer references that you can contact and then follow through by contacting the references provided.

- What is your experience working with organizations of our size? Have you worked with organizations focusing mostly on services or product development?

- What is your experience working with organizations targeting the profile we're hoping to achieve in terms of capability and/or maturity?

- What is your experience getting an improvement program started with our resource profile (if that's the stage where you are in your improvement)?

- What is your experience solving x kinds of problems? X could be anything from leadership problems to configuration management library problems and everything in between.

Some consultants specialize in teaching topics related to process improvement, others specialize in running workshop events, and still others specialize in providing hands-on daily help for your effort. Obviously, these different modes of interacting with the consultant will cost different amounts of money and various amounts of effort on your part.

The SEI uses a model for thinking about how you want or need to interact with a consultant based on a consulting grid that differentiates responsibility for project results from responsibility for client growth. The roles that are defined in the nine blocks of the grid reflect different levels of intervention that would be expected from the consultant. Figures 13-1 and 13-2 illustrate the degrees of intervention and briefly describe the roles for each block of the grid. SuZ regularly uses this grid with collaborators and pilot sites to

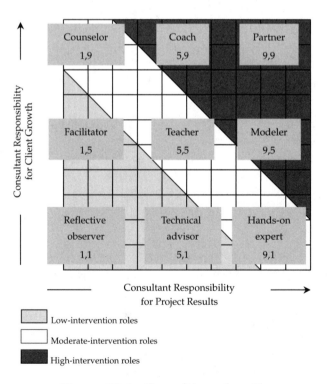

Figure 13-1: *Consulting role grid*

Counselor	Coach	Partner
"You do it; I will be your sounding board. "	"You did well; you can add this next time."	"We will do it together and learn from each other. "
Facilitator	**Teacher**	**Modeler**
"You do it; I will attend to the process. "	"Here are some principles you can use to solve problems of this type. "	"I will do it; you watch so you can learn from me. "
Reflective observer	**Technical advisor**	**Hands-on expert**
"You do it; I will watch and tell you what I see and hear. "	"I will answer your questions as you go along."	"I will do it for you; I will tell you what to do."

Figure 13-2: *Sample role statements*

clarify what's expected in the working relationship, not just what is expected in terms of the deliverables of the collaboration. This grid is discussed in the SEI's Mastering Process Improvement course.

13.3 Deploying practices to the targeted organizational scope

Having determined the target projects and arranged for the appropriate help, now you need to actually deploy the changes. This is the point where many of the psychological aspects of process improvement show up. In the next sections, we present several tools to enable more effective and efficient deployments.

13.3.1 Dealing with people issues involved in managing change: The Satir Change Model and beyond

In Chapter 8, when we were talking about building and sustaining sponsorship, we introduced the Satir Change Model. We provided some ideas on how paying attention to that cycle could help sponsors understand why the members of their organization are at a different place than they are (in terms of readiness to adopt) with regard to process improvement. In this section, we'll go a little further with the Satir model as a way to help the facilitators of the improvement effort work more effectively with those who are being asked to change.

Figure 13-3 shows a more detailed view of the Satir change cycle, highlighting some of the different things you'll see in organizations as they successfully and unsuccessfully navigate it.

When you look at the kinds of things going on in the Chaos block of Figure 13-3, you start to understand why performance during the Chaos period can be so variable. When energy in the organization is spent trying to deny the existence of the foreign element or is spent trying to make it go away, there won't be a lot of energy left for executing the primary tasks of the organization. And when a Transforming Idea is found, integrating it into the personal and work group's practices requires energy, as does practicing the new way of doing things until people become as skilled at it as they were with the old (attain Alistair Cockburn's fluency stage). Another thing to note in this diagram is that if a significant amount of time goes by after a change has been successfully integrated, the New Status Quo will become the Old Status Quo, and making changes to *that* set of practices

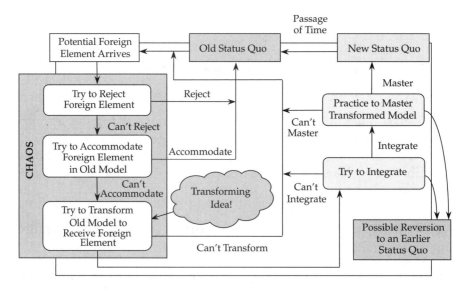

Adapted from G. Weinberg, *Quality Software Management, Vol. 4: Anticipating Change.*

Figure 13-3: *Flow chart of Satir Change Model*

will involve some of the same struggles as the first time you changed the practices.

One of the main functions of a process improvement group is to help the parts of the organization going through change successfully navigate both the Chaos and Integration & Practice stages of the Satir model.

Figure 13-4 shows graphically some of the things you're likely to observe in a group going through chaos in an improvement effort that affects it. One of the things you almost immediately see is that old feedback mechanisms—measurements, reports, meetings, and so on—are changed, making it difficult for the group members to know the "who, what, when, and where" associated with reporting information. They need to provide information back to management on how the new process is going, as well as whatever information is called for by the new process. This often leads to wild-looking performance and a desire by the group members to find some kind of stability. This is, in essence, the search for a Transforming Idea. However, not all the choices for stability are good, and this is another reason you see performance fluctuations in this stage. When stability is sought from inappropriate sources (OK, maybe the "tea-leaf readers" choice is a little extreme), you'll end up farther away from a Transforming Idea, not closer to one.

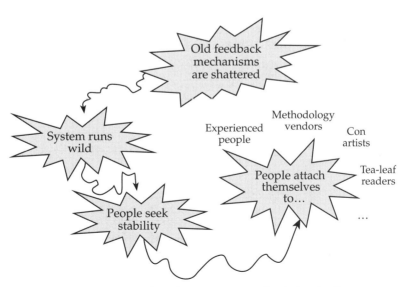

Adapted from G. Weinberg, *Quality Software Management, Vol. 4: Anticipating Change*

Figure 13-4: *What Chaos is like*

So how do you help the people in your organization get through their chaos? Jerry Weinberg (in QSM volume 4, *Anticipating Change*) has some ideas of what's needed as well as what's *not* needed during this stage.[4]

What's needed:

- Consistent, compassionate offers of reliable information
- Active listening (an oldie, but a goodie!)
- Empathy

What's *not* needed:

- Brutal versions of the facts that will destroy confidence
- Feel-better placating that will provide an excuse to stay in denial
- Actions that allow a temporary return to the old status quo (thus encouraging the hope that the foreign element can be successfully rejected)

When you're involved in this type of communication, another model from Satir—her Communication model—is also useful. It is covered pretty comprehensively in Weinberg's *QSM* volume 3, *Congruent Action*,[5] as well as his *Secrets of Consulting*.[6] And if you find personality typing a useful way of analyzing your communications with others, many in the process improvement field find the Myers-Briggs Type Indicator (MBTI) to be a very useful way of helping groups understand some of the issues they are dealing with as they go through improvement activities.[7] MBTI can be particularly useful to a process improvement team that comprises diverse roles from across the organization. There is a whole community of certified MBTI practitioners; if you're going to get involved with using MBTI, it shouldn't be too difficult to find one in your region and business domain. There are also several books that deal specifically with using MBTI in a work setting, such as *Type Talk at Work*.[8] Another reference that is particularly useful for people within the software industry is Tom DeMarco and Tim Lister's *Peopleware*.[9]

13.3.2 Using technology adoption approaches effectively

Technology adoption research can be easily and profitably applied to process deployment. Processes are similar to new technology in that they often represent change; they have associated knowledge transfer (for example, training); and they impact the way people accomplish their work and interact with co-workers. In addition to those we've already introduced, this section highlights some ways we've seen technology adoption approaches applied successfully to process improvement.

Among the first things to think about when deploying a new process or tool are the people you are asking to use it and any pertinent characteristics of the way that group tends to approach change. We discussed one aspect of analyzing the "who" when we talked about adopter analysis earlier in this chapter. Now we'll talk about another powerful technique: value networks.

13.3.3 Value networks

One way of deciding who needs to be enlisted, and in what time frame, is to construct a value network. The idea of a value network is to determine who (in terms of role and, where feasible, defined individuals and groups) needs something from you—a value you provide to them—and who you need things from—a value they provide to you. For example, as the process improvement group, you need money and access to labor resources from other departments and from your management sponsors. They need progress against PI infrastructure and deployment goals from you, as well as status reporting of the overall improvement effort from you.

Value networks were developed at the SEI, primarily by Eileen Forrester, as part of a technique called TransPlant. Their original use was to help technology developers identify what kinds of actions need to be taken with which groups to enable faster uptake of a technology within its intended community. The technique also works where you're trying to identify the players in adopting a particular technology or set of practices that you're deploying.

You start a value network by putting your improvement group in the middle of a diagram and identifying nodes in the network that represent different stakeholder groups. Then you identify what value is exchanged among the different nodes. In CMMI-based improvement, some of the nodes might be:

- Pilot projects
- Project managers
- Senior managers
- PI steering group
- External customers
- External consultants
- Training/education group
- SEI

When you think of the kinds of value that could be exchanged between the PI group and these stakeholders, or among the nodes themselves, you might think about:

- Different kinds of data
- Resources
- Special skills
- Project measurements
- Lessons learned
- Process assets
- Process appraisal results

Figure 13-5 shows the beginnings of a value network for a group transitioning to CMMI from another model. When a value network starts to become complex, you can move to a table form to make it easier to capture the information, especially if you have particular nodes within a particular stakeholder group that will have different value exchanges from the main category.

When you've developed a value network, you can start analyzing it in many ways, asking questions like

- What nodes do you have the capability of serving now?
- What is the priority for serving the nodes you're not capable of serving now?

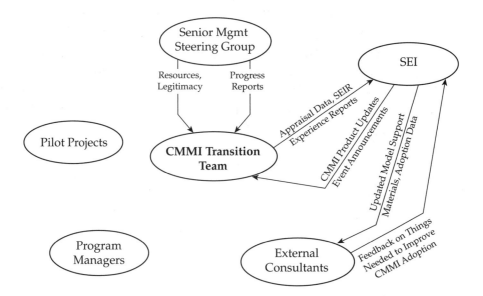

Note: Interactions occur both between the transition team and stakeholders as well as among the stakeholders.

Figure 13-5: *Beginnings of a CMMI value network*

- What is needed for you to be able to serve the priority nodes?
- Are there adopter type similarities that you can leverage among different nodes?

Look for future publications from the SEI on this technique as it gets used in a broader array of contexts.

13.3.4 Developing/obtaining appropriate transition mechanisms

At various points in your improvement activities, you will need to figure out what kinds of support people in different groups are likely to need to accelerate their adoption of the new practices. The model we use to help understand what kinds of things need to be created/deployed is called the Adoption Commitment Curve.[10] The version of this model that the SEI uses (Figure 13-6) is slightly different from the original but captures the resource commitments a little more realistically, based on our experience.

The idea of the Adoption Commitment Curve is that each individual or group moves through a series of learning stages while navigating a change.

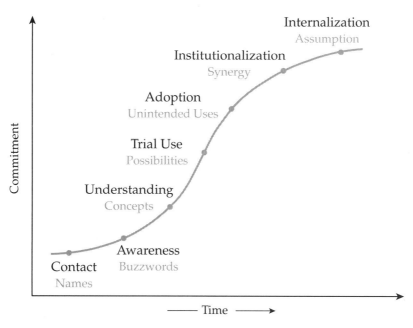

Adapted from Patterson & Conner, 1982 "Building Commitment to Organizational Change"

Figure 13-6: *Adoption Commitment Curve*

You can relate this curve back to the Satir model as well. The first three stages of this curve—Contact, Awareness, and Understanding—reflect the recognition of a foreign element and some of the Chaos stage that goes along with trying to understand the new process/technology to get to the Transforming Idea. Trial Use and Adoption reflect the stage of Integration and Practice, where you're actually using the new practices and finding ways to make them stick. Institutionalization is putting the final mechanisms in place to get to the New Status Quo. And Internalization is akin to moving over time to the Old Status Quo.

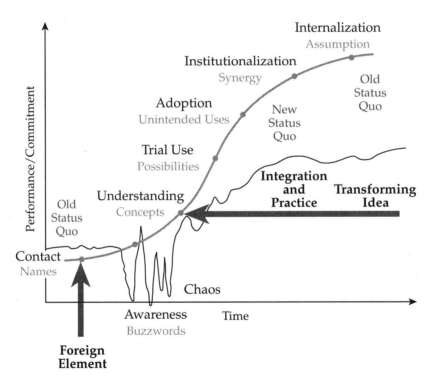

Figure 13-7: *Satir model plus Adoption Commitment Curve*

13.4 Communication

How you communicate with the stakeholders in a process improvement initiative is crucial. Everyone needs to at least know what chapter you're reading, even if they're not quite on the very same page. At a minimum, the implementation team should develop some approach for figuring "who needs to know what." Often, it helps to specifically identify the communications that are critical to success in your organization. Table 13-2 shows an example of a communication plan in a simple, tabular form. The headers in the table are

- Objective—the purpose the communication is meant to achieve
- Responsibility to Report Information—who needs to make sure it gets communicated
- Member(s) Receiving Information—who needs to get it
- Receiving Information Mechanism—what the communication event/ artifact is called
- Medium Used—how the material should be transmitted
- Frequency—how often this kind of communication should occur

13.4.1 Lessons from agile methods

One of the best discussions on how humans communicate in work environments is found in an unlikely place. The first chapters of Alistair Cockburn's *Agile Software Development*[11] focus entirely on this subject. His insights, based on keen observation of technical activities in several countries, are just as applicable to process improvement as they are to software development. Here's a summary of what he (and other agile proponents) have learned.

People parse complex experiences in very different ways.

In general, we all perceive information in somewhat different orders. We "parse" it—that is, break it into little pieces—and then reconstruct it according to the patterns we recognize. The best example for the truth of this statement is the graphic tests of perception often used in communications courses. The two most prevalent are a cup-versus-vase picture and a young woman-versus-crone picture. Depending on how you parse images—usually light to dark or vice versa, but sometimes according to your mood—you see one or the other. It takes an effort of will to see the second image, because your mind holds on to the first patterns you detect. Alistair indicates that

Table 13-2: *Example Communications Table*

Objective	Responsibility to Report Information	Member(s) Receiving Information	Receiving Information Mechanism	Medium Used	Frequency
Provide status on schedules and issues	Project manager	Implementation team	Risk review/mitigation meeting	Meeting	Monthly
Obtain guidance and resolution on issues					
Document status on schedules and issues	Project manager	Implementation team	Project status/milestone report (e.g., Gantt chart)	E-mail or file transfer	Biweekly
Provide status on schedules and issues	Implementation team	Department managers	Progress report	Paper or e-mail	Monthly
				Supervisors' meeting	
Provide status on schedules and issues	Department managers	Staff	Progress summary	Department meetings	Monthly
Provide high-level summary of achievements	Implementation team/project manager	Staff	"Temperature chart"	Poster board (companywide)	Monthly at minimum; interim updates as significant events occur

Table 13-2: *Example Communications Table* (Continued)

Objective	Responsibility to Report Information	Member(s) Receiving Information	Receiving Information Mechanism	Medium Used	Frequency
Ensure that staff know how to provide input related to the MES implementation	Implementation team	Staff	Problem-report process	E-mail	Quarterly reminders
Communicate and document any needed project adjustment	Department managers, staff	Start with immediate supervisor, then project manager, SEI, implementation team	Problem report/change request	E-mail to project manager, or talk to department representative for implementation team	As needed
Communicate and document status of all change requests	Implementation team	Project manager, SEI, department managers, originator	Disposition change request	Excel spreadsheet	As needed
Report issues as soon as possible	Project manager	Implementation team	Significant problems or issues	E-mail, voice mail, in person	ASAP

Adapted from INTRo, an SEI Web resource available at www.sei.cmu.edu/INTRo.

listening to how people tell a story about their work will often give you clues as to how they parse information.

Understanding includes internal information restructuring and shared experience.

Another way we understand is by developing models of what we're hearing that are constantly updated as more facts or descriptions are gathered. Have you ever found yourself interrupting someone to finish their sentence for them? If so, you should recognize that you have used your inner model to structure the information you heard and extrapolated the complete information from the fragments received. (Rich often inflicts this rather bad habit on his wife, Jo, usually missing her point completely.) Communication of any idea requires such internal restructuring and often leads to erroneous understanding, because we all build these internal models differently.

A corollary to this is communication based on shared experiences. Families and others in long-time relationships nearly always develop private languages of words, gestures, or expressions. Their use is incomprehensible to those outside the family, because they are usually shorthand for a long set of shared memories. An example of this in Rich's family is listening for a rhythm in some phrase that matches the first phrase of "Fascinating Rhythm." (You younger folks may need to look up this Gershwin tune and have a listen to appreciate this example.) The memory is based on going to the circus and the kids becoming hysterical when Jo noted that she could sing the animal trainer's name to the music that was playing (**Gun**-ther **Ge**-ble-**Wil**-liams). Twenty years later, "the fam" can still lapse into paroxysms of laughter when someone happens to recognize a matching rhythm. (For example, **di**-ver-**ti**-cu-**li**-**tis** resulted in our almost being asked to leave a quiet restaurant; it goes without saying that "asked to leave" is another long family story.)

So our communication with team members and stakeholders can either use or abuse these principles. They can draw a team together if you can find a shared experience but can also leave folks feeling that they are on the outside looking in if they are not "clued in" to the context.

You can never really know what you are experiencing, and you can't ever communicate it.

Although this sounds like an existential exercise, it is extremely important when working with all the diverse people and roles in process improvement initiatives. We understand what we hear or read based on the experiences and training we have received and our particular purpose at the time. In the same way, when we try to describe knowledge to others, we draw our language and thought constructions from the same reference sources. Because these references are essentially unique to us and vary with the task and thought priorities at hand, communication is always incomplete and misinterpreted.

The three stages of learning behavior—following, detaching, and fluent— are critical in communicating.

There are three stages that describe how comfortable or understanding people are with concepts and procedures. These would reflect "individual learning" in the learning model we talked about in Chapter 2. People in the first stage, *following,* are ready to hear about one thing that works. In the second phase, *detaching,* people parse an idea and look for places where it doesn't hold true or can't work. When they are *fluent,* people generally can't recognize that they are following any particular process at all, because they understand the desired end effect and move toward it based on their integration of experience using several different techniques.

This is important to understand when teaching people about process improvement or training them in processes. *Following*-stage people, for example, will not be interested in how many variations of a particular process there are; they want to understand one way that works and will become frustrated with too many options. People in the *detaching* phase can make very good quality-control people for your evolving process assets. If the majority of the team is already at the *fluent* stage, minimal process guidance can keep them aligned.

13.4.2 Communication and implementation support mechanisms

Although you can see that the Satir Change Model and the Adoption Commitment Curve are complementary, one of the particular things we use the Adoption Commitment curve for is to plan the transition mechanisms that need to be created to help people of different adopter types navigate an adoption process. *Transition mechanisms* are events or job aids that are usually meant to support either communication activities or implementation activities.

Communication mechanisms are transition mechanisms focused on improving understanding of the new practices/technology. They primarily serve to help move you from Contact through Understanding. *Implementation mechanisms* are transition mechanisms focused on actually assisting you in the implementation of the practices. They are used primarily for Trial Use, Adoption, and Institutionalization. Table 13-3, adapted from many sources by Eileen Forrester,

Table 13-3: *Typical Transition Mechanisms Categorized by Adoption Commitment Curve Category*[12]

Commitment Stage	Typical Mechanisms	Notes
Contact and Awareness	"Elevator speech" Standard 45-minute pitch; road show FAQ Magazine articles Conference briefings Flash cards with objectives, benefits, URL, and so on Web site devoted to the technology, with links and dialogue Successful ROI stories, case studies Executive summary of policy	Focus on concept, not the buzzwords
Understanding	One-day seminars, symposia for various vendors Detailed case studies Technical brief Identified and authorized champions Identified stakeholder roles, responsibilities, and interrelationships	

(continued)

Table 13-3: *Typical Transition Mechanisms Categorized by Adoption Commitment Curve Category* (Continued)

Commitment Stage	Typical Mechanisms	Notes
Trial Use	Pilot programs Carefully identified focused pilots (or "experiments") Defined incentives for pilot participation Small working group to support pilots Special authorities for pilots Documented pilot results Communication, education, and support Defined measures of success Two- to three-day course for pilots and interested others Users' group (may be external, such as SPINs); share experiences Lessons learned from Innovators and Early Adopters Case exercise for transitioning from one set of work practices to one with the new technology support Technology-use startup and coaching Identified barriers and workarounds	Questions to consider: How big do you need to be to consider pilots? How do small organizations conduct pilots? Protect and support the pilots

(continued)

Table 13-3: *Typical Transition Mechanisms Categorized by Adoption Commitment Curve Category* (Continued)

Commitment Stage	Typical Mechanisms	Notes
Adoption	Strong set of incentives; rewards and consequences	Ensure that CMMI sustainment infrastructure is in place and resourced
	Refined guidance on CMMI usage choices and implementation	
	Education: mature courses, modularized for just-in-time (JIT) delivery	
	In-process aids	
	Repository on business cases and lessons learned	
	Sample implementation plan with impact analysis	
	Job aids: process guides, startup guides, coaching, JIT training, guidebooks	
	Policies or standards	
Institutionalization	Fully realized curriculum of training for different types of users	Continuous improvement of adoption artifacts (such as guides)
	New-employee training/ orientation	
	Stability in leadership use of CMMI data	
	Grandfathering versus cutover policy	

shows typical Communication and Implementation support transition mechanisms for CMMI adoption.

One thing Table 13-3 can help you with is timing your development of process guidance and other work products that need to be developed or acquired. As you look through each stage and determine which of the types of mechanisms would work in your organization, you will start to see what kind of lead time you need before each activity (for example, start a pilot with Early Majority types of adopters). In many cases, your Innovators and Early Adopters will be willing to co-develop transition mechanisms with you. However, be aware that one characteristic of Early Adopters and Innovators is that they typically don't need the same kinds of communication and implementation support mechanisms that Early Majority and later adopter types do. One further warning: Don't try to use/develop all of the possible mechanisms. These are representative of several different organizations; you need to choose a subset and think about what other kinds of things work well in your environment.

When you've built a few transition mechanisms, it's time to take the "what" to the "who." Remember all those transition mechanisms that you started thinking about when planning your deployment? We hope you've been spending at least some of your time developing the job aids, training, and other communication and implementation support mechanisms that will be used by those slated to adopt your new processes.

The most popular transition mechanism, based on the people we talk to, is still training. We've seen both wonderful and abysmal training events, and one thing that almost always distinguishes the really good training events we've participated in or observed is that they are tuned to the roles of the people who are using the training to perform their jobs. This is not as important for Contact or Awareness types of training as it is for training meant to get adopters through the Understanding phase.

One of the fundamental tasks for an adopter in moving through the Understanding phase is to make the connection between the technology and work/activities. Anything your training can do to support making that connection is appreciated by potential adopters, and often this is one of the things that can make a huge difference in the success of your process adoption effort. SuZ and Shawn Presson's tutorial, "Beyond Death by Slides," introduces many techniques related to this.[13]

1. Chrissis, Mary Beth, et. al. *CMMI: Guidelines for Process Integration and Product Improvement.* 2d ed. (Boston: Addison-Wesley, 2006). All references to CMMI components in this chapter are from this source.

2. Rogers, Everett. *Diffusion of Innovations.* (New York: The Free Press, 1995).

3. Moore, Geoffrey. *Crossing the Chasm: Marketing and Selling Technology Products to Mainstream Customers.* (New York: Harper Business, 1991).

4. Weinberg, Gerald. *Quality Software Management Volume 4: Anticipating Change.* (New York: Dorset House Publishing, 1997).

5. Weinberg, Gerald. *Quality Software Management Volume 3: Congruent Action.* (New York: Dorset House, 1994).

6. Weinberg, Gerald. *Secrets of Consulting: A Guide to Giving and Getting Advice Successfully.* (New York: Dorset House, 1985).

7. Keirsey, David. *Please Understand Me II: Temperament, Character, Intelligence.* (Del Mar, Calif.: Prometheus Nemesis Books, 1998).

8. Kroeger, Otto, et al. *Type Talk at Work (Revised): How the 16 Personality Types Determine Your Success on the Job.* (New York: Random House, 2002).

9. DeMarco, Tom, and Timothy Lister. *Peopleware: Productive Projects and Teams.* 2d ed. (New York: Dorset House, 1999).

10. Patterson, R., and D. Conner. "Building Commitment to Organizational Change." In *Training & Development Journal* 36:4, pp. 18–30.

11. Cockburn, Alistair. *Agile Software Development.* (Boston: Addison-Wesley, 2002).

12. Forrester, Eileen. Omaha SPIN Meeting Tutorial, 2003.

13. Garcia, S. and Presson, S. "Beyond Death by Slides," tutorial, SEPG Conference 2004 (Pittsburgh, Carnegie Mellon University, 2004).

Chapter 14

Looking Ahead

In the preceding chapters, we have made our way through philosophy, practicality, applicability, and survivability, not to mention creativity, to arrive here at possibility. What is possible for you and your organization in your environment? What does the future hold for the practice of process improvement? What's the possibility that you can sell this book used? (Just kidding.)

In this chapter, we try to answer the above questions and help you chart your own path toward better, more effective, and more efficient processes.

14.1 What's next for you?

Now that you have learned about our approach to surviving CMMI and process improvement, it's time to look at your own future. You understand the rationale and difficulties behind process improvement. You have access to tools, techniques, and resources for implementing process improvement. You have several approaches and models to choose among. You even have a case study to help visualize your entire initiative. So don't sit there lollygaggin'; get up and do something!

14.1.1 Figure out where you are in your own decision cycle

As Watts Humphrey has said more times than he can count, "If you don't know where you are, any map will do." So the *first* next step is to find out where you are in your considerations of process improvement:

- Are you still considering a process improvement initiative? Have you made that list of reasons, pro and con?

- Has such an initiative been mandated? If so, have you looked at how best to integrate the required improvement activity with meeting your existing business goals?

- Do you have sponsorship? If not, reread Chapter 8, and look for strategies that seem to fit your situation. Do the sales techniques provide insight into how you could move forward? Are there particular executives who might be experiencing pain that your process improvement effort could ease?

14.1.2 Proceed from there

When you've figured out your location vis-à-vis process improvement decision making, you'll be able to start moving in some direction. Here are some pointers:

- Be realistic about where you are and what you can achieve in the near term. Don't promise things you can't deliver to sell your PI initiative. It's much better to not do PI right now than it is to fail at it and possibly jeopardize any future efforts. If the time just doesn't seem right, pursue other activities that will support later improvement, such as measurement programs and quality-assurance practices.

- Figure out where you need consulting versus training versus other kinds of resources. Know how much you are going to need to spend so that you can get the right amount of funding and other resources from the sponsor.

- Be bold with your approach. It is equally wrong to underestimate what you can do if there is a high probability of significant impact.

14.1.3 Find the right resources

You've got a location and a direction, and possibly some tasks. Now you need to make sure you've got the right "team" working for you. Our quick tips for resources:

- Read the next chapter carefully.

- SEI Partner Network is a safe place to start for consulting. These companies have been through all the required training and met the rigorous standards established by the SEI.

- Don't try to learn everything yourself. Even smart engineers and managers can't expect to get all the nuances of some of the models and life cycles without some support. If nothing else, you can save time and energy struggling to solve problems that have already been solved in dozens of other places.

- Use the SEPG Conference, NDFA CMMI Conference, and SPIN resources in your area to check up on consultants and share lessons learned. If there is someone in your company who has done PI before, find out what challenges and enablers he or she found.

We want you to succeed. If that means succeeding in process improvement, and we have helped in that journey, we are happy. If, however, PI isn't in the stars for you, follow the signs and guides of your environment, and look for other ways to improve. There are many roads to success, and we hope you find the one that's straightest and broadest for you.

14.2 What's next for process improvement?

Although this section will become dated at some point (given today's acceleration of technology development, probably by the time this book is published), we thought it was still worthwhile to provide some insights as to where we see the process movement going as of the writing of this edition. Just like the organizations that embrace process improvement, the process improvement movement itself must evolve and learn to remain vibrant lest we become what Barry Boehm calls "change-averse change agents." Here are a few of the things going on that may be of interest to you as you look beyond your individual organization's improvement journey.

14.2.1 International Process Research Consortium (IPRC)

The IPRC is a consortium of researchers and forward-thinking companies that are working together to build a road map of future research needed to further the ability of process to support businesses. Through a series of six workshops facilitated by the Software Engineering Institute, this group of researchers from around the world has explored current research directions, as well as possible future needs for process support. The first road map from the consortium is scheduled to be published in the fall of 2006. Other activities that are possible are a working group on implementing processes in small settings and one for e-health systems. Check the SEI Web site, www.sei.cmu.edu/iprc, for details and ongoing information about the IRPC and its products and events.

14.2.2 CMMI constellations

With the publication of CMMI version 1.2, more information is becoming available about some future directions for CMMI that the CMMI Steering Group has established. One of the most interesting and possibly far reaching of these is the concept of a set of CMMI constellations.

The idea of these constellations is that a core of CMMI practices is generally useful no matter what model context is being used. These practices are supplemented by groups of Process Areas that reflect a cluster, or *constellation*, of practices particular to a broad, but not all-inclusive, context. The three constellations that have been identified so far are

- *Product Development.* This is the baseline and is the one reflected in the current model content.
- *Services.* This one is in the works and is expected to cover the kind of operations/services delivery context consistent with an Information Technology operation or an engineering services organization, among others.
- *Acquisition.* This constellation is also in the works and is expected to cover the practices common in organizations that primarily contract for and accept products, rather than develop and integrate them.

Conceptually, organizations would be able to choose one or more constellations to work from and be appraised against. While retaining the core practices across all their contexts, they would be able to use the constellations to improve the fit of the CMMI practices to particular parts of their organization. This constellation concept is consistent with CMMI ideas going back to the CMM standards work that was done in the mid-'90s and has the potential for improving CMMI's utility even more than what we're seeing today.

14.2.3 ISO Working Group on Life Cycles for Very Small Enterprises

In October of 2005, the committee within ISO that has been working on process-focused standards for the past dozen years[†] commissioned a new working group, Working Group 24, to address Life Cycle Processes for Very Small Enterprises (VSE). What makes this effort noteworthy is that the group does *not* intend to create another compliance-oriented standard. Rather, it is looking at using existing ISO standards to create a "profile" of practices to recommend to VSEs, along with a guidebook to help users interpret and make more effective use of existing ISO standards, most of which were not created with VSEs in mind. Claude Laporte, the project editor for the working group, plans to establish a Web site to solicit community input on the intermediate efforts of the working group. We suggest that you search for *ISO SC7 Working Group 24 and Claude Laporte,* or something similar, to find it. For a presentation on this working group's plans/efforts, look on the SEI Web site for the *Proceedings of the 1st International Researcher's Workshop on Process Improvement in Small Settings.*[1]

The presentation is one of the items included in the technical report.

14.2.4 Integration of different process improvement–related technologies

One of the many challenges for people in the improvement field is to help organizations understand which of the various improvement approaches are relevant and useful for different situations and contexts. With the Software Engineering Process Management (SEPM) program of the SEI, integrating process improvement support technologies like PSP, TSP, and CMMI is being actively addressed, as well as integrating techniques like Six Sigma into SEI approaches to measurement. You can expect to see new courses and other support materials as these efforts progress.

14.3 Summary of Part IV

Part IV is certainly the richest part of the book, but we hope it has answered many of your questions about how to approach the common challenges of establishing and sustaining an improvement effort, especially when you're

---

[†] SC7, for those of you who speak ISO-ese

dealing with a resource-constrained environment. Part IV could have been even more dense (the other term we've heard for *content-rich*) if we had put all the details of some of the techniques we've introduced into it. Instead, we chose to move procedural detail for techniques like CMMI-based Business Analysis and Readiness and Fit Analysis into their own chapter, Chapter 15. When you're ready for them, they'll be there for you.

You have now journeyed (vicariously at least) through most of the common challenges you'll face as you get started, and you have some idea of what to do about them. From establishing sponsorship to understanding what a transition mechanism is and why you should care, you have navigated the landscape of process improvement and have started to use CMMI as your guide, not only for your organization but also for your own process improvement tasks. We can't emphasize enough how much difference leading by example makes in an improvement effort. It's much more powerful to be able to say to someone, "I've done this, and here's how it works," than to say, "I've read about this, and here's how it's supposed to work."

This is the close of the main parts of the book. Here, we brought you back to "What are you going to do now?" because we hope that this book will truly become a guide for your efforts, not just a book on your shelf. We also shared some of the things going on that we find interesting in the world of process improvement, even though we know that Chapter 14 will be out of date even before this book completes production. The point is not so much what *exactly* is going on, but that there is always *something* going on, and staying up to speed with process improvement research and practice is a never-ending activity.

---

1. Garcia, Suzanne, et al. *Proceedings of the 1st International Researcher's Workshop on Process Improvement in Small Settings.* CMU/SEI-2006-SR-001. (Pittsburgh: Carnegie Mellon University, 2006).

Illustration from *The Travels of Marco Polo*
by Witold Gordon (1885–1968)

Part V

―――

Outfitting Your Expedition (PI Resources)

Scholars are a nation's treasure; learning is like a delicious feast.
Chinese proverb

*Common experience is the gold reserve which confers an exchange value
on the currency which words are; without this reserve of shared experiences,
all our pronouncements are cheques drawn on insufficient funds.*
René Daumal (1908–1944)

*Life is constantly providing us with new funds, new resources, even when we are
reduced to immobility. In life's ledger there is no such thing as frozen assets.*
Henry Miller (1891–1980)

*Innovation is the specific instrument of entrepreneurship . . . the act that
endows resources with a new capacity to create wealth.*
Peter F. Drucker

Surviving using CMMI or any other process improvement initiative is truly dependent on the kind of help you can get. As we said in Part 1, process improvement isn't trivial. Breadth of knowledge and depth of experience are significant factors in a smooth journey. Because many of us don't have either (at least when we're getting started), we need to get help from every place we possibly can. We recommend that you equip your team with as much good, solid information as you can find from those who have gone before. In Part V, we provide instructions or references to many of the resources we believe will be useful to you.

The resources come in various forms. Books, articles, and Web sites provide basic understanding. Conferences and workshops highlight lessons learned and new ways to approach difficult problems. Organizations, people, and services provide more personal consulting and training. Tools and techniques help you leverage others' experience.

Obviously, this is not an exhaustive list (although we were pretty exhausted by the time we finished it). The resources we present are only a subset of the ones we know about, but we do believe they can help until you find something that works better for you.

If at this point you feel a bit overwhelmed, we invite you to visit the Addison-Wesley Web page for this book, www.awprofessional.com/title/0321422775, and enjoy some Process Improvement humor: "The Stout Maturity Model."

Have fun!

Chapter 15

Tools and Techniques

In this chapter, we provide more detailed procedures for several of the tools and techniques we discussed in earlier parts of the book, as well as a bibliography. Remember, these are selective, noninclusive lists. Just because something isn't on our particular list doesn't mean that it isn't worth looking into. Our experiences have exposed us to a subset of the literature and events in the process improvement world, and that's what's reflected here. Like all of you, we don't have infinite time to read and review every article, book, presentation, or report that is released about CMMI and process improvement. We have even fewer opportunities to try new approaches—although we try very hard to do so whenever we possibly can. But the references that we rely on in our work are the ones included here. The only certain thing about this list is that it will expand and change over time as our own understanding improves and we continue to learn nuances of different aspects of process improvement.

15.1 An example of setting SMART goals

When an organization has established a set of SMART goals for its business, deriving process improvement goals is usually fairly obvious. Consider the following based on the Balanced Scorecard:

- *Customer-quadrant business goal:* Add at least two new customers to our portfolio.

An improvement goal associated with that business goal might be:

- *Customer-quadrant improvement goal*: Ensure that all our customer-facing processes are visibly responsive and cost-effective for existing customers.

The premise is that if our customers see responsive, cost-effective processes, they will recommend us to new customers.

But is this a SMART goal? Let's look at each element.

Specific: The goal addresses customer-facing processes rather than all processes, and it's looking at two specific attributes: "visibly responsive" and "cost-effective." If we actually know which processes are customer facing, that could be sufficient, or if there are really too many customer-facing processes for us to deal with at once, we might want to change that to one that we know needs to be improved. We may also want to be more specific about existing customers. So maybe we'll modify it to:

- Ensure that our customer requirements management process is visibly responsive and cost-effective for existing product development customers.

What about *measurable?* The two measurement-related aspects are "visibly responsive" and "cost-effective." The first question here is, "Cost-effective for who? Customers? Or us? If for them, 'cost-effective' might mean that they never have to pay for a change after the requirements are agreed to . . . but that could be devastating for us if they change their minds all the time! And how do we measure 'visibly responsive'? Maybe that means that they can always tell the status of any change that they have initiated with us?"

Let's assume that this is what we mean. So the next mod might be:

- Ensure that our customer requirements management process allows customers to have 24-hour access to their requirements-change status and that this access doesn't cost them anything additional.

Whoa! Did we really mean that "cost-effective" was related to status, or did we mean that our whole requirements management process is cost-effective?

If the former is the case, this goal probably works. If the latter, we probably have a different goal we need to create related to the cost-effectiveness of the overall requirements management process. Let's say we decide to create a second goal, but we actually like the fact that our improvement goal for responsiveness has a cost element to it, so we'll keep it too.

Is this goal *achievable/attainable?* At this point it probably is, although when it was more general, it may have been too vague to determine what the actions would be to achieve this goal. One action we might envision (not the only possibility) would be to establish an 800 number that is staffed 24 hours a day by someone who has access to our internal change database and who will answer questions for customers about their change. Another action might be to create a customer-accessible, password-protected Web site for customers to use. Thus the goal is actionable and no further changes are needed at this point.

Now let's talk about *realistic.* We established the goal's *relevance* when we said this was a way to attract new customers. Note that both of the above actions assume that we *have* an accessible requirements change database. If that's true, one of the actions could be reasonable, and if we think we have the resources to do either one of them, we'd say that it's a realistic goal. In the search for realism, we may also come up with some other actions/solutions that would be more reasonable than these two. If, on the other hand, our internal requirements-change process status is *not* available for access, this may not be a realistic goal for us yet. A related enabling goal might be to:

- Understand the status of any requirements change at any point in time, from its request through its completion and incorporation into a new release of the product.

If we need to pursue this derivative goal first, we should do the same SMART analysis on it and improve it to where we can use it.

But let's assume that the first goal is still useful. The last thing to check on is *time-basis,* or tangibility. For this goal, a time basis is probably relevant. We already have one time-basis in the goal when we say that customers should have 24-hour access. The other aspect of time we should think about is when this needs to be done. Within the next week? Next month? Next year? Most business/improvement cycles do goal setting every year or so unless there's some particular environmental pressure we have to respond to. So let's change our goal to:

- Ensure that our customer requirements management process will allow our product development customers to have 24-hour access to their requirements-change status by September 2007, and that this access doesn't cost them anything additional.

At this point, let's compare our original goal to this one. Remember, it started out as:

- Ensure that our customer requirements management process is visibly responsive and cost-effective for existing customers

Which of these two would you rather sign up for if your bonus depended on it? We'd rather sign up for the revised goal if we agreed that it's realistic (that is, we agree that we have the basis internally for doing this and will get the resources to create a solution that's reasonable). Even if we didn't think it was realistic, we could probably negotiate some parameter changes on this goal that would make us and our sponsors happy, because we can actually understand what's being asked of us.

We would want to accept the original goal only if we would be the ones to establish *all* the success parameters. Otherwise, we could make some really great improvements, but the sponsor could say, "That's not cost-effective for *us*, even though it's cost-effective for our customers," or any other number of things related to the ambiguity of this goal.

15.2 Performing a CMMI-based Business Analysis

To run a CMMI-based Business Analysis (CBA), first assemble the following:

- A facilitator who understands implementation of the model (probably a consultant who has worked in CMMI implementation successfully).
- Your sponsoring team and opinion leaders within the groups that are planning to adopt CMMI.
- A conference room with a good amount of wall space (enough room for at least ten flip-chart sheets hanging on the walls).
- Sticky notes. (We use 3-inch by 3-inch notes, for the most part; they give you enough room to write a phrase but not a paragraph.)
- Flip charts (preferably the stick-to-the-wall type).
- A representation of the model that provides just the Purpose, Goals, and Specific Practices for each Process Area you'll be talking about; for example the appendixes in *CMMI Distilled* or the *Mini CMMI* available from www.cooliemon.com or Amazon.com in either staged or continuous representation.[1]

Before doing the analysis, you may want to meet with your facilitator to decide on an initial scope. Rather than take people through all 22 PAs, you may decide (as many people do) that just going through the Maturity Level 2 and 3 PAs is enough to get started. If you are working in an organization that has already been doing process improvement and you're looking at "what's next," you may have a different subset of PAs that you want to work with for the analysis.

When you've decided on the scope and acquired the participants, perform the setup and execution procedures in Tables 15-1 and 15-2.

When you've completed this analysis, you should have a set of around three CMMI Process Areas to work.

Table 15-1: *Instruction for CBA Room Setup*

Role (Who Does It)	Task (What They Do)	Outcome (What's Expected)
Facilitator	Create one flip chart per Process Area, with its title. Add one more flip chart for "Other" to capture items that are not covered by the current set of PAs being analyzed. Post these around the walls of the room.	Walls with flip charts with readable PA titles
Facilitator	Create a scoring flip chart by drawing a table with the following headings and as many rows as you have PAs to work on in the analysis scope: –Process Area Initials –Importance –Problem Level	Table set up for scoring

Table 15-2: *Execution of a CBA*

Role (Who Does It)	Task (What They Do)	Outcome (What's Expected)
Facilitator	Introduce the activity to the group. Even if participants know one another, ask for introductions with name, role in the organization, and reason for attending this workshop.	Shared understanding of expectations of the activity Group awareness of each person's role within the activity
Facilitator	Conduct an overview of CMMI that includes each of the Process Areas within the scope of the analysis. For each PA, discuss the symptoms that would indicate that you're having problems in the area covered by this PA and the business consequences that are likely to result if the current problems continue.	Group awareness of the model contents within scope of the analysis and possible relationships to their problems
Facilitator and participants	As you finish discussing each PA, ask for a "thumb vote" of PA Importance, followed by PA Problem Level (thumb up = high, thumb sideways = medium, thumb down = low). Count the votes in each category, and post to the appropriate block on the scoring flip chart.	High, medium, and low ratings posted to scoring flip chart for PA Importance and PA Problem Level. We usually use $x/y/z$ format in the block, where x is number of highs, y is number of mediums, and z is number of lows.
Facilitator	Note on the scoring flip chart the PAs that ranked highest on Importance and Problem Level.	Initial prioritization of PAs

Table 15-2: *Execution of a CBA* (Continued)

Role (Who Does It)	Task (What They Do)	Outcome (What's Expected)
Facilitator	Cut the list of candidate PAs down to around ten. If initial scope was ten or fewer, cut the list down to around five. If initial scope was five or fewer, skip this step.	
Facilitator and participants	Go back through the material, making sure that participants have access to an abbreviated version (PAs with required and expected elements) of the model. Ask, "What are the business or project issues you're experiencing in relation to this topic?" for each Process Area. Ask participants to answer the question by writing one succinct statement of the issue on a 3-by-3 sticky note and handing it to the facilitator. The facilitator checks to see that the issue properly belongs in that PA. If it doesn't, put the sticky note in question off to the side, and put it on the PA you think it applies to when it comes up.	PA flip charts with sticky notes of problems occurring in the organization that are associated with that PA
Facilitator	When all the issues are posted, review them with the group and do a first cut at affinitization (putting similar items in a group together).	Scoring chart with voting dots allocated by participants

(continued)

Table 15-2: *Execution of a CBA* (Continued)

Role (Who Does It)	Task (What They Do)	Outcome (What's Expected)
Facilitator (cont.)	Come back to the scoring flip chart with the top PAs after reviewing the contents of the Issues flip charts, and conduct a dot vote to get a sense of initial perception of priorities. Use three dots per person to emphasize that the groups of potential PAs need to be cut down to three. Encourage participants to "walk the wall" of the group's issues as they consider how to allocate their votes.	
Facilitator/ participants	When the dot vote is complete, see where the natural break point in the vote groupings occurs. Discuss the top four or five vote-getters, and start talking about possible pilot projects that would fit in terms of timing or personnel within each of the areas. After consensus is reached on PAs and projects, assign pilot team leaders from among the project personnel, and discuss the next steps going forward.	List of agreed upon PAs, projects, and leaders

A few tips on selecting projects:

- For best timing, it's best to match up projects with PAs that are relevant to the kinds of work the project is doing in the next few weeks. Assigning a project that is almost completed to work on the Project Planning Process Area might not be the best choice.

- If it's convenient, having more than one project to work on the same PA can produce synergy among the projects and achieve some team building. If this is your first cycle through, don't demand that the group come up with the identical solution for each project. There are likely to be environmental differences and team differences that drive some different, but equally valid, solution approaches. If you can get the projects to follow the same format for process guidance, that's actually enough for the first time through.

- If you have a choice between a project with a short life cycle and one with a longer duration, choosing the shorter project is generally better; you will be able to see the results of your improvements faster and can determine whether you want to deploy further, or do more refinement before further deployment.

15.3 Performing a Readiness and Fit Analysis

To perform your own Readiness and Fit Analysis (RFA), you need to assemble the following:

- Someone who understands implementation of the model (probably a consultant who has worked in CMMI implementation successfully).
- Your sponsoring team and opinion leaders within the groups that are planning to adopt CMMI.
- A conference room with a good amount of wall space.
- Sticky notes. (We use 3-inch by 3-inch notes, for the most part; they give you enough room to write a phrase, but not a paragraph!)
- A facilitator who understands how to perform clustering or affinity diagramming.
- Flip charts (preferably the stick-to-the-wall type).
- Sufficient forms similar to Figure 15-1 to allow participants to record their scoring.

When you've gathered the participants and prepared the room, Table 15-3 provides the basic procedure.

Factor	Your Score*	Comments
Strategy		
WP1	N/A	
WP2	N/A	
...		
Reward System		
Sponsorship		
Values		
Skills		
Structure		
History		

*Note 1: 1 = low fit; 5 = high fit
Note 2: For individual risks or issues, write them on sticky notes, one per sticky note.

RISKS: Something that *might* happen that would have a defined consequence. Nominal form: Given that <condition>, there is a possibility that <consequence>.

ISSUES: Something that is happening right now and needs to be dealt with to improve the fit.

Figure 15-1: *RFA form*

Table 15-3: *Procedure for Performing Readiness and Fit Analysis*

Role (Who Does It)	Task (What They Do)	Outcome (What's Expected)
Facilitator	Introduce the purpose of the activity and the process that will be used. Pass out the forms for scoring and the sticky notes.	Shared understanding of the purpose and process by all participants
Model expert	Explain the RFA questions and the CMMI assumptions table.	Shared general understanding of the content to be processed

Table 15-3: *Procedure for Performing Readiness and Fit Analysis* (Continued)

Role (Who Does It)	Task (What They Do)	Outcome (What's Expected)
Model expert and participants	Go through each question, and give participants time to score the fit and record any issues or risks for that factor (one per sticky note).	Individual forms filled out with fit scores Pile of sticky notes with issues and risks
Facilitator or model expert	Compile fit scores into a profile.	RFA profile
Facilitator and participants	Put up all the risks/issues generated during step 4, and cluster them into themes; create a header for each cluster.	Clustered sticky notes with theme headers
Facilitator and participants	Prioritize the clusters based on their perceived impact (either positive or negative) on the improvement effort.	Prioritized list of issues and risk themes
All	Discuss whether there are any "show stoppers" in the themes that would argue for postponing starting the effort (if that's a valid choice for your implementation).	Go/no go decision on improvement effort based on RFA
Facilitator	Get commitments for recording RFA info and passing it along to the implementation team so it can plan mitigation strategies as part of the improvement planning.	Recorded data set from RFA

15.4 One-Hour Process Description method

Our favorite technique for creating, integrating, and verifying/validating your process descriptions is called the One-Hour Process Description method. It's aptly named because you need only about one hour of time from the subject-matter experts for the process you want to define. Of course, the team working on documenting the processes for improvement and future use will have a good bit more than an hour's work to prepare and to follow up after the definition session.

The goals for this kind of workshop are to:

- Quickly create a first-level *draft* of as-is or to-be processes based on a defined process architecture that is ready to be transcribed for future review by stakeholders.
- Identify areas where process guidance exists or doesn't exist for sub-process or tasks.

So what can you actually do in one hour? Experience shows that from two to eight three-person teams creating/reviewing their descriptions can create a 70-80 percent complete draft of a well-bounded life-cycle stage or support process. To accomplish this, ahead of the session, you will need to:

- Identify the process architecture (how you want the process descriptions broken into sections).
- Identify two to three subject-matter experts for each topic. This can become limiting on the process when you're in a small organization, you have only one or two people who know multiple processes well, and very few others to draw on as subject-matter experts in even one process.
- Establish a candidate-roles list, with definitions for each role. (These are the role names you will use in the definition session.)
- Gather, and make available to the subject-matter experts, current process guidance artifacts to help jog their memories if they get stuck and to help solve disputes that may come up.

The general approach is to use two- to three-person teams of process "owners"/subject-matter experts to define processes they are knowledge-able about and to review processes in their customer/supplier chain that are being defined in the same session. This is a very low-tech technique; you just need flip charts or mural paper, multiple colors of sticky notes (different colors for Roles, Tasks, and Deliverables), and pens. There are three main roles in the process: the Facilitator, the Champion or Engineering Process Group Lead (the person sponsoring the event), and the Participants. Figure 15-2 is a summary diagram of the workshop.

This method is useful as the basis for a model-based "mini-appraisal" by someone who knows the reference model being used. It is also useful as a generator of a first draft as-is or to-be process description in a medium-size or larger organization. It is particularly useful where subject-matter experts are difficult to schedule for continuous periods of time.

This method is not as useful when you are at the stage of generating detailed procedures and job aids, or when subject-matter experts are not available. It is also not meant to provide rigorous appraisal results (for example, for a SCAMPI A against CMMI) or in the event that there is no process architecture available as guidance for breaking up the process into chunks.

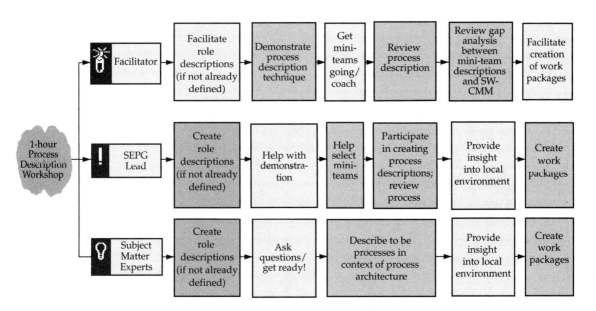

Figure 15-2: *One-Hour Process Description summary diagram*

15.4.1 Critical success factors

Here are a few facilitation hints that make this technique more effective:

- Plenty of physical space should be available for team work.
- Use sticky notes on flip charts or mural paper to make it fast and easy to move things around during the definition session and force definers to keep it simple.
- Use three 15-minute description and 5-minute review cycles to keep the process description focused and relevant.
- Team members need to accept the 15-minute deadline.
- Team members should be assigned only to processes they understand.
- The Facilitator needs to be capable of spotting "too high/too low" descriptions and performing course correction on the fly.
- Descriptions produced in the workshop should be thoroughly reviewed by other stakeholders after the workshop.

People frequently ask "How many teams should we use?" The answer usually depends on how many appropriate process owners/subject-matter experts are available:

- If you have a small number of teams and/or a large number of processes, you will need several sessions.
- Even with just two teams, six processes can be described in one afternoon.
- If you have a large number of teams (and a large room), you can do as many as seven or eight processes in one session.

15.4.2 Workshop preparation

So that you can minimize the impact on the participants' schedules, there are several things to complete before you begin the workshop. You want to "hit the ground running" when the players arrive, instilling confidence in the participants that you are there to help, not waste their time.

Process "architecture" is needed to organize the description.

Before the workshop session, you need to decide on a process architecture, the high-level structure of the content that will be described. Most organizations start with a time-phased or life cycle-based architecture. If you're getting started and don't have an architecture that is easily identifiable, you'll probably use the as-is process to get started. Here's some simple architecture guidance:

- For as-is process descriptions:
  - ➤ Often, CMMI Process Areas or existing local life-cycle phases are selected.
- For to-be process descriptions:
  - ➤ Subprocesses should relate to the desired implementation focus, usually *not* Process Area-based.
  - ➤ Subprocesses should integrate with parent life cycles, where applicable.

The architecture will be used, at its highest level, to create the mini-teams.

Deciding on names for the roles in your organization.

Before the workshop, you also need to identify the major roles involved in the processes and decide on the names you will use for them in the workshop. This may sound like a trivial step, but if you do *not* do this, when you try to sequence the different subprocesses, you will spend a lot of unnecessary time resolving whether "project leader" and "project manager" are really the same role.

When you have a set of role names defined, send it out to the workshop participants for review and questions. If you can answer their role-based questions before the workshop, things will go more smoothly.

Preparing your "demo" subprocess.

The most effective way to get participants comfortable with the process and speed of the description task is to demonstrate it by using one of the simpler processes, preferably one that most of the workshop attendees participate in. If you don't have any other ideas, Requirements Management is usually a good one.

Create a table on a flip chart with role sticky notes across the top or down the side. If roles are across the top, your task flow will be top to bottom. If roles are down the side, your task flow will be left to right. SuZ's preference is for roles to go down the side; that's probably because her knees are starting to object to working down by the floor as she gets to the end of a process.

Assuming that you have put your roles down the side, fill in task sticky notes by the primary role(s) involved in the task, along with the work products or events that result from the task. If another role is involved in the task at that time, give it its own sticky note. If there's a dependency relationship, draw an arrow from the task providing the input to the task producing the output. Continue adding sticky notes and workflow arrows.

When you're satisfied with your description, copy it (through a digital photograph or the old-fashioned pencil-and-paper method) on a 8½ × 11" or A4 sheet of paper. Set up a second flip chart with just the roles and no tasks, deliverables, or arrows. When you do the demonstration, do it with this empty flip chart. Demonstrate two or three tasks, and when you think the participants have the idea, bring out the finished flip chart(s) to show them the level of granularity you're looking for.

15.4.3 Basic process for workshop

The following steps describe the flow of the workshop.

Entry criteria for workshop

- Room is prepared.
- Mini-teams and processes are selected.
- Role names are defined and sent out to the mini-team participants.
- Existing process artifacts are gathered and available in the room for mini-teams to use.
- Demonstration materials have been prepared.

Approach for process descriptions

Form teams related to process topics. (Use local process architecture as a guide.)

Each team uses color-coded sticky notes to identify the major:

- Tasks
- Roles
- Deliverables (work product or event)

As an option, teams may also be asked to identify (with a different-color sticky note, of course) process guidance available related to their assigned process/subprocess.

Assigned review teams "switch" with the primary team to review evolving drafts, based on a customer–supplier chain. Figure 15-3 illustrates the recommended cycles.

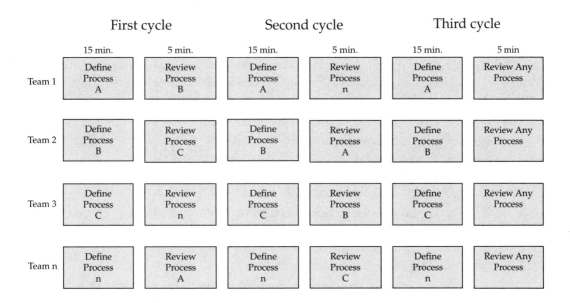

Figure 15-3: *Process description cycles*

Ground rules for process description

This is a set of ground rules that we give each mini-team:

- Use one task, role, or deliverable per sticky note.
- Make sure that you look at your assigned process throughout the entire product life cycle (initiation > retirement). Generally, use one table or flip chart per life-cycle phase unless the activity during a phase is really minor. (This is most relevant for processes, such as Configuration Management, that have different activities that are expected to occur at different times in the life cycle.)
- Keep it simple!
- If capturing "as-is,"
  - ➤ Post ONLY current practice (do capture ideas for the future elsewhere).
  - ➤ You may want to capture "barriers to this step."
- Use a maximum of ten tasks per subprocess.
- If you're in doubt as to level of granularity or other such questions, don't hesitate to ask the facilitator.

Incorporating process guidance into your process description

If you're exercising this option, chances are that you will go over the one-hour mark. (Don't extend the work sessions longer than 15 minutes; instead, add another session.) This step could also be done after the main workshop by a smaller team that knows what process guidance is and is not available.

Assign different colors to small sticky notes (we usually use 1 × 2" notes) to represent "guidance available" and "no/inadequate guidance."

For tasks or work products that clearly have current process guidance:

• Use "guidance available" sticky-note color.

For tasks or work products you're unsure about:

• Start with "no guidance" sticky-note color.
• The Facilitator reviews to identify documentation that may be missing.

Don't obsess! If you're unsure, mark what you think the answer is, but put a question mark on that sticky note so you know to review it with someone who knows the guidance better.

You're done, but you're just getting started!

If you are the Facilitator, you have several important postworkshop tasks:

• One minor but important detail is to number all the sticky notes before taking down the flip charts so that any sticky notes that fall down can be replaced. A good way to do this is to use a convention we call *RNX*, where *R* = Role, *N* = subprocess, and *X* = task. We also tend to use clear tape to do a gross "tape down" of the sticky notes on the flip charts or mural paper. It is also useful to circle each task cluster and number the clusters so that they can be re-created from sticky notes that fall down.

• Transcribe flip charts into diagrams or tables, using your preferred process-visualization tool. (Microsoft Visio has a nice template that we often use; sometimes we just use a Microsoft Word table.)

• When the materials are transcribed, review them with the participants to make sure nothing went awry and to allow them to refine their descriptions based on what they've thought about in the meantime.

• When the participants are satisfied with the descriptions, bring both the transcribed files *and* the flip charts to scheduled review meetings with the different roles called out in a particular subprocess and with other stakeholders you know will add value. Reviewing the flip charts themselves is very interactive and best for a "meeting"-type review rather than an e-mail round robin. Keep in mind that the reviews are highly likely to take longer than the original draft.

- During the reviews, look for "must include/must not include" types of conflicts. Translation: Some people will say, "It's not correct unless you include *x*" or, conversely, "It's correct only if you delete *x*." This gets thorny though when one role says a task must be included while another says it must not be included. If these kinds of conflicts come up in the review-session meeting, commit to take the parties in the conflict offline to resolve the issue. If you don't get the issue resolved, your description will lose credibility with those who are relying on your accuracy, and when it comes time to derive the to-be process, you are likely to get less-than-stellar participation.

Next steps

The next steps you engage in depend on your original goal:

- For mini-appraisal, CMMI gap analysis can be performed after the initial session, even before stakeholder review.
- For an as-is process, desired improvements to the process are identified.
- For a to-be process, work packages of process guidance can be formulated for assignment or production.

15.5 Infusion and diffusion measurement

In Chapter 9, we introduced the concept of adoption progress measurement. This type of measurement attempts to provide indicators of progress toward your adoption goals for CMMI (or any other technology you want to apply it to). We wish we could tell you that there are "standard" indicators for measuring adoption progress, but so far we haven't found any. The ones we present here have been used in pilot settings but should still be considered somewhat experimental. The work to improve and evolve them is continuing, although at a slow pace. In particular, the diffusion measurements exhibit a "break" in the type of measurement that, from a researcher's viewpoint, makes them irregular. (You move from measuring numbers of individuals completing events to measuring existence of particular organizational artifacts/practices.) So far, this hasn't created much of a problem in practice, but we hope that in future editions, we'll have more evolved indicators for you. In any case, the premise that you need to measure adoption progress before you can know when it's "safe" to calculate ROI is a sound one, both from a research and a field perspective. Even if you don't find our approach useful, we hope you'll take the time to decide on some indicators of your own.

15.5.1 Infusion measurement

Infusion, as illustrated in Figure 15-4, defines the "depth" of the adoption:

- How integrated are the new practices into the existing work practices and culture of the organization?
- How integrated should they be?
- Which roles need to be have a "deeper" Level of Use (and, therefore, understanding) than others?

Establishing *Level of Use goals* is one way to establish measurements for gauging infusion. In addition to helping with understanding your adoption success, establishing Level of Use goals helps you scope the need for training and other transition mechanisms needed to support adoption for different subsets of your adoption population.

The first thing to think about in defining Level of Use goals is what roles are critical for adoption of these practices. When you are deploying a new process, be it a new project planning process, a new services integration process, or a new proposal process, it is useful to ask, "What are the different roles that are likely to be involved?" Typical roles for process deployment include someone who will

- be in charge of developing the process
- control changes to the process
- use all the aspects of the process
- use only one aspect or some aspects of the process
- manage those who use the process

When you have an idea of the roles that need to be accounted for in the development and deployment of the process, think about what level of understanding/use of the process is necessary for each role's success. Think in terms of the needed understanding of the improvement process as well as the process content. For example, the process developer typically needs more depth of understanding of the PI activities than an end user of the process. This typically varies from broad and deep knowledge to narrow and

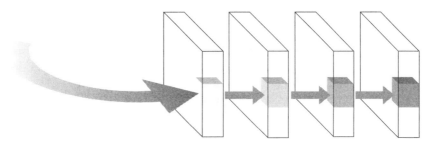

Figure 15-4: *Conceptual view of infusion*

cursory. In this context, understanding CMMI or another model's content would be a "specialty" knowledge area just for those developing the process to be seen by others.

Next, think in terms of how many people are in each role group that you've defined. The number of people may impact training or communication mechanisms implementation choices you make based on the level of understanding you have specified. If only one or two people are in the Process Developer role, for example, and they need to understand CMMI deeply, you may want them to attend an SEI CMMI course. It will probably be cheaper to send the two of them to a public course than to bring in an on-site course designed for 24 people who don't really need that depth of knowledge about the model.

Once Level of Use goals are established, you need to establish criteria for accomplishment of that Level of Use. (Essentially, you're creating an explicit success condition.) Many of the same events you're tracking for diffusion measurement will be part of the criteria for Level of Use. For an end-user role, for example, there may be a general orientation course required, followed by a specific Web presentation on using the new process. In addition, there may be a checklist that records the results of process completion to be turned in when the process is completed. When two checklists (or three, or however many you think establish regular use of the process) have been completed, that end user is considered to have met his or her Level of Use goals. This information will also be helpful in tracking diffusion of the process.

When you have criteria for each goal, and you know which of your staff fit into each role category, you can track achievement against the criteria you've established. Figure 15-5 illustrates a profile as one way of tracking. Note that not all use/role categories have lots of people who are part of that category.

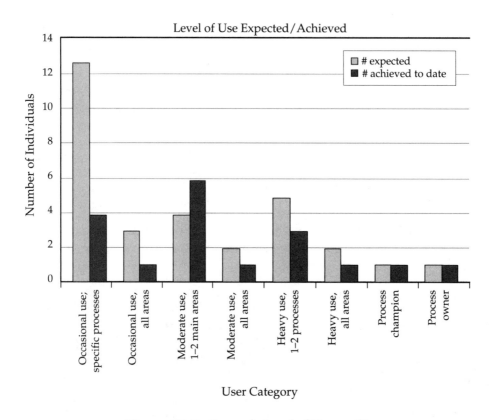

Figure 15-5: *Example Level of Use profile*

For some categories, you may need or want only one or two people to be in a usage category.

In Table 15-4, we provide an example set of Roles and their respective Level of Use understanding goals. From this table, you could derive the criteria that would confirm that role has met the understanding and usage goals. Note that you are likely to have different names for these roles within your own organization and that the actual usage goals may differ for different settings. In some settings, for example, the Process Developer may also be required to be a User "Doer," so he or she would be expected to use the processes he or she develops. In other organizations, those roles may not be combined.

The following is a suggested set of Level of Use categories for process improvement:

Casual 1. Casual use of a single, or only a couple, of the processes being improved

Casual 2. Casual use of many of the processes being improved

Moderate 1. Moderate use (probably would be in the approval cycle related to at least one process) of one or two processes being improved

Moderate 2. Moderate use of several of the processes being improved

Heavy 1. Heavy, probably daily, use of one or two processes being improved

Heavy 2. Heavy, probably daily, use of several of the processes being improved

Expert 1. Subject-matter expert, capable of defining and improving one or two of the processes being improved

Expert 2. Subject-matter expert capable of defining and improving several of the processes being improved

Expert 3. Versed in process improvement techniques and a process subject-matter expert.

Expert 4. Expert in process improvement techniques

When you've established Level of Use goals, you can derive the transition mechanisms that will be needed to support achieving them and add them to your infrastructure planning.

15.5.2 Diffusion measurement

Diffusion, as illustrated in Figure 15-6, measures how broadly the process improvement has been adopted by the organization. The approach documented here is an expansion of an idea from Kim Caputo's book *CMM Implementation Guide: Choreographing SW Process Improvement.*[2] Even though Kim focuses on her experience of SW-CMM adoption at Unisys, most of what she talks about is easily adapted to CMMI, so it's worth reading. She uses a choreography metaphor throughout the book to illustrate her points. Some people don't relate well to that metaphor, but the content of the book is good enough that it's worth reading even if you skip the choreography parts.

As you might guess, infusion and diffusion are independent measures. Diffusion measures are most useful in larger populations. In smaller settings,

Table 15-4: *Example Roles and Levels of Use*

Role Name/Definition	Expected Level of Use of Technology (Process Improvement)	Assigned Level of Use Category
Process Owner (the person responsible for a particular process being accomplished)	Detailed understanding of "the process" Understanding of the approach to PI Heavily uses "the process"	Heavy 1
Process Champion (the person(s) trying to promote the improvement of the processes)	Broad understanding of "the process" Broad understanding of the PI approach Light to moderate use of process elements depending on his or her other roles within the organization	Expert 3
Customer (of the process being improved)	Broad understanding of "the process" Light use of a few process elements relevant to him or her	Casual 1
User Manager (manager of the group where the process being improved is actually performed)	Broad understanding of "the process" Overview of all business processes Broad understanding of PI Moderate use of the process elements within his or her purview	Moderate 1

(continued)

Table 15-4: *Example Roles and Levels of Use* (Continued)

Role Name/Definition	Expected Level of Use of Technology (Process Improvement)	Assigned Level of Use Category
User "Doer" (practitioner within the group where the process being improved is performed)	Detailed understanding of his or her elements of "the process" Broad understanding of PI Heavy use of the process elements relevant to his or her role	Heavy 1
Facilitator (member of the improvement team working with both users and Process Developers to improve the process)	Detailed understanding of PI approach Broad overview of all processes No use of "the process" likely	Expert 3
Process Developer (member of the improvement team responsible for codifying the improved process)	Detailed understanding of PI process Broad understanding of "the process" No use of "the process" likely	Expert 4

you can probably assess diffusion informally. However, you'll still want to establish and use more formal Level of Use (infusion) goals.

To measure diffusion, first you have to identify key transition mechanisms for your process improvement effort. Then you can use the concept of *phased* transition mechanisms to help build a profile of adoption progress:

- Define the key events that constitute evidence of movement from one commitment state to another.

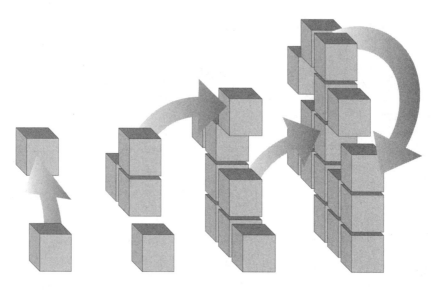

Figure 15-6: *Conceptual view of diffusion*

- Create measures that allow you to know when those events have occurred.
- Gather and chart the measurements.

The example that follows provides "notional" profiles as an organization progresses through a process improvement effort. In the following charts, on the X axis, *C/A* stands for Contact/Awareness, *U* stands for Understanding, *TU* stands for Trial Use, *A* stands for Adoption, and *I* stands for Institutionalization.

Let's say that the main Contact and Awareness event being measured is attendance at an all-hands meeting where the process improvement effort is being announced and introduced. When everyone has attended that meeting or has read the presentation as a makeup if he or she was absent, your profile would look like Figure 15-7. One hundred percent of the relevant staff have completed that event.

If you've defined Understanding events as a set of role-based training events that people would be expected to attend and Trial Use as participating in a pilot, you would collect information on who has attended those classes and who has participated in pilots, and add those numbers. At some defined point, maybe three months from the initial meeting, you look at the numbers again and get a different profile (Figure 15-8). About 25 percent of your population has moved from Contact/Awareness to Understanding or Trial Use. Questions that a graph like this does not answer are "Is this fast enough?" and

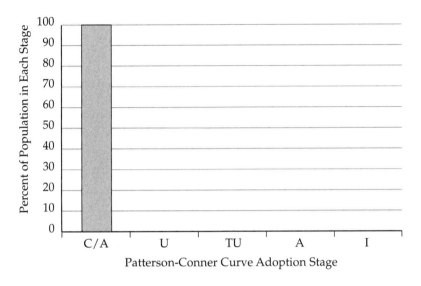

Figure 15-7: *After the all-hands meeting*

"Are the right people attending the training classes so that we progress as expected with the pilots?" If you've established Levels of Use goals and are tracking data for those, you may already be able to answer these questions. When you've gone through the improvement cycle a couple of times, you can

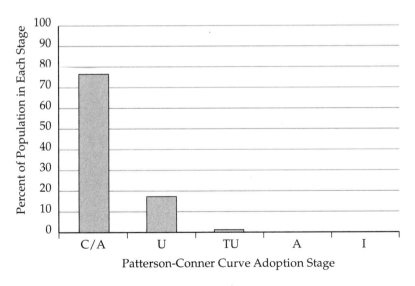

Figure 15-8: *Basic classes for key roles held*

set targets for different profiles at different points in time as you go through your improvement activities. Initially, it's usually enough just to look at the actual data and start asking questions.

In Figure 15-9, we're seeing that more people are attending the classes and participating in the pilots. Depending on when this snapshot was taken, this may be good progress, or it may be slower than anticipated. If you think that progress toward adoption is slower than it should be, it's a good idea to ask why. Why aren't more people attending classes? Why aren't more people participating in pilots? The answers to those questions could highlight barriers you weren't aware of before that need to be removed.

In Figure 15-10, we're starting to see some of the population move into Adoption and Institutionalization. The measures for Adoption might include how many employees have been through the new process more than once, or how many employees have responded to a project-retrospective questionnaire that gathers data about the new process. Some of the other measures you might use for Adoption are not so much about the number of employees as about the existence and use of particular mechanisms by defined audiences. One measure of Adoption, for example, might be the use of a particular set of project review questions by Project Managers. In this case, it's not the entire population you're after, but it's more a Level of Use measure that's also used to support diffusion measures. For Institutionalization, the measures tend to be around the existence and use of certain policies

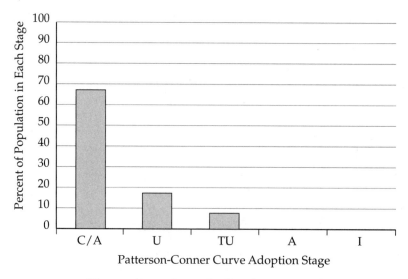

Figure 15-9: *Several pilots have started*

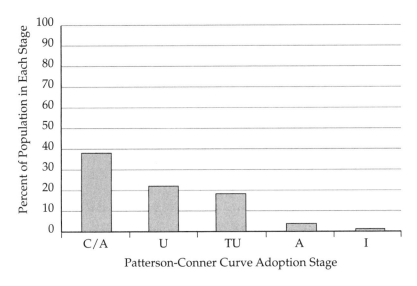

Figure 15-10: *Widespread adoption has begun*

and specific types of training (for example, new-employee orientation). This conflation of different types of measures makes this more of a heuristic measurement.

In Figure 15-11, we're seeing more people completing the Understanding training events, more people using the improved processes for the first time, and more people using the processes routinely, as well as the appearance of some of the indicators that we're institutionalizing the processes. This is probably the first point in our example where asking the question, "What's our ROI for this change?" would make sense, although you would probably want to see more people actually using the processes (at least 40 percent) before seriously looking at ROI. Why 40 percent? In Everett Rogers's diffusion research,[3] 37 percent was the point at which self-sustaining adoption was seen to occur, so we use 40 percent as our heuristic.

In Figure 15-12, we're definitely at a place where calculating ROI would be a reasonable thing to do, provided you have actually measured some of the things we suggest in our section on business value. There are still some laggards who haven't finished training or started using the processes, but it's hard to tell just from this chart whether it's because they don't want to use the process or whether they may be part of the population that doesn't encounter these processes very often. You can see from this how you can make a better interpretation of the diffusion information if you also have some infusion information to pair it with.

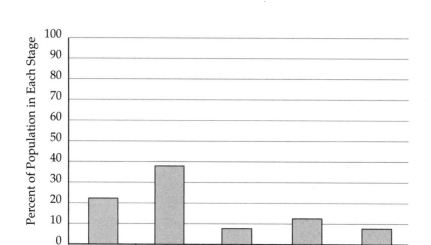

Figure 15-11: *Starting to see Institutionalization*

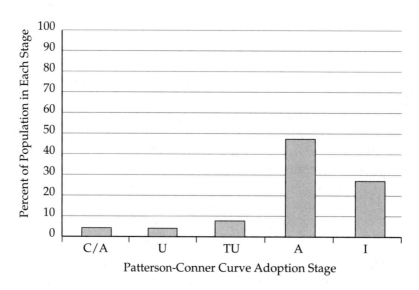

Figure 15-12: *Moving into widespread use*

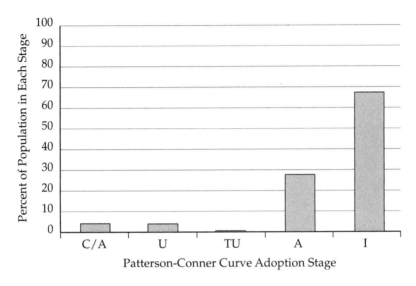

Figure 15-13: *Improvement is the new status quo!*

In Figure 15-13, the processes should be firmly in place and the risk of back-sliding should be relatively low. You will always have some percentage of your population moving through the earlier stages of adopter commitment if you're experiencing any kind of growth or turnover, because your population is likely to be expanding. We would never expect to see a graph that showed only populations in Adoption and Institutionalization unless the population were static or declining.

We've already mentioned that the character of diffusion measures changes as you move from Trial Use into Adoption and Institutionalization. Here's a bit of guidance on selecting measures.

For Contact, Awareness, Understanding, and Trial Use:

- You typically count the numbers of the target population who have attended some event or received some communication.

For Adoption and Institutionalization:

- You typically count the existence or absence of specific artifacts, such as a policy, that affects a subset of the population or the use of a particular mechanism, such as measurements, with a specific subset of the population (for example, senior management).

Note that because you're counting percentages of the population, you don't automatically know from this graph the actual numbers of people going through the process. You may find it useful to graph actual numbers; however, if you're comparing different parts of an organization, the percentages may give you a better view of the diffusion progress, even though the sizes of the different parts of the organization are different.

It is very important to remember that *this type of data collection can be overkill for very small organizations.* If you have only 20 people affected by a change, it's pretty easy to see who's missing from the training events and who is actually using the new processes, and this kind of explicit diffusion measurement would not be as necessary. It's most useful in a larger organization, where it's more difficult to have a broad view of the actual participation in different improvement activities designed to promote adoption of the new processes.

15.5.3 Establishing events for adoption diffusion measurement

Table 15-5 provides more detail on exit criteria for the Adoption Commitment Curve categories covered in Chapter 13 and suggests some events you might consider as measurable events for your diffusion profile.

Table 15-5: *Diffusion Events Suggestions*

Stage	Key Question	Successful Exit Criteria	Potential Events to Measure
Contact/ Awareness	What is it (in this case, the model you're using for your improvement effort)?	Can concisely answer "What is it, why should I use it, who is it for, how is it different from current practice?"	Attended awareness meetings Received newsletters with articles on improvement effort
Understanding	What does it mean to us? How will we have to change?	Detailed knowledge of what it will take to use new processes	Participated in working meetings to define work practice changes

Table 15-5: *Diffusion Events Suggestions* (Continued)

Stage	Key Question	Successful Exit Criteria	Potential Events to Measure
		Beginning to think through changes to work practices and environment needed for new processes to be successful Level of Use goals defined	End user: Attended detailed user course for his or her role in the new process PI specialist: Attended detailed course on model used as basis for developing improved processes
Trial Use	How will we implement it?	Explicit decision to go forward with widespread adoption	Participated in at least one pilot activity Has tried the new process for at least one cycle of typical tasks
Adoption	Are we really using it?	Initial Levels of Use goals achieved (assumes that they've been specified) Not using the improved processes an exception to general work practices	Not using the improved processes noted in reviews/audits Individuals routinely completing their work assignments using the improved processes

(continued)

Table 15-5: *Diffusion Events Suggestions* (Continued)

Stage	Key Question	Successful Exit Criteria	Potential Events to Measure
Institutionalization	What do we need to keep it in place?	Long history of worth, durability, continuity of new processes Defined negative consequences for *not* using new processes	All infrastructure (such as licenses) needed to support the improved processes provided/kept up to date Use of the improved processes visible in relevant policies/procedures Reference to the process use included in performance metrics

Table 15-6 provides a template for recording your own diffusion events. One possible use for this template is to have all the members of the improvement team fill it out separately, and then look at the responses as a group and discuss the similarities and differences in the events that were chosen. A good question to get people going is, "What kinds of events or evidence would be appropriate for a user of the new processes to go through to transit each stage of the commitment curve?"

Table 15-6: *Blank Diffusion Events Template*

Stage	
Contact/Awareness	
Understanding	
Trial Use	
Adoption	
Institutionalization	

15.6 CSI (Crime Scene Investigation) technique + Chaos Cocktail Party

This section combines two techniques that work very well together: the CSI (Crime Scene Investigation) and the Chaos Cocktail Party. SuZ learned both of these techniques at a NASAGA (North American Simulation and Gaming Association) conference a few years ago and has had generally wonderful responses to both techniques.

The purpose of the CSI exercise is to get people to think beyond symptoms to root causes. The device of a taped-out "body" is used to represent whatever failure is being analyzed. The way we usually frame the question to think about is "Why did X [X is the topic of interest] die?" So you could have "Why did the process improvement effort die?", "Why did the training event die?", and so on. Participants are asked to review the "evidence" (sticky notes with the symptoms being observed in the organization) and think about the possible root causes for the "death." CSI can be used with a small or large group. If the group is larger than 20 people, you may want to tape out two bodies so that people can actually see the sticky notes. Figure 15-14 shows an example of a "body" set up for this exercise.

When people have written their root causes, ask each participant to exchange his or her index card with someone else in the group. On the back of the new index card, each participant writes his or her preferred solution to the identified root cause. We also instruct them to put a line through the root cause so that it's easy to tell which one is intended as a cause versus which one is intended as a solution. Then you can use any prioritization scheme you like to discuss and prioritize the solutions. Our favorite follow-on at this point is the Chaos Cocktail Party.

The purpose of the Chaos Cocktail Party is to actively and quickly prioritize a large number of ideas without losing broad visibility into the ideas. Use index cards to get people's answer to the focus question and then give them brief amounts of time (around 30 seconds) to exchange their index cards with others in the group. Each time they exchange, they read the card and then exchange the card with someone else for a different card. At about 30-second intervals, the facilitator stops the exchange, and people pair up to do a forced binary rating of the two cards. The number of rounds of exchange/rate depend on the number of participants—usually three or five. After the exchange rounds, participants add up the score for each card, and the facilitator counts down scores and collects the highest-scoring items for further discussion.

Figure 15-14: *Example "body" for CSI exercise*

15.6.1 CSI (Crime Scene Investigation) Example Instructions for Participants: Why the Training Module Died

1. Get one index card from the back table, one of the instructors, or one of the room monitors.

2. Get up and go to one of the crime scenes. Take your index card with you.

3. Look at the clues. They're all related to "why the training module died."

4. Write on the index card the *one* possible "cause of death" for the training module that you think is most important to investigate.

5. Exchange your cause of death with someone else.

6. On the opposite side of the card you received, write what you think is the one most promising solution to prevent that cause of death.

15.6.2 Chaos Cocktail Party: Follow-on from CSI

1. Cross out the cause of death on your index card.
2. From now on, focus only on the solution side.
3. Repeat the following exchange-review cycle three to five times (the facilitator will tell you how many):
4. Exchange-review cycle:
   a. When the instructor calls time, exchange cards as many times as possible with others, glancing at the solution but not discussing it.
   b. When the instructor calls time, find a partner, and look at the two prevention actions (one on each of your current cards).
   c. Together, allocate seven points between the two cards according to your opinion as to the value of each solution and write the values on the appropriate cards.
5. Tally the score of the index card you were left holding at the end of the last round.
6. The instructor will call out scores, going down from 35 (if five rounds were used), asking for items that fall in that score range.
7. The top five to ten items go on flip charts for discussion.

The cartoons shown in Figure 15-15 can also be used in conjunction with a CSI exercise; they were prepared by Shawn Presson for our tutorial on active learning, and they provide a bit of dark humor for a group that is dealing with a failure-analysis process.[4] Think of this as being like the *U.S. Army Survival Manual* metaphor; get participants to think up PI-relevant analogies to the causes shown here.

Figure 15-15: *Archetypal death cartoons*
(adapted from Garcia and Presson's "Beyond Death by Slides" tutorial)

15.7 Additional resources

In this section, we list some additional resources you may find interesting. Some are mentioned in earlier chapters, but we thought that having them in a single place might help you explore a bit more.

15.7.1 Conferences of Interest

One of the best places to learn about what process improvement techniques really work and how to approach real-world problems is at a conference. You can attend sessions or just network informally. We list some of the better-known conferences that address process improvement issues.

SEPG (System and Software Engineering Process Group) conferences
SEPG conferences are currently held annually in four locations: United States (usually March), Europe (usually June), Australia (usually September),

and Latin America (usually November; primarily Spanish and Portuguese-language submissions). All conferences are co-sponsored by the SEI and one or more partners.

These conferences are among the best sources of information on implementation issues and solutions for model-based process improvement, and they're great places to network with like-minded individuals who are facing problems similar to yours. The largest, in the United States, typically hosts upward of 1,500 individuals. The other locations have fewer than 500 attendees per conference so far.

PSQT (Practical Software Quality and Testing) conferences

PSQT conferences are held in the northern United States (usually June) and southern United States (usually October). Most conferences have at least one model-based improvement track.

ICSP (International Conference on Software Process)

ICSP is sponsored by the same folks as PSQT and focuses on both theoretical and practical aspects of process improvement.

Software Guru conference

This is a new conference, holding its first event in Mexico City in September 2006. It is primarily a Spanish-language conference, sponsored by the Mexican software-quality association AMCIS.

ISQC (International Software Quality Conference)

ISQC is sponsored by the American Society for Quality. Although it frequently has a process improvement track, it focuses more on software quality and testing practitioners.

PSM (Practical System and Software Measurement)

The annual PSM conference, usually in July, is a forum for the measurement aspects of process improvement and project management. Check its Web site (www.psmsc.com) for the latest information.

SE2 (South East Software Engineering conference)

SE2 is a small conference held in Huntsville, Alabama every year at the beginning of April. Its primary host is the Software Engineering Division of the U.S. Army Research, Development, and Engineering Command, and although there will be some distinctly DoD-focused presentations, there are often some really good sessions on process improvement–related topics. It's a smaller conference, which can be nice if you want to have more interaction with people.

SSTC (Systems and Software Technology Conference)

SSTC is hosted annually by the Software Technology Support Center at Hill Air Force Base. Although it has been traditionally held in Salt Lake City, usually at the end of April or beginning of May, the U.S. Department of Defense is now considering moving the venue annually. This conference has a strong DoD focus, but there are usually a number of good process improvement-related presentations. Check for the latest information at www.stsc.hill.af.mil.

CMMI Technology Conference and Users Group

This conference is co-sponsored by the National Defense Industrial Association (NDIA) and the SEI. It is the premier conference for CMMI-specific research, development, and practice. It is usually held in Denver in the fall. Check the SEI Web site for more information.

AYE (Amplifying Your Effectiveness) conference/workshops

The AYE conference, usually held in November in Phoenix, Arizona, is a conference centered on humanistic change management. It's a nice change of format from the usual 45-minute presentation. Each session is a half-day tutorial, so you get a chance to actually do something, and the sessions are generally very participative. Many of the sessions focus on various aspects of techniques based on Virginia Satir's work, as translated into organizational settings by Jerry Weinberg and others.

NASAGA (North American Simulation and Gaming Association)

The NASAGA conference is usually held in the autumn somewhere in North America. The focus of this conference is participative, active techniques for supporting various organizational development and process improvement settings. Some of SuZ's favorite techniques have come from this conference. If you have any interest in active learning, this is a great conference to attend and participate in. Most of the sessions focus on demonstrating a technique more than on presenting slides.

15.7.2 Web sites of interest

Here are the Web sites we mention in the text, as well as some additional ones to surf for a wide variety of process improvement and CMMI information.

The CMMI Survival Guide Site

www.awprofessional.com/title/0321422775
This is our site where you can find additional information on this book.

SEI-Related Sites

www.sei.cmu.edu

The Software Engineering Institute site has a multitude of material, such as:

- CMMI models, specifications, and other aids to applying CMMI
- Hundreds of process-related technical reports, many of which are useful and some of which have been written by your favorite authors (us, of course!)

www.sei.cmu.edu/seir

If you haven't already discovered the Software Engineering Information Repository, now's the time. It's a free resource, managed by the SEI, that accepts submissions from sources worldwide on many topics related to software engineering and process improvement. It's a very rich resource set and sometimes can be daunting to navigate, but it has resources that don't show up in a lot of other places, so it's usually worth looking through the site.

www.sei.cmu.edu/tip/publications/toolkit

This is the CMMI in Small Settings Pilot Toolkit Web site.

www.sei.cmu.edu/cmmi/appraisals

The home page for information on SCAMPI, the standard appraisal method for CMMI.

https://bscw.sei.cmu.edu/pub

The CMMI Transition Aids BSCW site is a repository of CMMI adoption aids moderated by Mike Phillips, program manager for CMMI. Phillips publishes job aids and presentations that have been made available for community use by individuals and organizations throughout the CMMI community. This is a place to find cross-model mappings; information about forthcoming CMMI project products; and "CMMI Today," a presentation on what's going on with CMMI that Phillips gives to SPINs and conferences. To access, go to the referenced url, click on "public area" and then click on "CMMI Transition Aids."

www.sei.cmu.edu/partners/

The SEI Partner Network Directory of process improvement consulting and training resources.

www.sei.cmu.edu/iprc

Here you can find information on the International Process Research Consortium and their work determining the future of process improvement.

Other Interesting Sites

www.gantthead.com

This is a public-plus-members site that focuses on project management in information technology settings and usually has good articles. The members-only area has lots of good templates and examples related to project management.

http://groups.yahoo.com/group/cmmi_process_improvement

This site has a wealth of information and conversations related to CMMI and process improvement.

www.grove.com

This is the Grove Web site for the Drexler-Sibbett Team Performance Model and other team-related information.

www.ieee.org and **www.computer.org**

These sites are the source of a great deal of engineering process information.

www.infomap.com

This site has information and training courses from the originators of the Information Mapping technique.

www.isixsigma.com

This site is a community resource for Six Sigma training, consulting, and articles.

www.iso.org

This site includes the ISO Standards Store.

www.ndia.org

Home for the National Defense Industrial Association. They sponsor scads of conferences on defense-related subjects, but of primary interest to you is the CMMI Technology Conference and Users Group. The proceedings and presentations from this conference are available here.

www.ogc.gov.uk

The UK organization that manages ITIL maintains this site.

www.sel.gsfc.nasa.gov

This is the site for one of the great achievements in process improvement. The Software Engineering Lab at NASA operated for 25 years as the first (and probably only) organization to approach process improvement based on focused empirical studies. You can find information about Goal-Question-Metric as well as other QIP-related methods.

15.7.3 Journals, magazines, and e-zines of interest

SPIP

This journal provides practical as well as theory-based articles on implementing software process improvement. It frequently has themed issues that explore a particular topic in depth.

SW Guru **(Spanish)**

This Spanish-language magazine (published in Mexico) focuses on many aspects of software and system development, including software process improvement and software standards.

Software Development

A commercially focused software development magazine that follows current trends in software methodologies and approaches, including material on process improvement.

IEEE Software

Published every two months, this is one of the highest regarded publicly available magazines for state-of-the-practice and state-of-the-art topics in the software field. The magazine includes frequent articles on process improvement.

CrossTalk

This magazine is published by the Software Technology Support Center (the U.S. Air Force organization that sponsors the SSTC). Because much of the research in process has been supported by the defense industry, this is often a place to find emerging authors and ideas. Issues are generally organized around a common theme, and process improvement is included in nearly every issue. Subscription is free.

Software Quality Professional (SQP)

Published by the American Society for Quality's software division, this magazine focuses on the issues faced by software quality professionals. It's a great resource for PPQA implementation, and it also has occasional process improvement articles.

Sticky Minds

Begun as a resource for software test professionals, this e-zine (www.stickyminds.com) also publishes book reviews and articles on process improvement, as well as other software quality topics.

1. Williams, Ralph, and Patrick Wegerson. *MINI CMMI (SE/SW/IPPD/SS Version 1.1) Continuous Representation.* (Harmony, Penn.: *Cooliemon* LLC, 2002).

2. Caputo, Kim. *CMM Implementation Guide: Choreographing Software Process Improvement.* (Reading, Mass.: Addison-Wesley, 1998).

3. Rogers, E. *Diffusion of Innovations.* (New York: The Free Press, 1995).

4. Garcia, Suzanne, and Shawn Presson. "Beyond Death by Slides." In *Proceedings of the Software Engineering Process Group Conference 2004.* (Pittsburgh: Carnegie Mellon University, 2004).

Bibliography

Adler, Paul. "Adapting Your Technological Base: The Organizational Challenge." In *Sloan Management Review,* Fall 1990, pp. 25–37.

Ahern, Dennis, et al. *CMMI Distilled: A Practical Introduction to Integrated Process Improvement.* 2d ed. (Boston: Addison-Wesley, 2004).

Ahern, Dennis, et al. *CMMI SCAMPI Distilled: Appraisals for Process Improvement.* (Boston: Addison-Wesley, 2004).

Assessment Methods Team. *Standard CMMI Appraisal Method for Process Improvement (SCAMPIS), Version 1.1: Method Definition Document.* CMU/SEI-2001-HB-001. (Pittsburgh: Carnegie Mellon University, 2001).

Basili, V. "The Experience Factory and Its Relationship to Other Improvement Paradigms." In *Proceedings of the Fourth European Software Engineering Conference (ESEC) in Garmish-Partenkirchen, Germany.* The Proceedings appeared as lecture notes in *Computer Science* 717 (September 1993).

Basili, V., G. Caldiera, F. McGarry, R. Pajerski, G. Page, and S. Waligora. "The Software Engineering Laboratory—An Operational Software Experience Factory." In *Proceedings of the Fourteenth International Conference on Software Engineering,* May 1992.

Basili, V., and S. Green, "Software Process Evolution at the SEL." In *IEEE Software,* vol. 11(4): 58–66, July 1994.

Bate, Roger. "Systems Engineering Coverage in Capability Maturity Models." In *Proceedings of the Software Engineering Process Group Conference 2006.*

Bergey, John, Jeannine Sivy, and Eileen Forrester, et al. *Results of Independent Research and Development Projects and Report on Emerging Technologies and Technology Trends.* CMU/SEI-2004-TR-018. (Pittsburgh: Carnegie Mellon University, 2004).

Boehm, Barry, and Richard Turner. *Balancing Agility and Discipline.* (Boston: Addison-Wesley, 2004).

Bosworth, Michael, et al. *Solution Selling: Creating Buyers in Difficult Selling Markets.* (Scarborough, ON: Irwin Professional Publishing, 1995).

BS ISO/IEC 20000-2:2005. *Information Technology—Service Management Code of Practice.* (British Standard/International Organization for Standardization/International Electrotechnical Commission, 2005).

BS ISO/IEC 20000-1:2005. *Information Technology—Service Management Specification.* (British Standard/International Organization for Standardization/International Electrotechnical Commission, 2005).

Card, David, et al. *Practical Software Measurement: Objective Information for Decision Makers.* (Boston: Addison-Wesley, 2001).

Cepeda, Sandra. "Generic Practices—What Do They Really Mean?" In *Proceedings of NDIA CMMI Technology and User Conference 2004.* NDIA, www.ndia.org, 2004.

Chrissis, Mary Beth, et al. *CMMI: Guidelines for Process Integration and Product Improvement.* (Boston: Addison-Wesley, 2003).

Conway, Melvin E. "How Do Committees Invent?" In *Datamation,* April 1968, pp. 28–31.

Demarco, Tom, and Timothy Lister. *Peopleware: Productive Projects and Teams.* 2d ed. (New York: Dorset House, 1999).

Fowler, Priscilla, and Stan Rifkin. *Software Engineering Process Group Guide.* CMU/SEI-90-TR-024. (Pittsburgh: Carnegie Mellon University, 1990).

Garcia, Suzanne. "Managed Technology Adoption Risk: A Way to Realize Better Return from COTS Investments." In *Proceedings of International Conference on COTS-Based Systems 2004.* (New York: Springer-Verlag, 2004).

Garcia, Suzanne. "Standardization as an Adoption Enabler for Project Management Practice." In *IEEE Software,* vol. 22, no. 5 (Sept./Oct. 2005), pp. 22–29.

Garcia, Suzanne. "Beyond Installation: Realizing Better Return from Your IT Investment" Tutorial. In *Proceedings of TIDE Conference 2002.* www.sei.cmu.edu/TIDE.

Garcia, Suzanne. "Beyond the Vendor's Checklist: Managing Risk in SW Technology Adoption" Tutorial. In *Proceedings of TIDE Conference 2002.* www.sei.cmu.edu/TIDE.

Garcia, Suzanne, and Shawn Presson. "Beyond Death by Slides." In *Proceedings of the Software Engineering Process Group Conference 2004.* (Pittsburgh: Carnegie Mellon University, 2004).

Garcia, Suzanne, and Charles Meyers. "Out from Dependency: Thriving as a Process Insurgent in a Sometimes Hostile Environment." In *Proceedings of SEPG 2003*. (Pittsburgh: Carnegie Mellon University, 2003).

Garcia, Suzanne, et al. *Proceedings of the 1st International Researcher's Workshop on Process Improvement in Small Settings*. CMU/SEI-2006-SR-001. (Pittsburgh: Carnegie Mellon University, 2006).

Goldenson, Dennis, and Diane Gibson. *Demonstrating the Impact and Benefits of CMMI®: An Update and Preliminary Results*. CMU/SEI-2003-SR-009. (Pittsburgh: Carnegie Mellon University, 2003).

Goldman, Daniel. *Emotional Intelligence: Why It Can Matter More Than IQ*. (New York: Bantam Books, 1995).

Grove Consulting. *Team Performance Creating and Sustaining Results*. www. grove.com.

ISACA. *Control Objectives for Information and Related Technology (COBIT)*. 4th ed. (Rolling Meadows, IL: ISACA, 2005).

ISO 9001:2000(E). *Quality Management Systems—Requirements. International Organization for Standardization*. 3d ed., 2000.

ISO/IEC 12207. *1995 Information Technology—Software Life Cycle Processes. Edition 1.0*. (International Organization for Standardization/International Electrotechnical Commission, 1995).

ISO/IEC 12207/Amd1:2002. *Information Technology—Software Life Cycle Processes—Amendment 1*. (International Organization for Standardization/International Electrotechnical Commission, 2002).

ISO/IEC 12207/Amd2:2004. *Information Technology—Software Life Cycle Processes—Amendment 2*. (International Organization for Standardization/International Electrotechnical Commission, 2004).

ISO/IEC 15288:2002. *Systems Engineering—System Life Cycle Processes*. (International Organization for Standardization/International Electrotechnical Commission, 2002).

ISO/IEC TR 15504-5:1999. *Information Technology—Software Process Assessment—Part 5: An Assessment Model and Indicator Guidance*. (International Organization for Standardization/International Electrotechnical Commission [technical report], 1999).

Kaplan, David, and Robert Norton. *The Strategy-Focused Organization*. (Cambridge, Mass.: Harvard Business School Press, 2000).

Keirsey, David. *Please Understand Me II: Temperament, Character, Intelligence.* (Del Mar, Calif.: Prometheus Nemesis Books, 1998).

Kerth, Norm. *Project Retrospectives: A Handbook for Team Reviews.* (New York: Dorset House, 2001).

Kroeger, Otto, et al. *Type Talk at Work (Revised): How the 16 Personality Types Determine Your Success on the Job.* (New York: Random House, 2002).

Leonard-Barton, D. "Implementation as Mutual Adaptation of Technology and Organization." In *Research Policy,* 1988, Vol. 17 (5): pp. 251–2.

Mayo, E. *The Human Problems of an Industrial Civilization,* Chapter 3. (New York: Macmillan, 1933).

McFeeley, Robert. *IDEAL: A User's Guide for Software Process Improvement.* CMU/SEI-96-HB-001. (Pittsburgh: Carnegie Mellon University, 1996).

Moore, G. *Crossing the Chasm: Marketing and Selling Technology Products to Mainstream Customers.* (New York: Harper Business, 1991).

Mutafelija, Boris, and Harvey Stromberg. *Systematic Process Improvement Using ISO 9001:2000 and CMMI.* (Boston: Artech House Publishing, 2003).

Oktaba, Hanna, ed. *Modelo de Procesos para la Industria de Software.* (Cartagena: C.F.C.E., 2003).

Patterson, R., and D. Conner. "Building Commitment to Organizational Change." In *Training and Development Journal,* 36:4 (April 1982), pp. 18–30.

Paulk, Mark, and Mary Beth Chrissis. *2001 High Maturity Practices Workshop.* CMU/SEI-2001-SR-014. (Pittsburgh: Carnegie Mellon University, 2002).

Project Management Institute. *A Guide to the Project Management Body of Knowledge (PMBOK® Guide).* 3d ed. (Newton Square, Penn.: Project Management Institute, 2000).

Reifer, Donald J. *Making the Software Business Case: Improvement by the Numbers.* (Boston: Addison-Wesley, 2002).

Roethlisberger, F. J., and W. J. Dickson. *Management and the Worker.* (Cambridge, Mass.: Harvard University Press).

Rogers, E. *Diffusion of Innovations.* (New York: The Free Press, 1995).

Rouillard, Larrie. *Goals and Goal Setting: Achieving Measured Objectives.* 3d ed. (Boston: Thomson Learning, 2003).

Rummler, Geary A., and Alan P. Brache. *Improving Performance: How to Manage the White Space in the Organization Chart*. (San Francisco: Jossey-Bass Business and Management Series, 1995).

Scholtes, Peter R. *The Team Handbook: How to Use Teams to Improve Quality*. (Madison, Wis.: Joiner and Associates, 1988).

Shull, F., C. Seaman, and M. Zelkowitz. "Quality Time: Victor R. Basili's Contributions to Software Quality." In *IEEE Software*, January 2006, pp. 16–18.

U.S. Army. *FM 21-76: U.S. Army Survival Manual*. (New York: Dorset Press, 1999).

Weinberg, Gerald. *Quality Software Management Volume 3: Congruent Action*. (New York: Dorset House, 1994).

Weinberg, Gerald. *Quality Software Management Volume 4: Anticipating Change*. (New York: Dorset House Publishing, 1997).

Weinberg, Gerald. *Secrets of Consulting: A Guide to Giving and Getting Advice Successfully*. (New York: Dorset House, 1985).

Wheeler, Donald. *Understanding Variation: The Key to Managing Chaos*. 2d ed. (Knoxville, Tenn.: SPC Press, 1999).

www.grove.com. *Strategic Vision Process Overview*. 2006.

Zmud, R., and L. E. Apple. "Measuring Technology Incorporation/Infusion." In *Journal of Product Innovation Management* 1992, vol. 9, pp. 148–155.

Williams, Ralph, and Patrick Wegerson. *MINI CMMI (SE/SW/IPPD/SS Version 1.1) Continuous Representation*. (Harmony, PA: Cooliemon LLC, 2002).

Index

A

Q

ESSENTIAL GUIDES TO CMMI

CMMI®, Second Edition: Guidelines for Process Integration and Product Improvement

Mary Beth Chrissis, Mike Konrad, and Sandy Shrum

0-321-27967-0

The definitive guide to CMMI—now updated for CMMI v1.2! Whether you are new to CMMI or already familiar with some version of it, this book is the essential resource for managers, practitioners, and process improvement team members who to need to understand, evaluate, and/or implement a CMMI model.

CMMI® Assessments: Motivating Positive Change

Marilyn Bush and Donna Dunaway

0-321-17935-8

Written for executives, managers, technical professionals, and assessors themselves, this book illuminates every phase of the assessment process, from planning through post-assessment follow-up.

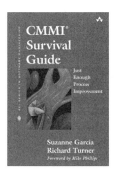

CMMI® Survival Guide: Just Enough Process Improvement

Suzanne Garcia and Richard Turner

0-321-42277-5

Practical guidance for any organization, large or small, considering or undertaking process improvement, with particular advice for implementing CMMI successfully in resource-strapped environments.

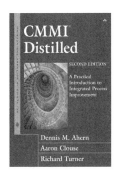

CMMI® Distilled, Second Edition: A Practical Introduction to Integrated Process Improvement

Dennis M. Ahern, Aaron Clouse, and Richard Turner

0-321-18613-3

This book is a compact, informative guide to CMMI for practitioners, executives, and managers and includes expanded coverage of how process improvement can impact business goals, and how management can support CMMI adoption.

CMMI® for Outsourcing: Guidelines for Software, Systems, and IT Acquisition

Hubert F. Hofmann, Deborah K. Yedlin, Joseph Elm, John W. Mishler, and Susan Kushner

0-321-47717-0

Best practices for outsourcing and acquiring technology within the CMMI framework, reflecting initial results from a joint General Motors-Software Engineering Institute project, and written for both vendors and suppliers needing to improve their processes.

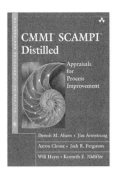

CMMI® SCAMPI Distilled: Appraisals for Process Improvement

Dennis M. Ahern, Jim Armstrong, Aaron Clouse, Jack R. Ferguson, Will Hayes, and Kenneth E. Nidiffer

0-321-22876-6

Offers concise, realistic guidance for every stage of the SCAMPI process, and demonstrates how to overcome the obstacles to a successful appraisal.

For more information on these and other books in The SEI Series in Software Engineering, please visit www.awprofessional.com/seiseries

Learn More About the Carnegie Mellon® Software Engineering Institute (SEI)

The 2005 SEI Annual Report is available at *www.sei.cmu.edu/annual-report*. It describes the accomplishments of the SEI during fiscal year 2005 (October 1, 2004 through September 30, 2005). The report features stories that exemplify how the SEI pursued its strategy of "Create-Apply-Amplify" to improve the practice of software engineering during the year.

The SEI Guide to Products and Services is available at *www.sei.cmu.edu/publications/guide.pdf*. It is a complete catalog of all the SEI's tools and methods, services, courses, conferences, credentials, books, and opportunities to collaborate with the SEI on research.

To obtain a hard copy of these documents, contact SEI Customer Relations at 1-888-201-4479 or *customer-relations@sei.cmu.edu*.

Software Engineering Institute
Carnegie Mellon

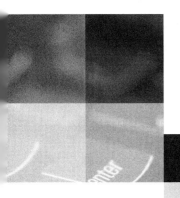

Safari

BOOKS ONLINE

ENABLED

THIS BOOK IS SAFARI ENABLED

INCLUDES FREE 45-DAY ACCESS TO THE ONLINE EDITION

The Safari® Enabled icon on the cover of your favorite technology book means the book is available through Safari Bookshelf. When you buy this book, you get free access to the online edition for 45 days.

Safari Bookshelf is an electronic reference library that lets you easily search thousands of technical books, find code samples, download chapters, and access technical information whenever and wherever you need it.

TO GAIN 45-DAY SAFARI ENABLED ACCESS TO THIS BOOK:

- Go to **http://www.awprofessional.com/safarienabled**

- Complete the brief registration form

- Enter the coupon code found in the front of this book on the "Copyright" page

Addison
Wesley

If you have difficulty registering on Safari Bookshelf or accessing the online edition, please e-mail customer-service@safaribooksonline.com.